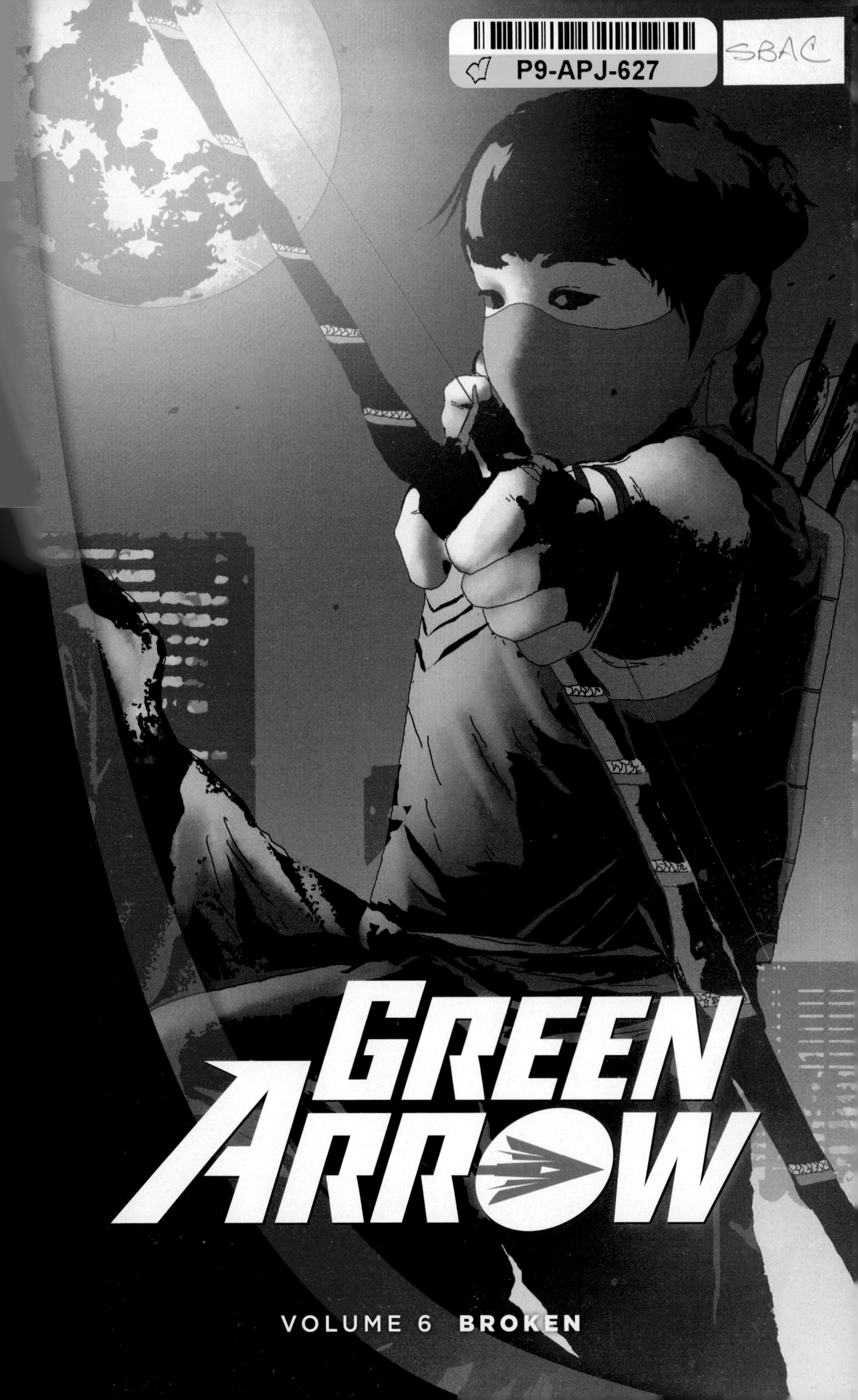
GREEN
ARROW
VOLUME 6 BROKEN

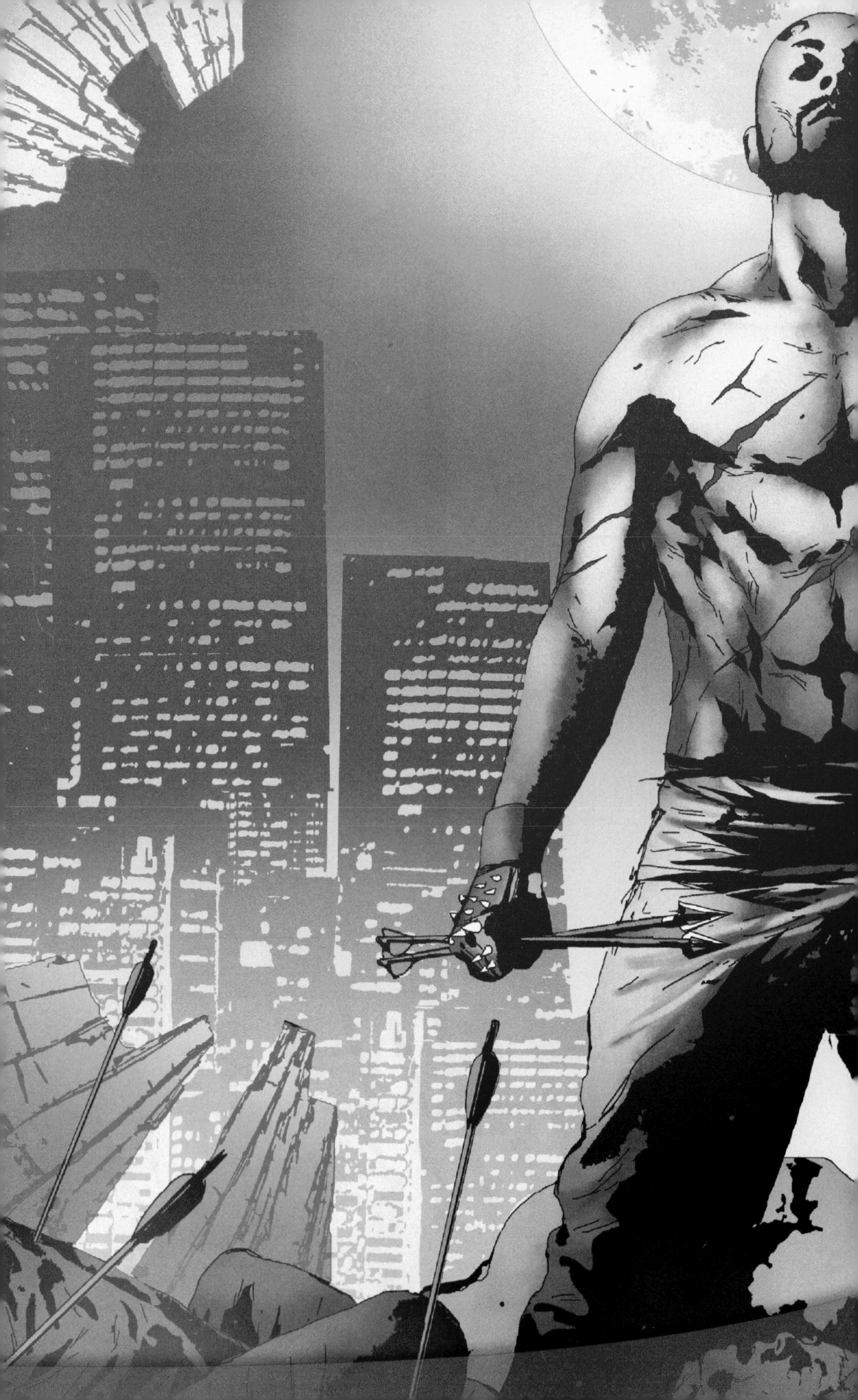

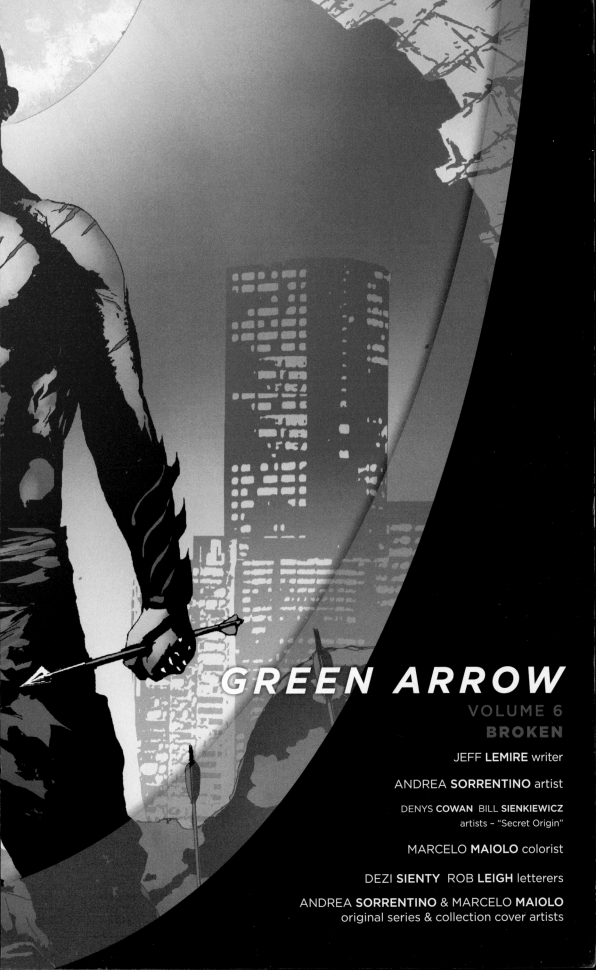

GREEN ARROW

VOLUME 6
BROKEN

JEFF **LEMIRE** writer

ANDREA **SORRENTINO** artist

DENYS **COWAN** BILL **SIENKIEWICZ**
artists – "Secret Origin"

MARCELO **MAIOLO** colorist

DEZI **SIENTY** ROB **LEIGH** letterers

ANDREA **SORRENTINO** & MARCELO **MAIOLO**
original series & collection cover artists

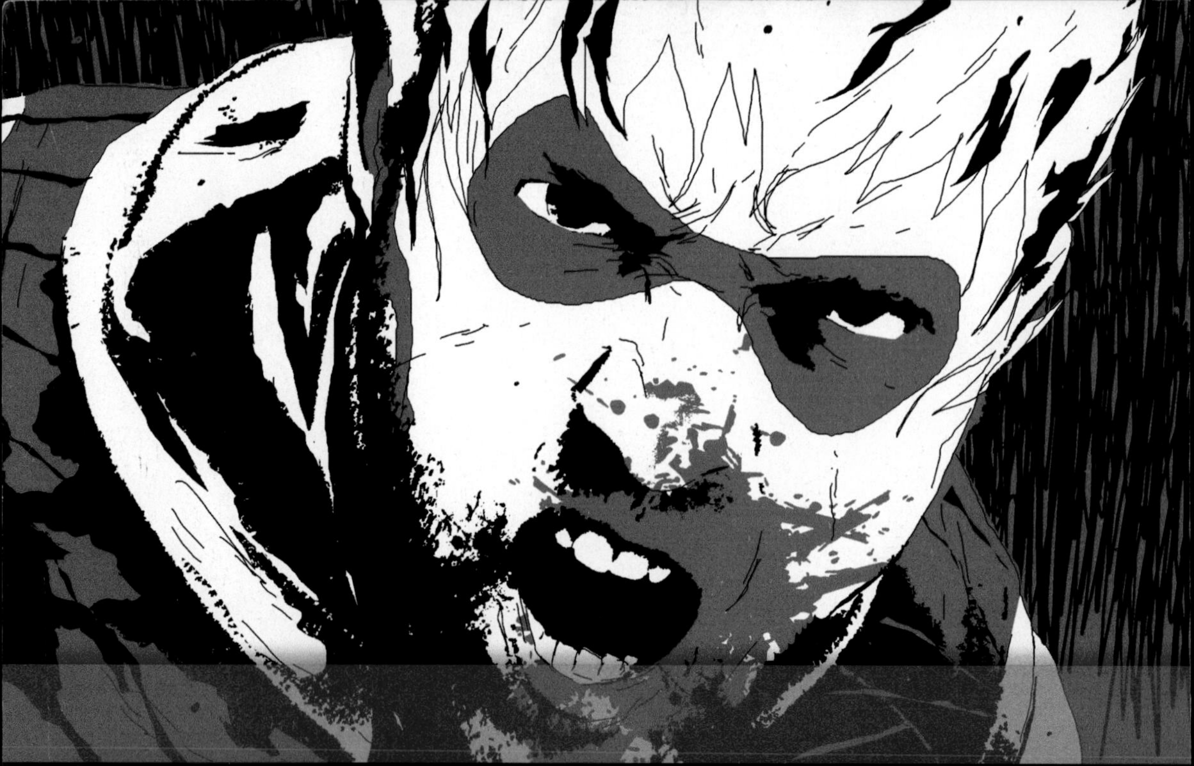

CHRIS CONROY Editor – Original Series HARVEY RICHARDS Associate Editor – Original Series ROBIN WILDMAN Editor
ROBBIN BROSTERMAN Design Director – Books ROBBIE BIEDERMAN Publication Design

BOB HARRAS Senior VP – Editor-in-Chief, DC Comics

DIANE NELSON President DAN DIDIO and JIM LEE Co-Publishers GEOFF JOHNS Chief Creative Officer
AMIT DESAI Senior VP – Marketing and Franchise Management
AMY GENKINS Senior VP – Business and Legal Affairs NAIRI GARDINER Senior VP – Finance
JEFF BOISON VP – Publishing Planning MARK CHIARELLO VP – Art Direction and Design
JOHN CUNNINGHAM VP – Marketing TERRI CUNNINGHAM VP – Editorial Administration
LARRY GANEM VP – Talent Relations and Services ALISON GILL Senior VP – Manufacturing and Operations
HANK KANALZ Senior VP – Vertigo and Integrated Publishing JAY KOGAN VP – Business and Legal Affairs, Publishing
JACK MAHAN VP – Business Affairs, Talent NICK NAPOLITANO VP – Manufacturing Administration SUE POHJA VP – Book Sales
FRED RUIZ VP – Manufacturing Operations COURTNEY SIMMONS Senior VP – Publicity BOB WAYNE Senior VP – Sales

GREEN ARROW VOLUME 6: BROKEN

DC Comics, 1700 Broadway, New York, NY 10019
A Warner Bros. Entertainment Company.
Printed by RR Donnelley, Owensville, MO, USA. 3/27/15. First Printing.

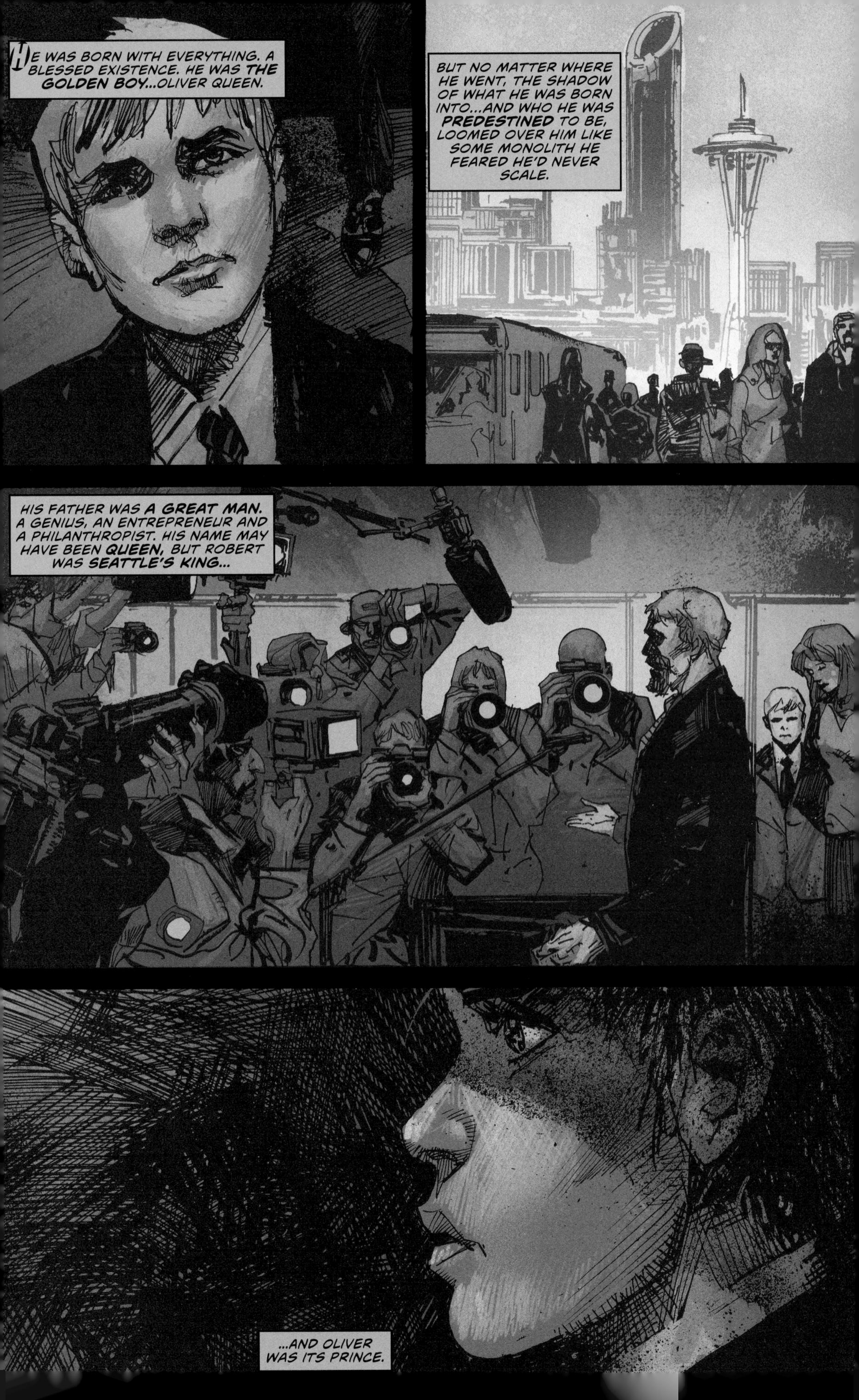
HE WAS BORN WITH EVERYTHING. A BLESSED EXISTENCE. HE WAS **THE GOLDEN BOY**...OLIVER QUEEN.
BUT NO MATTER WHERE HE WENT, THE SHADOW OF WHAT HE WAS BORN INTO...AND WHO HE WAS **PREDESTINED** TO BE, LOOMED OVER HIM LIKE SOME MONOLITH HE FEARED HE'D NEVER SCALE.
HIS FATHER WAS **A GREAT MAN.** A GENIUS, AN ENTREPRENEUR AND A PHILANTHROPIST. HIS NAME MAY HAVE BEEN **QUEEN,** BUT ROBERT WAS **SEATTLE'S KING...**
...AND OLIVER WAS ITS PRINCE.

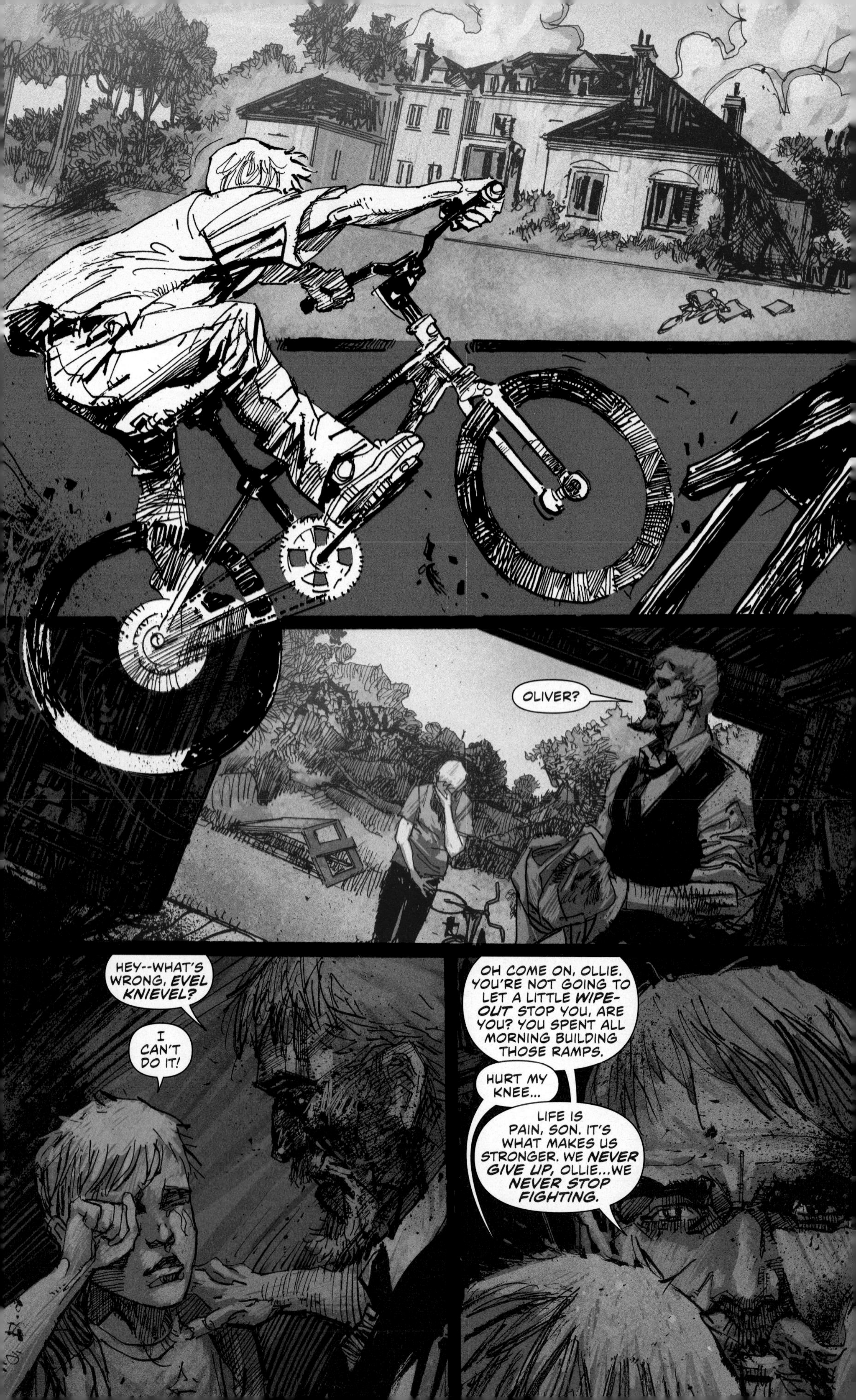
OLIVER?
HEY--WHAT'S WRONG, EVEL KNIEVEL?
I CAN'T DO IT!
OH COME ON, OLLIE. YOU'RE NOT GOING TO LET A LITTLE WIPE-OUT STOP YOU, ARE YOU? YOU SPENT ALL MORNING BUILDING THOSE RAMPS.
HURT MY KNEE...
LIFE IS PAIN, SON. IT'S WHAT MAKES US STRONGER. WE NEVER GIVE UP, OLLIE...WE NEVER STOP FIGHTING.

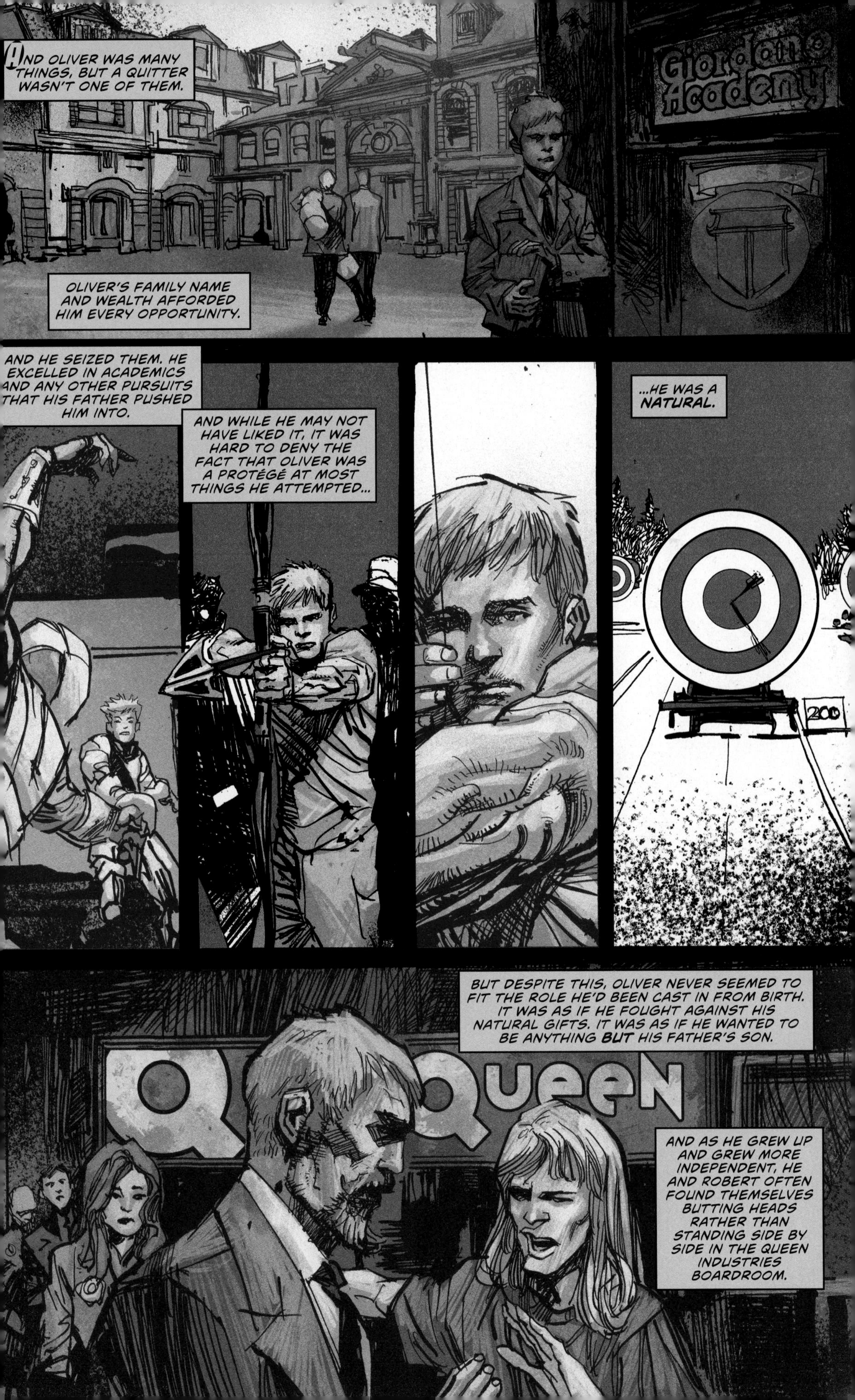
AND OLIVER WAS MANY THINGS, BUT A QUITTER WASN'T ONE OF THEM.
Giordano Academy
OLIVER'S FAMILY NAME AND WEALTH AFFORDED HIM EVERY OPPORTUNITY.
AND HE SEIZED THEM. HE EXCELLED IN ACADEMICS AND ANY OTHER PURSUITS THAT HIS FATHER PUSHED HIM INTO.
AND WHILE HE MAY NOT HAVE LIKED IT, IT WAS HARD TO DENY THE FACT THAT OLIVER WAS A PROTÉGÉ AT MOST THINGS HE ATTEMPTED...
...HE WAS A **NATURAL.**
200
BUT DESPITE THIS, OLIVER NEVER SEEMED TO FIT THE ROLE HE'D BEEN CAST IN FROM BIRTH. IT WAS AS IF HE FOUGHT AGAINST HIS NATURAL GIFTS. IT WAS AS IF HE WANTED TO BE ANYTHING **BUT** HIS FATHER'S SON.
Q Queen
AND AS HE GREW UP AND GREW MORE INDEPENDENT, HE AND ROBERT OFTEN FOUND THEMSELVES BUTTING HEADS RATHER THAN STANDING SIDE BY SIDE IN THE QUEEN INDUSTRIES BOARDROOM.

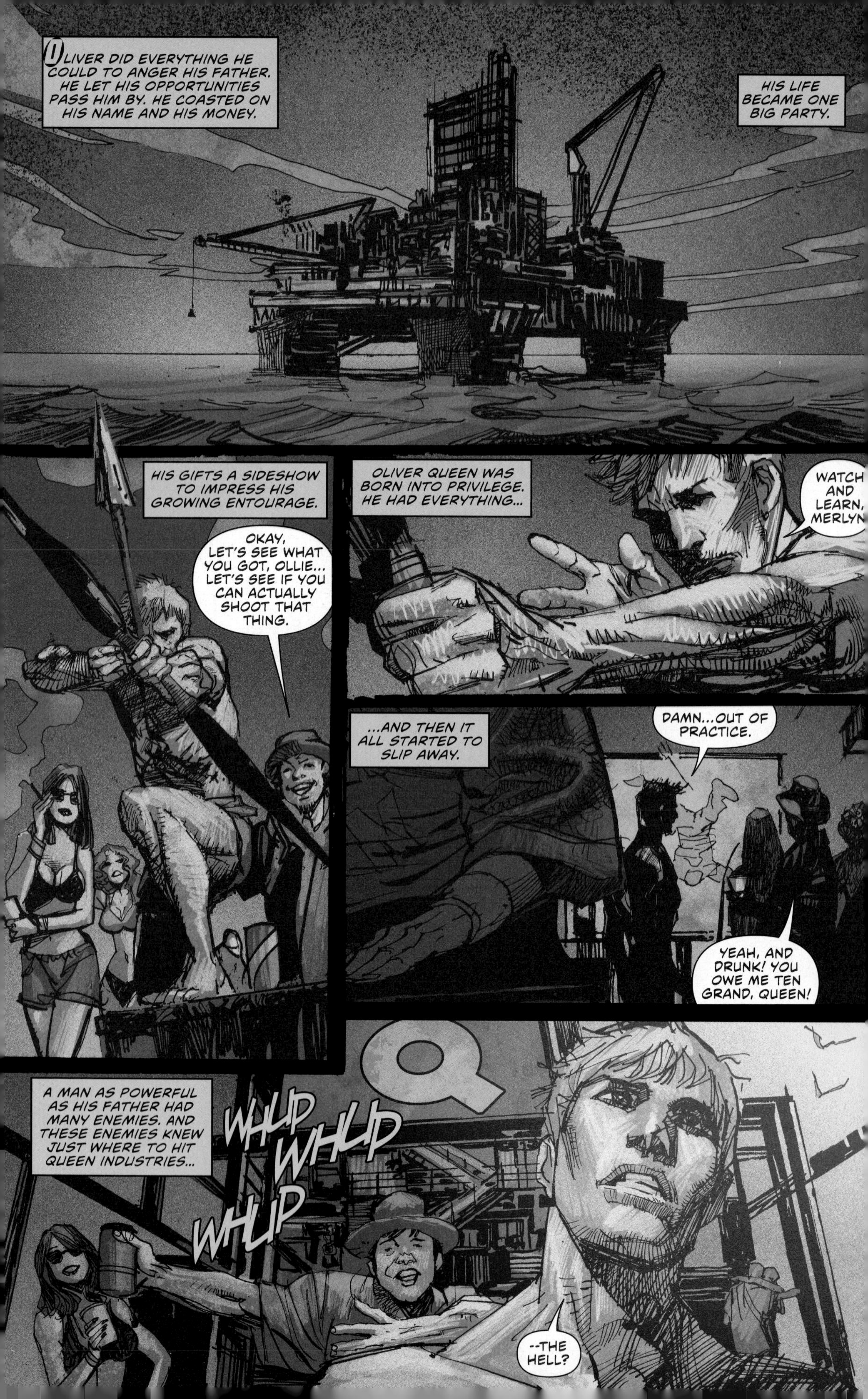
OLIVER DID EVERYTHING HE COULD TO ANGER HIS FATHER. HE LET HIS OPPORTUNITIES PASS HIM BY. HE COASTED ON HIS NAME AND HIS MONEY.
HIS LIFE BECAME ONE BIG PARTY.
HIS GIFTS A SIDESHOW TO IMPRESS HIS GROWING ENTOURAGE.
OKAY, LET'S SEE WHAT YOU GOT, OLLIE... LET'S SEE IF YOU CAN ACTUALLY SHOOT THAT THING.
OLIVER QUEEN WAS BORN INTO PRIVILEGE. HE HAD EVERYTHING...
WATCH AND LEARN, MERLYN
...AND THEN IT ALL STARTED TO SLIP AWAY.
DAMN...OUT OF PRACTICE.
YEAH, AND DRUNK! YOU OWE ME TEN GRAND, QUEEN!
A MAN AS POWERFUL AS HIS FATHER HAD MANY ENEMIES. AND THESE ENEMIES KNEW JUST WHERE TO HIT QUEEN INDUSTRIES...
WHUP WHUP WHUP
--THE HELL?

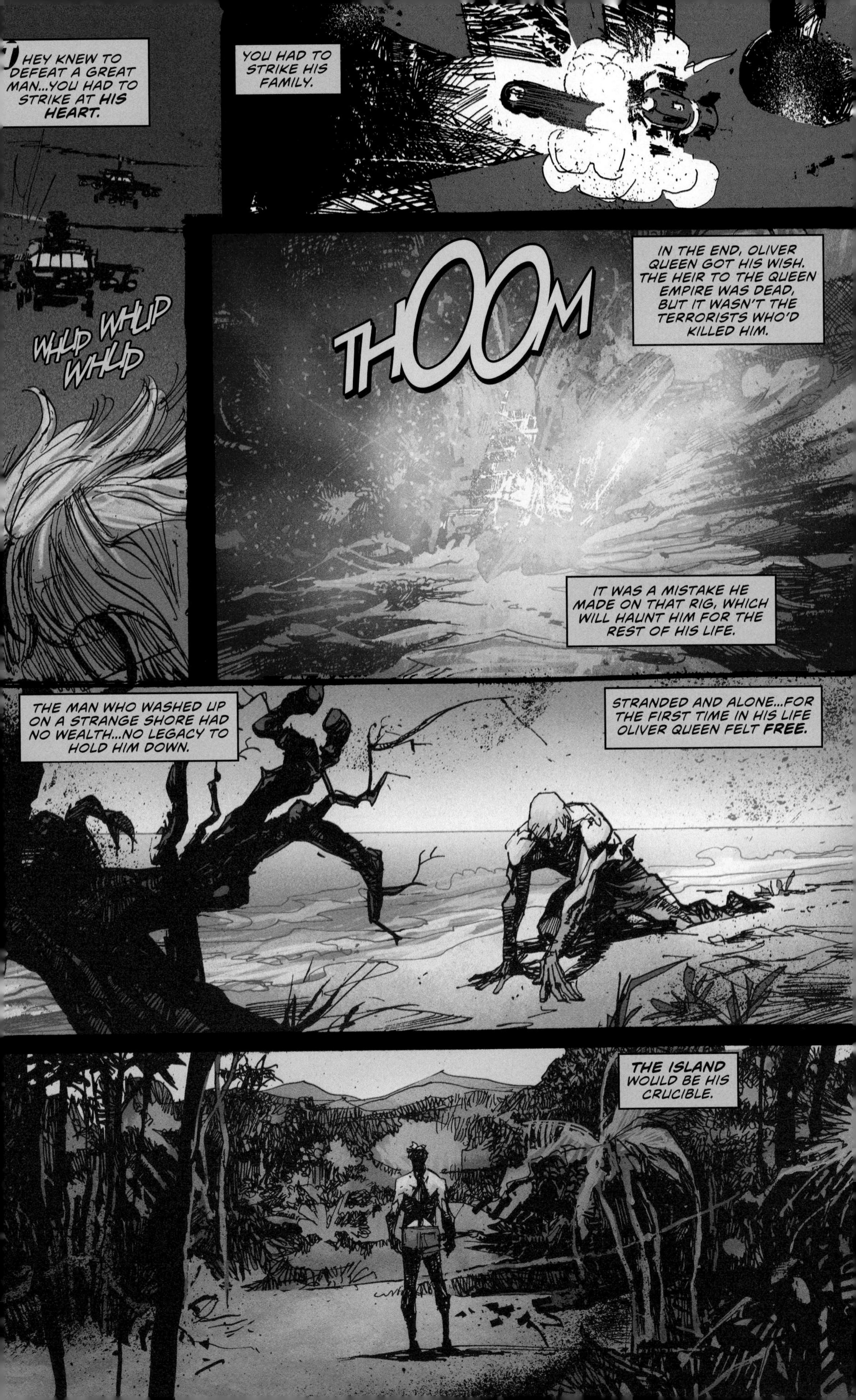
THEY KNEW TO DEFEAT A GREAT MAN...YOU HAD TO STRIKE AT HIS HEART.
YOU HAD TO STRIKE HIS FAMILY.
WHUP WHUP WHUP
THOOM
IN THE END, OLIVER QUEEN GOT HIS WISH. THE HEIR TO THE QUEEN EMPIRE WAS DEAD, BUT IT WASN'T THE TERRORISTS WHO'D KILLED HIM.
IT WAS A MISTAKE HE MADE ON THAT RIG, WHICH WILL HAUNT HIM FOR THE REST OF HIS LIFE.
THE MAN WHO WASHED UP ON A STRANGE SHORE HAD NO WEALTH...NO LEGACY TO HOLD HIM DOWN.
STRANDED AND ALONE...FOR THE FIRST TIME IN HIS LIFE OLIVER QUEEN FELT FREE.
THE ISLAND WOULD BE HIS CRUCIBLE.

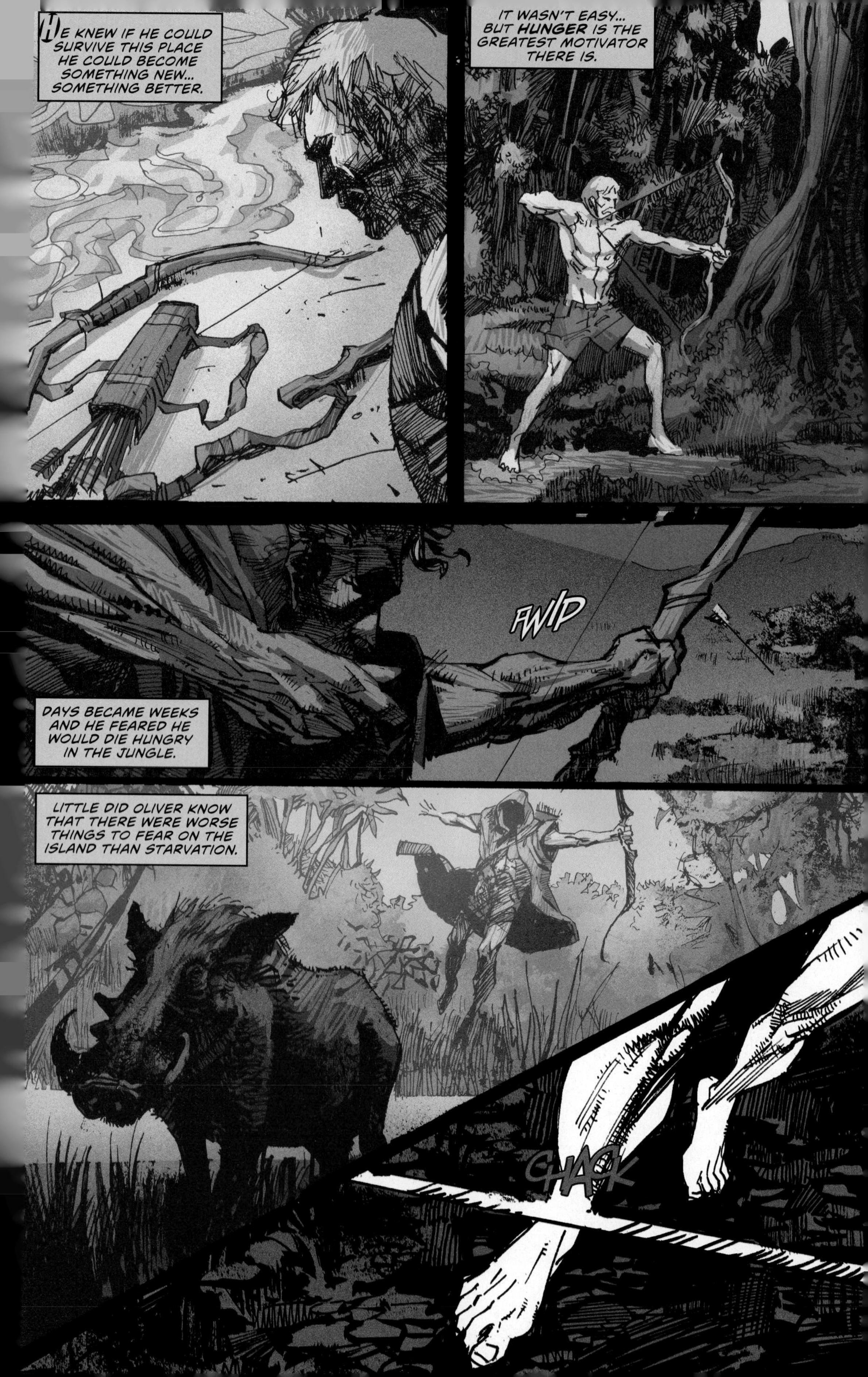
HE KNEW IF HE COULD SURVIVE THIS PLACE HE COULD BECOME SOMETHING NEW... SOMETHING BETTER.
IT WASN'T EASY... BUT HUNGER IS THE GREATEST MOTIVATOR THERE IS.
FWIP
DAYS BECAME WEEKS AND HE FEARED HE WOULD DIE HUNGRY IN THE JUNGLE.
LITTLE DID OLIVER KNOW THAT THERE WERE WORSE THINGS TO FEAR ON THE ISLAND THAN STARVATION.
CHACK

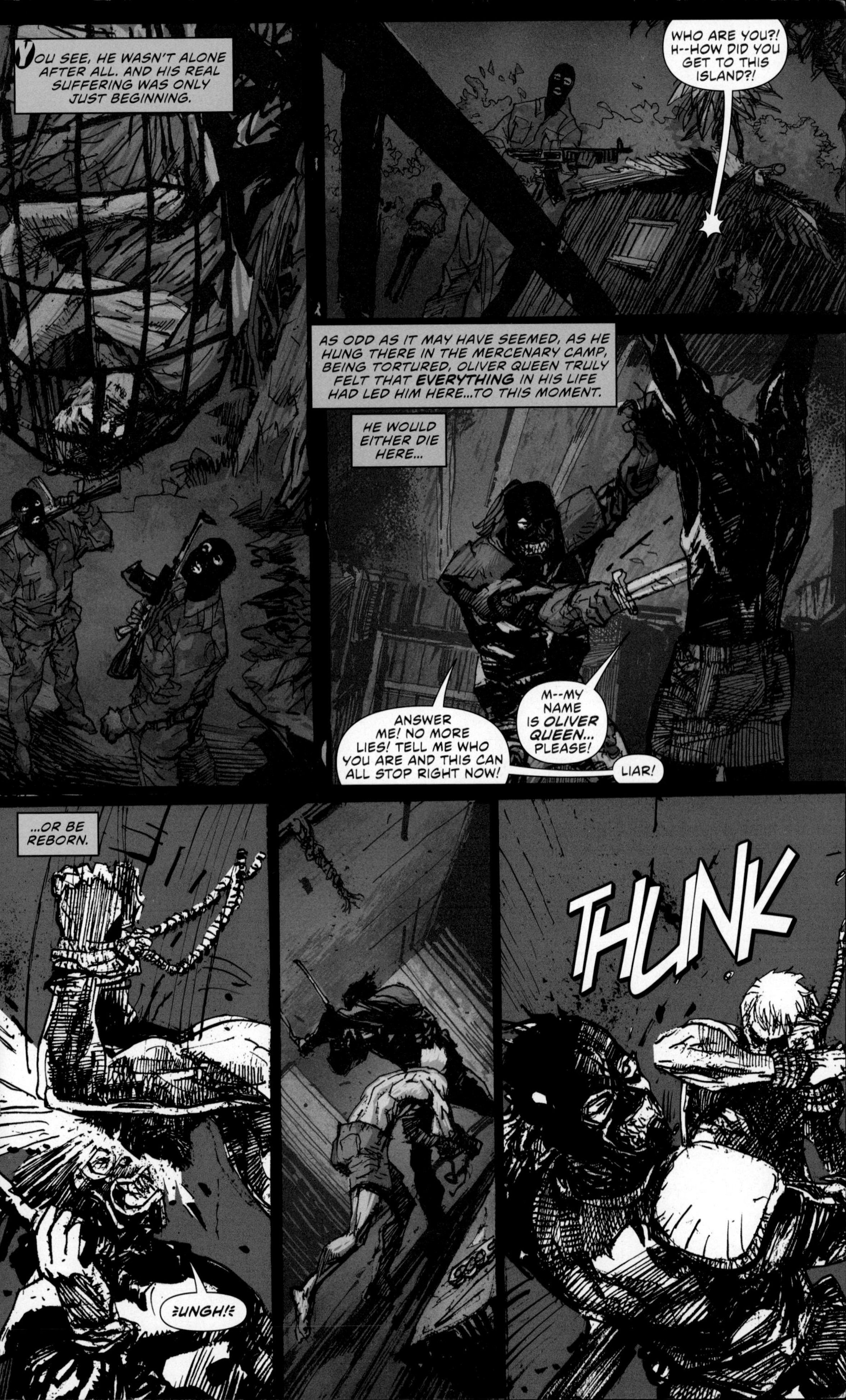
YOU SEE, HE WASN'T ALONE AFTER ALL. AND HIS REAL SUFFERING WAS ONLY JUST BEGINNING.
WHO ARE YOU?! H--HOW DID YOU GET TO THIS ISLAND?!
AS ODD AS IT MAY HAVE SEEMED, AS HE HUNG THERE IN THE MERCENARY CAMP, BEING TORTURED, OLIVER QUEEN TRULY FELT THAT EVERYTHING IN HIS LIFE HAD LED HIM HERE...TO THIS MOMENT.
HE WOULD EITHER DIE HERE...
ANSWER ME! NO MORE LIES! TELL ME WHO YOU ARE AND THIS CAN ALL STOP RIGHT NOW!
M--MY NAME IS OLIVER QUEEN... PLEASE!
LIAR!
...OR BE REBORN.
UNGH!
THUNK

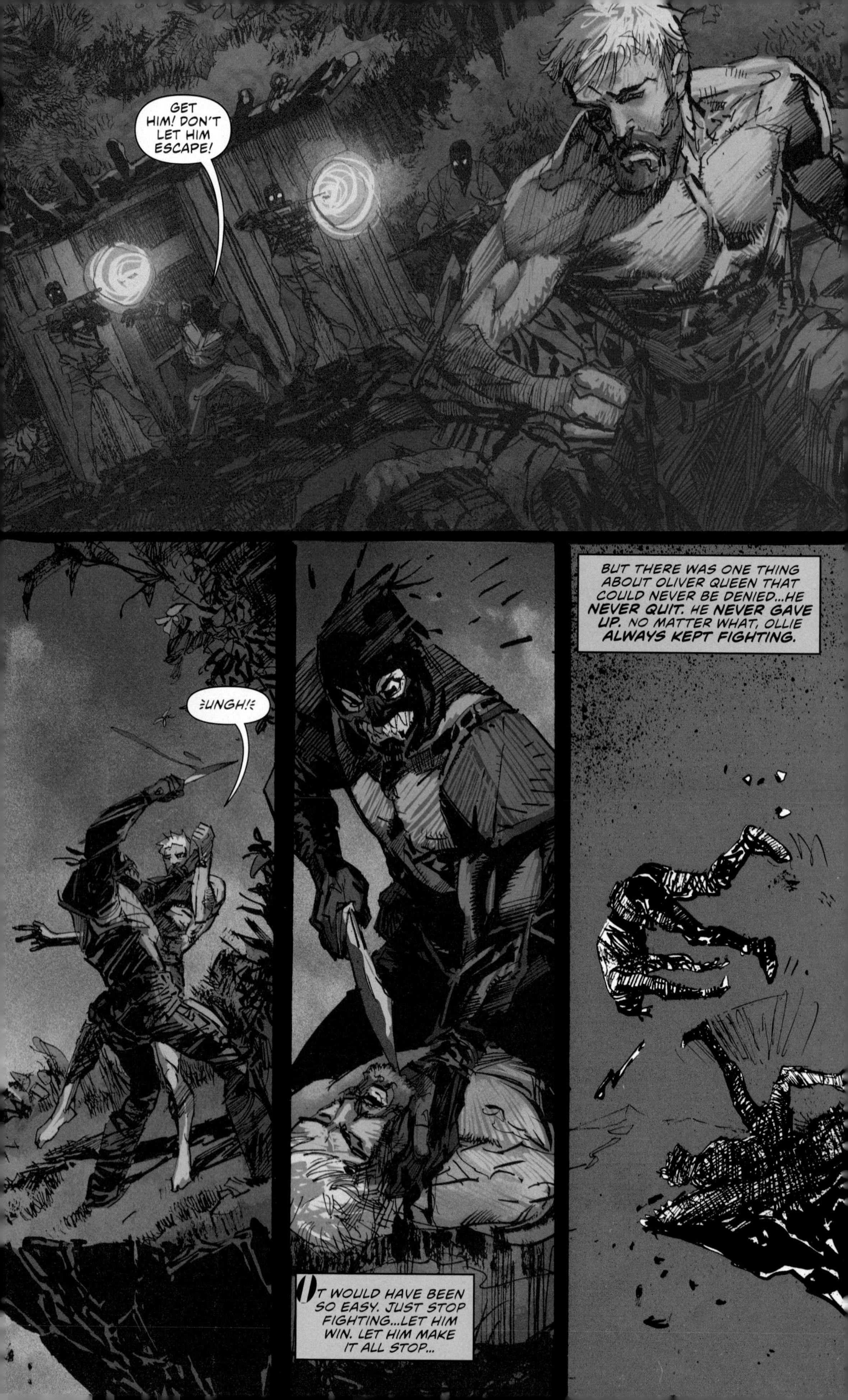
GET HIM! DON'T LET HIM ESCAPE!
UNGH!
IT WOULD HAVE BEEN SO EASY. JUST STOP FIGHTING...LET HIM WIN. LET HIM MAKE IT ALL STOP...
BUT THERE WAS ONE THING ABOUT OLIVER QUEEN THAT COULD NEVER BE DENIED...HE NEVER QUIT. HE NEVER GAVE UP. NO MATTER WHAT, OLLIE ALWAYS KEPT FIGHTING.

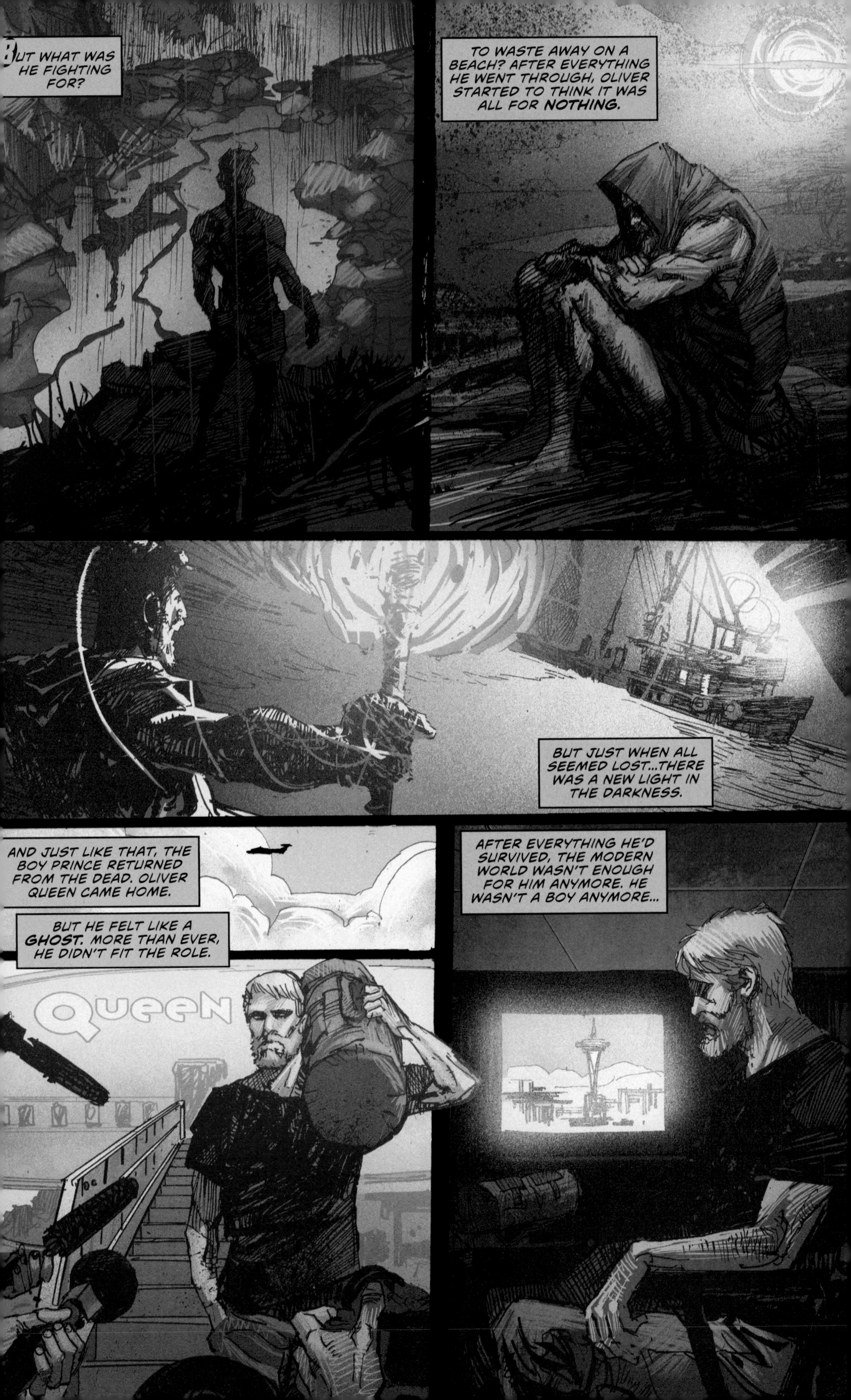
BUT WHAT WAS HE FIGHTING FOR?
TO WASTE AWAY ON A BEACH? AFTER EVERYTHING HE WENT THROUGH, OLIVER STARTED TO THINK IT WAS ALL FOR NOTHING.
BUT JUST WHEN ALL SEEMED LOST...THERE WAS A NEW LIGHT IN THE DARKNESS.
AND JUST LIKE THAT, THE BOY PRINCE RETURNED FROM THE DEAD. OLIVER QUEEN CAME HOME.
BUT HE FELT LIKE A GHOST. MORE THAN EVER, HE DIDN'T FIT THE ROLE.
QUEEN
AFTER EVERYTHING HE'D SURVIVED, THE MODERN WORLD WASN'T ENOUGH FOR HIM ANYMORE. HE WASN'T A BOY ANYMORE...

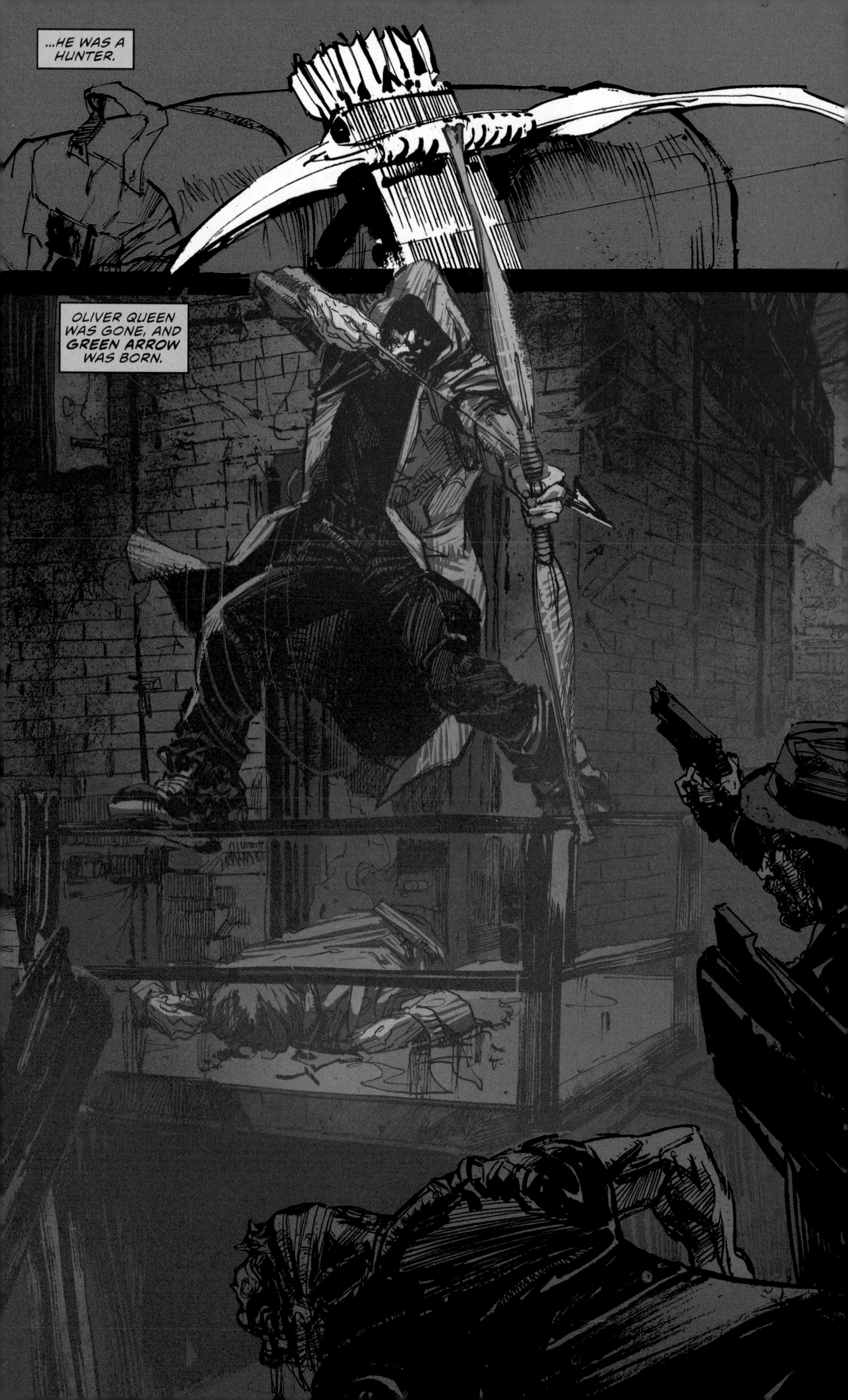
...HE WAS A
HUNTER.
OLIVER QUEEN
WAS GONE, AND
GREEN ARROW
WAS BORN.

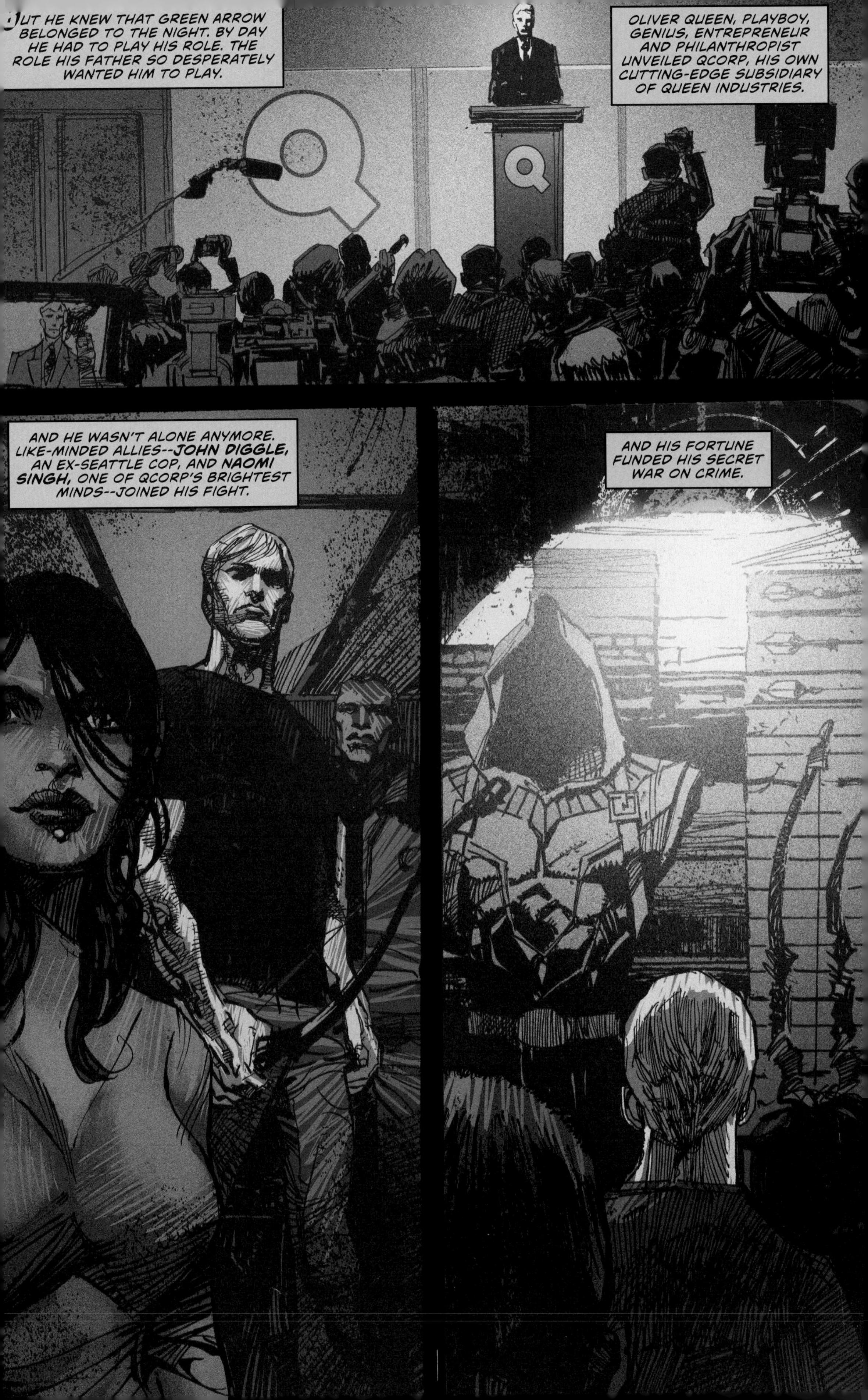

BUT HE KNEW THAT GREEN ARROW BELONGED TO THE NIGHT. BY DAY HE HAD TO PLAY HIS ROLE. THE ROLE HIS FATHER SO DESPERATELY WANTED HIM TO PLAY.
OLIVER QUEEN, PLAYBOY, GENIUS, ENTREPRENEUR AND PHILANTHROPIST UNVEILED QCORP, HIS OWN CUTTING-EDGE SUBSIDIARY OF QUEEN INDUSTRIES.
AND HE WASN'T ALONE ANYMORE. LIKE-MINDED ALLIES--JOHN DIGGLE, AN EX-SEATTLE COP, AND NAOMI SINGH, ONE OF QCORP'S BRIGHTEST MINDS--JOINED HIS FIGHT.
AND HIS FORTUNE FUNDED HIS SECRET WAR ON CRIME.

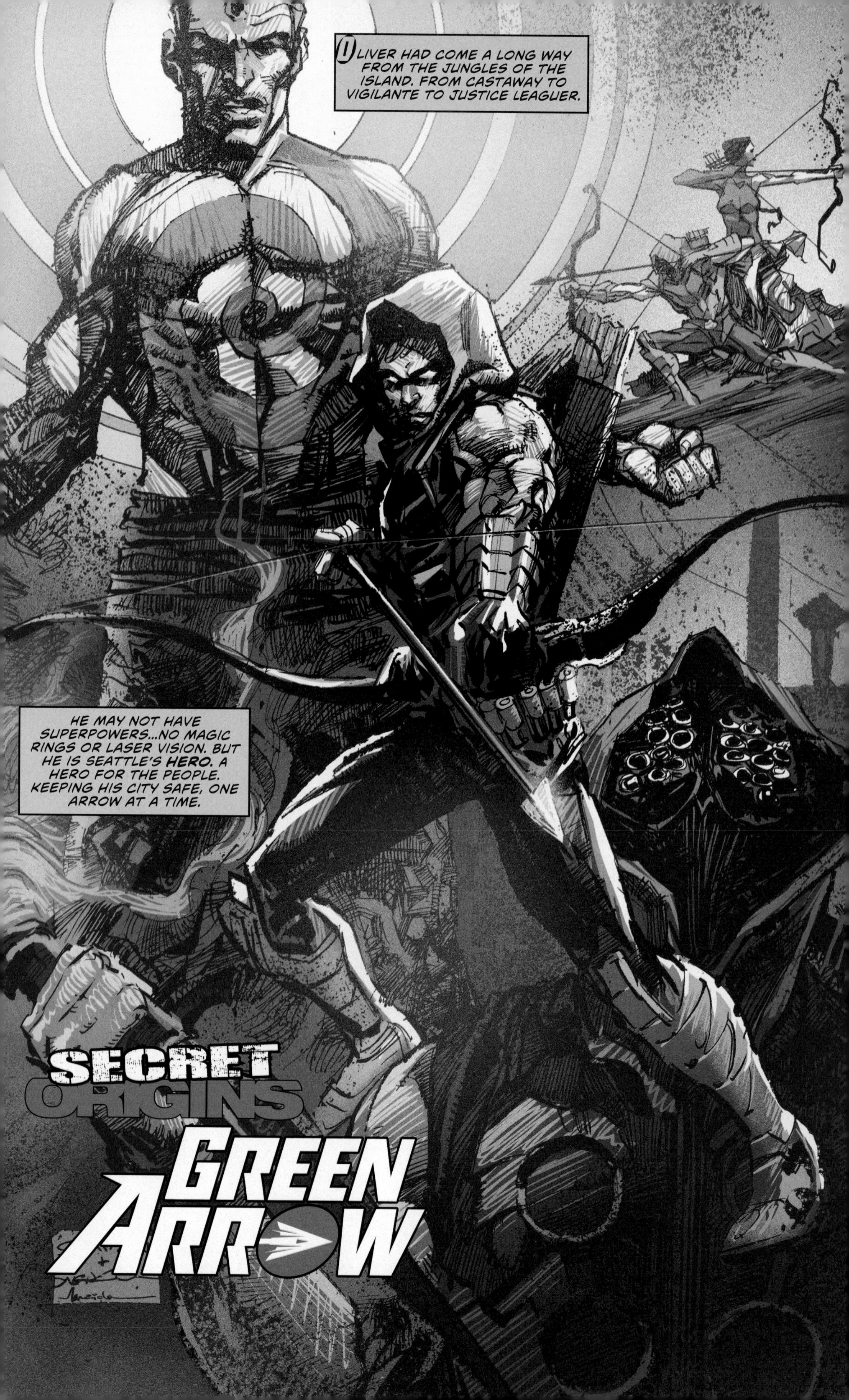
OLIVER HAD COME A LONG WAY FROM THE JUNGLES OF THE ISLAND. FROM CASTAWAY TO VIGILANTE TO JUSTICE LEAGUER.
HE MAY NOT HAVE SUPERPOWERS...NO MAGIC RINGS OR LASER VISION. BUT HE IS SEATTLE'S **HERO**. A HERO FOR THE PEOPLE. KEEPING HIS CITY SAFE, ONE ARROW AT A TIME.
SECRET ORIGINS
GREEN ARROW

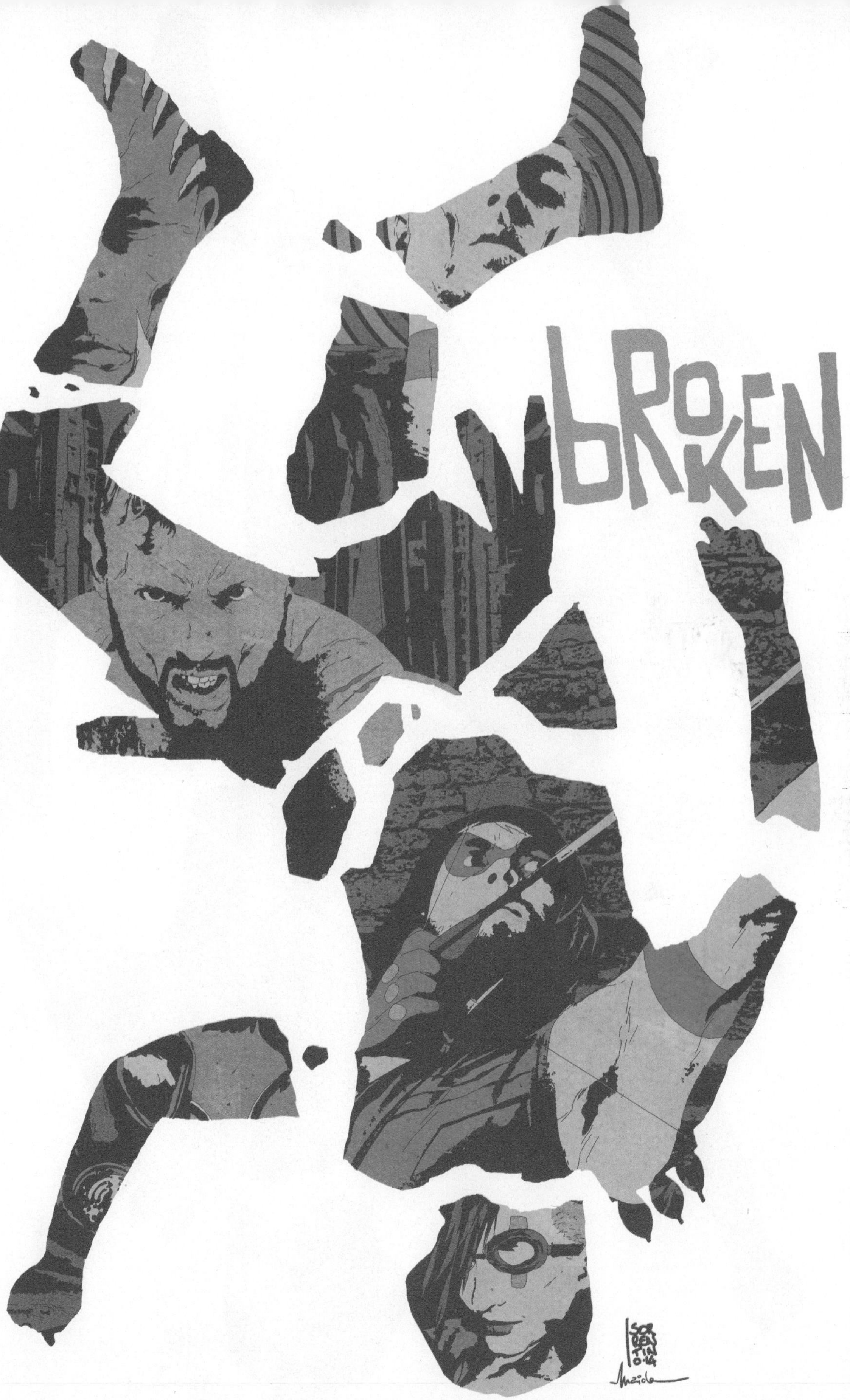
bROKEN

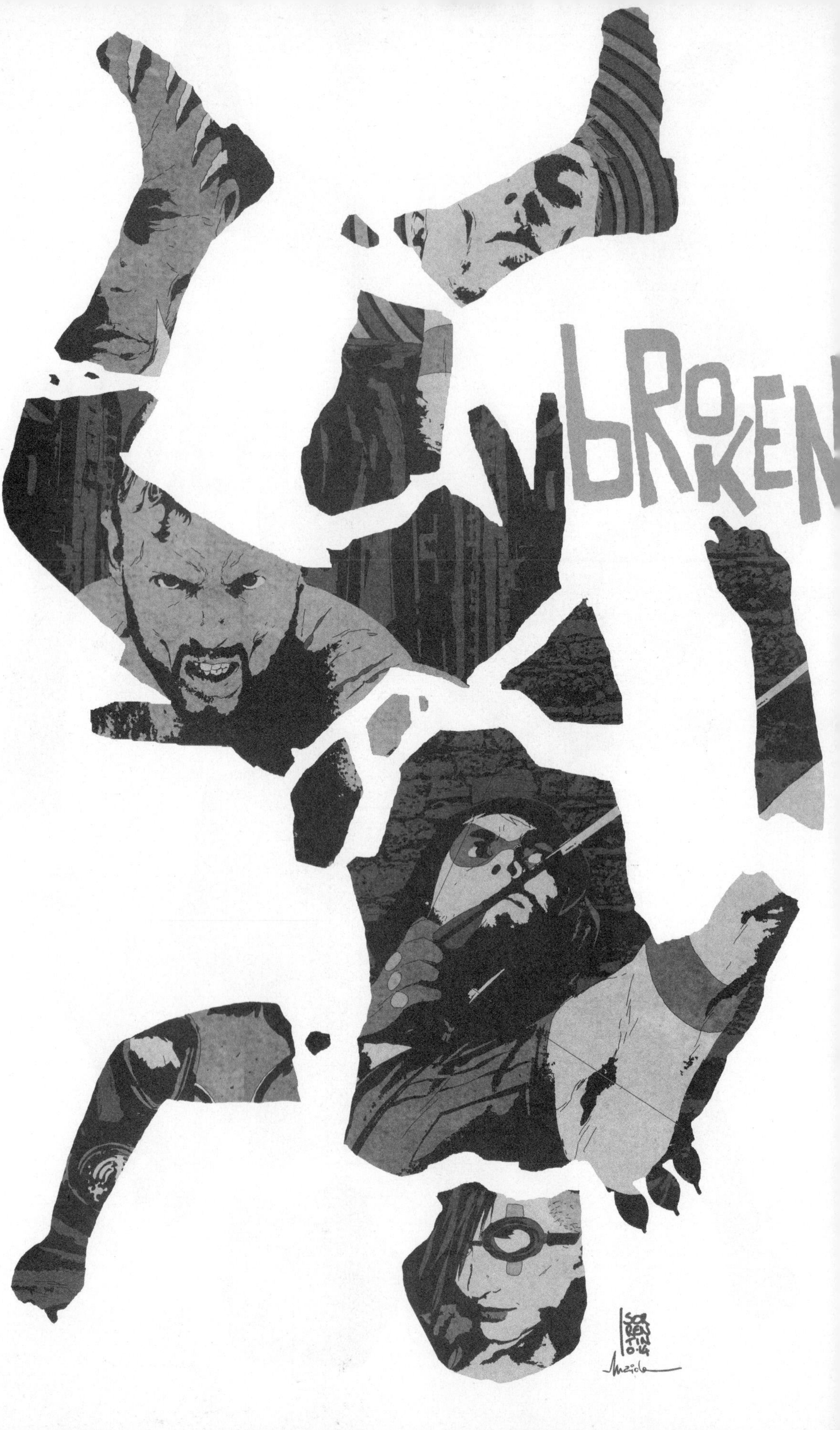
bROKEN

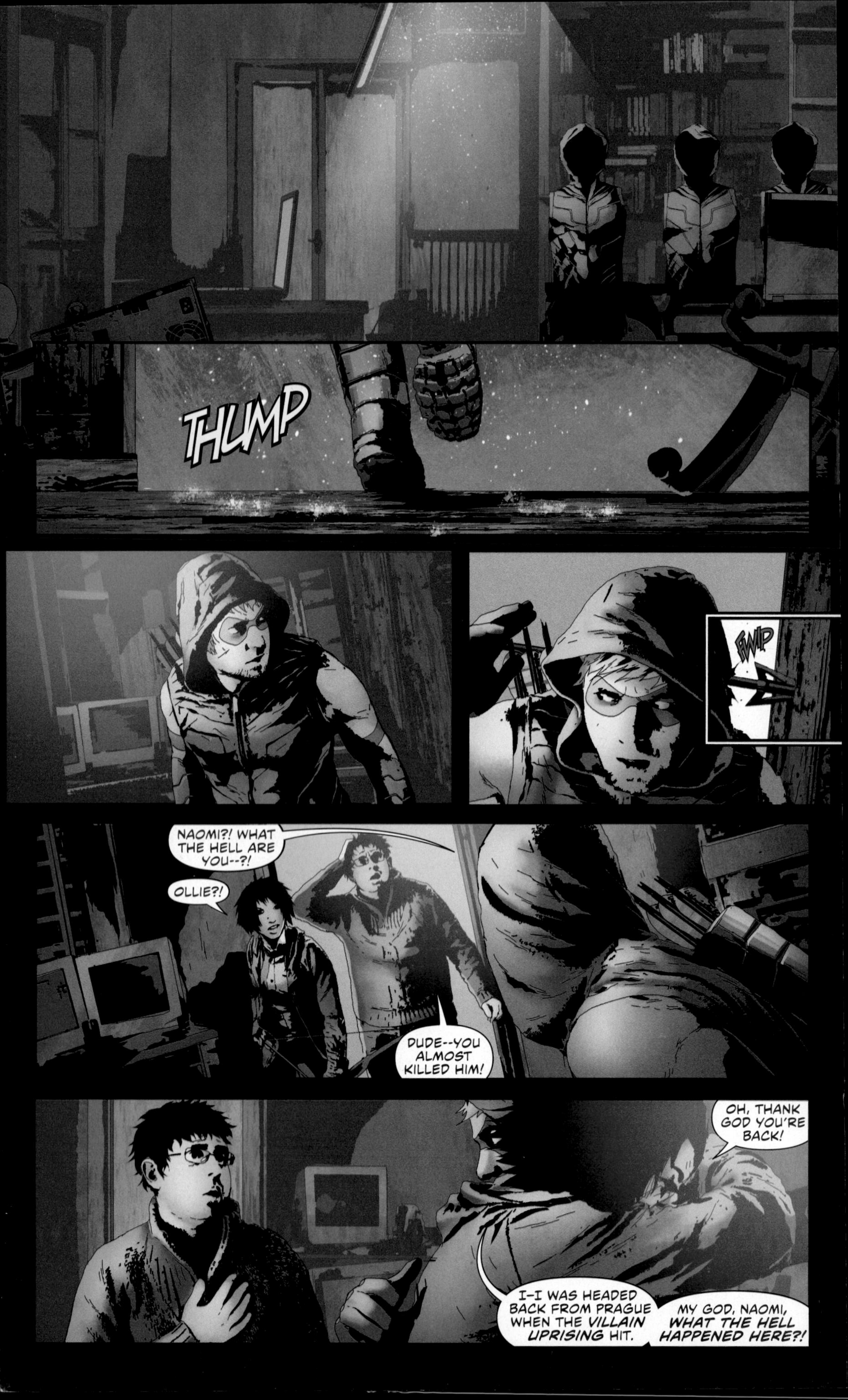
THUMP
FWIP
NAOMI?! WHAT THE HELL ARE YOU--?!
OLLIE?!
DUDE--YOU ALMOST KILLED HIM!
OH, THANK GOD YOU'RE BACK!
I-I WAS HEADED BACK FROM PRAGUE WHEN THE VILLAIN UPRISING HIT.
MY GOD, NAOMI, WHAT THE HELL HAPPENED HERE?!

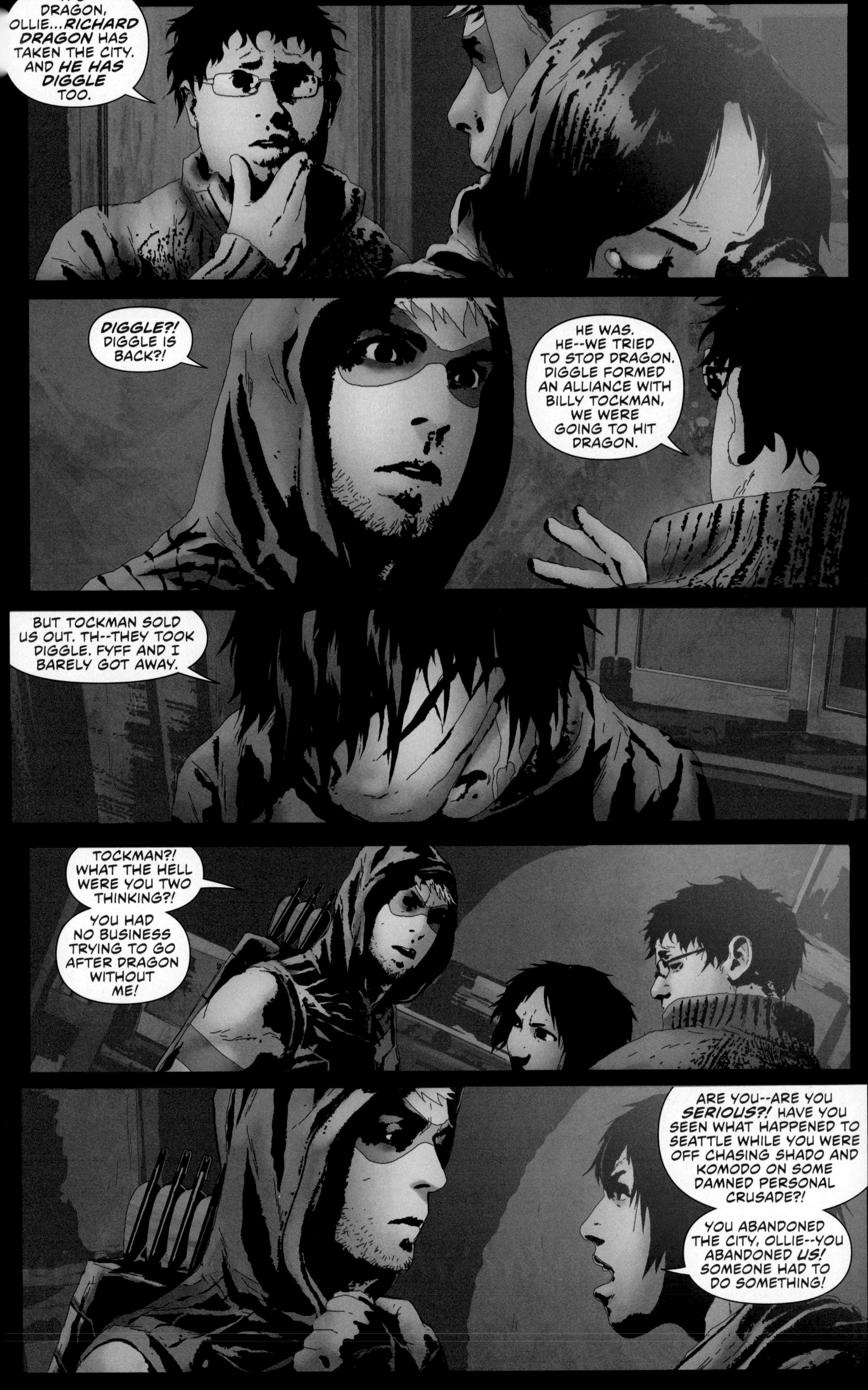
IT'S DRAGON, OLLIE...RICHARD DRAGON HAS TAKEN THE CITY. AND HE HAS DIGGLE TOO.
DIGGLE?! DIGGLE IS BACK?!
HE WAS. HE--WE TRIED TO STOP DRAGON. DIGGLE FORMED AN ALLIANCE WITH BILLY TOCKMAN, WE WERE GOING TO HIT DRAGON.
BUT TOCKMAN SOLD US OUT. TH--THEY TOOK DIGGLE. FYFF AND I BARELY GOT AWAY.
TOCKMAN?! WHAT THE HELL WERE YOU TWO THINKING?!
YOU HAD NO BUSINESS TRYING TO GO AFTER DRAGON WITHOUT ME!
ARE YOU--ARE YOU SERIOUS?! HAVE YOU SEEN WHAT HAPPENED TO SEATTLE WHILE YOU WERE OFF CHASING SHADO AND KOMODO ON SOME DAMNED PERSONAL CRUSADE?!
YOU ABANDONED THE CITY, OLLIE--YOU ABANDONED US! SOMEONE HAD TO DO SOMETHING!

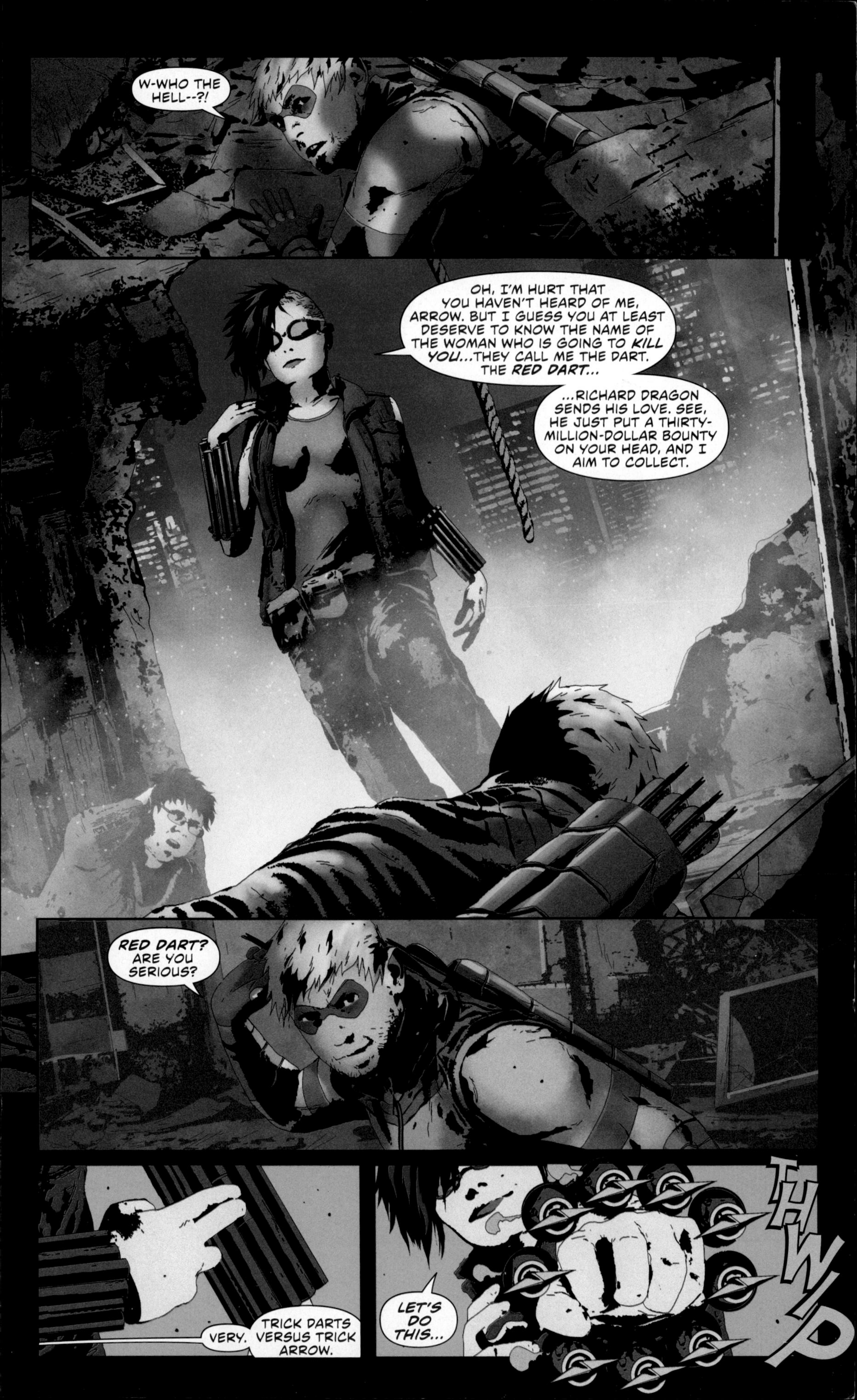
W-WHO THE HELL--?!
OH, I'M HURT THAT YOU HAVEN'T HEARD OF ME, ARROW. BUT I GUESS YOU AT LEAST DESERVE TO KNOW THE NAME OF THE WOMAN WHO IS GOING TO KILL YOU...THEY CALL ME THE DART. THE RED DART...
...RICHARD DRAGON SENDS HIS LOVE. SEE, HE JUST PUT A THIRTY-MILLION-DOLLAR BOUNTY ON YOUR HEAD, AND I AIM TO COLLECT.
RED DART? ARE YOU SERIOUS?
VERY.
TRICK DARTS VERSUS TRICK ARROW.
LET'S DO THIS...
THWIP

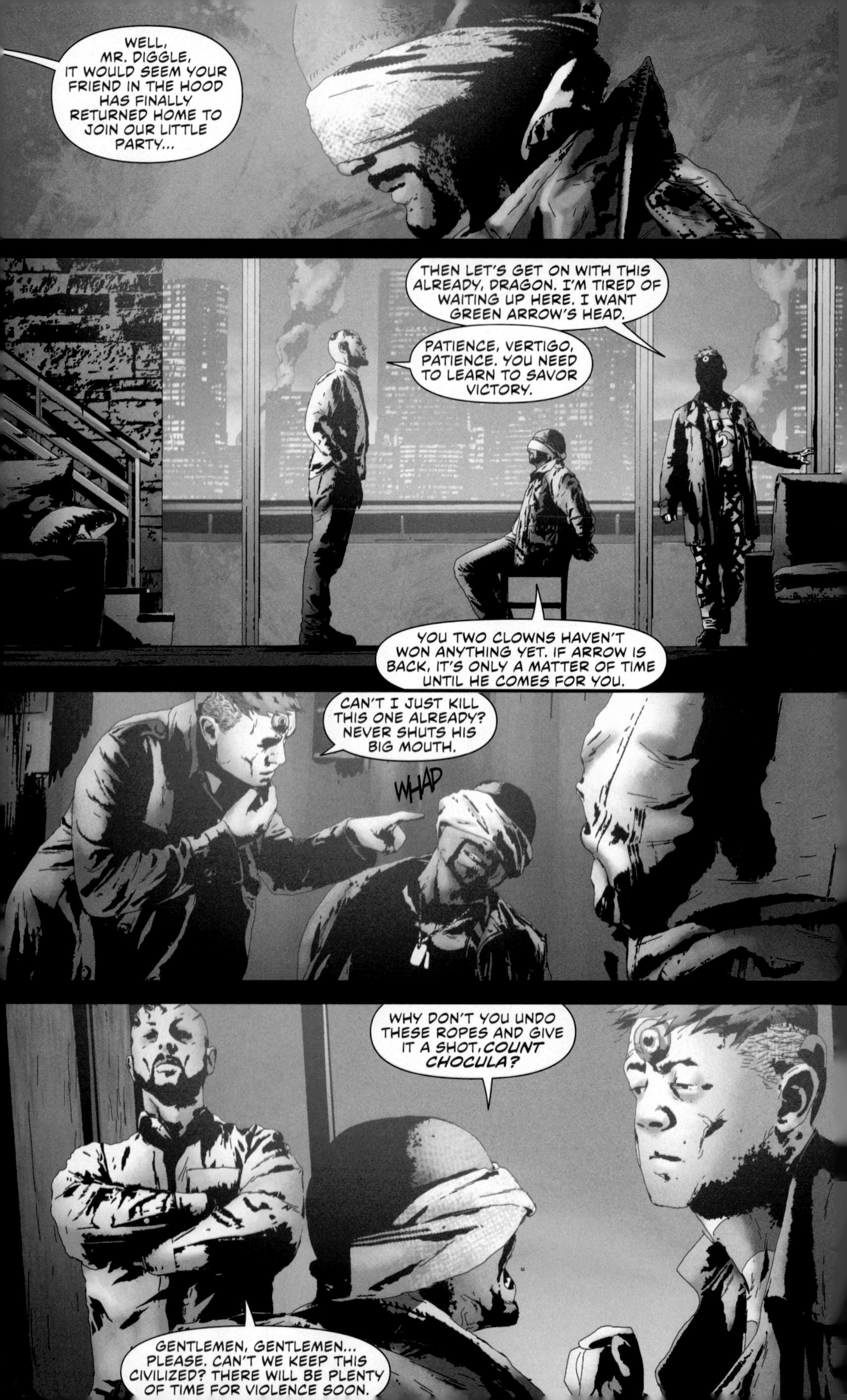
WELL, MR. DIGGLE, IT WOULD SEEM YOUR FRIEND IN THE HOOD HAS FINALLY RETURNED HOME TO JOIN OUR LITTLE PARTY...
THEN LET'S GET ON WITH THIS ALREADY, DRAGON. I'M TIRED OF WAITING UP HERE. I WANT GREEN ARROW'S HEAD.
PATIENCE, VERTIGO, PATIENCE. YOU NEED TO LEARN TO SAVOR VICTORY.
YOU TWO CLOWNS HAVEN'T WON ANYTHING YET. IF ARROW IS BACK, IT'S ONLY A MATTER OF TIME UNTIL HE COMES FOR YOU.
CAN'T I JUST KILL THIS ONE ALREADY? NEVER SHUTS HIS BIG MOUTH.
WHAP
WHY DON'T YOU UNDO THESE ROPES AND GIVE IT A SHOT, COUNT CHOCULA?
GENTLEMEN, GENTLEMEN... PLEASE. CAN'T WE KEEP THIS CIVILIZED? THERE WILL BE PLENTY OF TIME FOR VIOLENCE SOON.

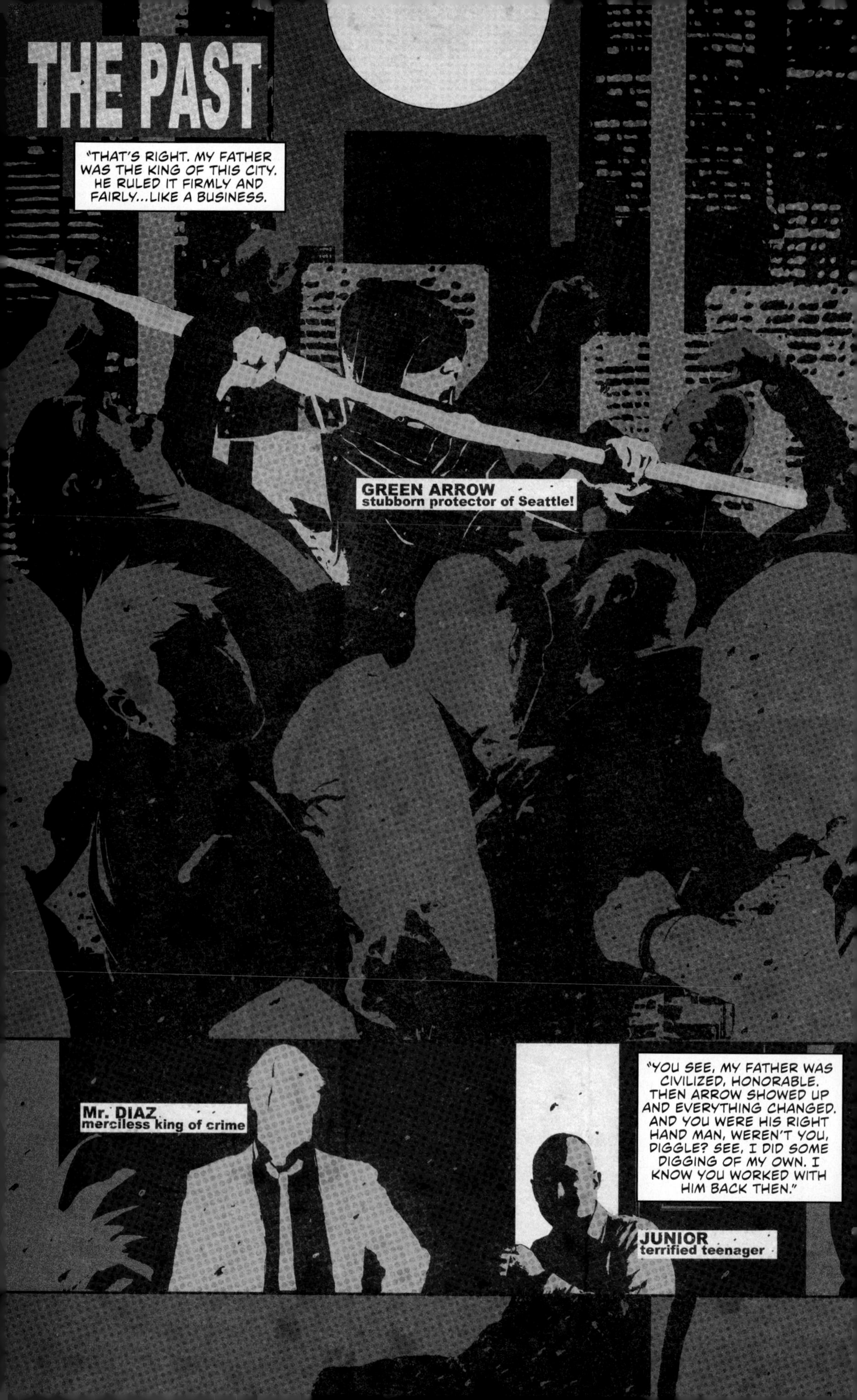
THE PAST
"THAT'S RIGHT. MY FATHER WAS THE KING OF THIS CITY. HE RULED IT FIRMLY AND FAIRLY...LIKE A BUSINESS.
GREEN ARROW stubborn protector of Seattle!
Mr. DIAZ merciless king of crime
"YOU SEE, MY FATHER WAS CIVILIZED, HONORABLE. THEN ARROW SHOWED UP AND EVERYTHING CHANGED. AND YOU WERE HIS RIGHT HAND MAN, WEREN'T YOU, DIGGLE? SEE, I DID SOME DIGGING OF MY OWN. I KNOW YOU WORKED WITH HIM BACK THEN."
JUNIOR terrified teenager

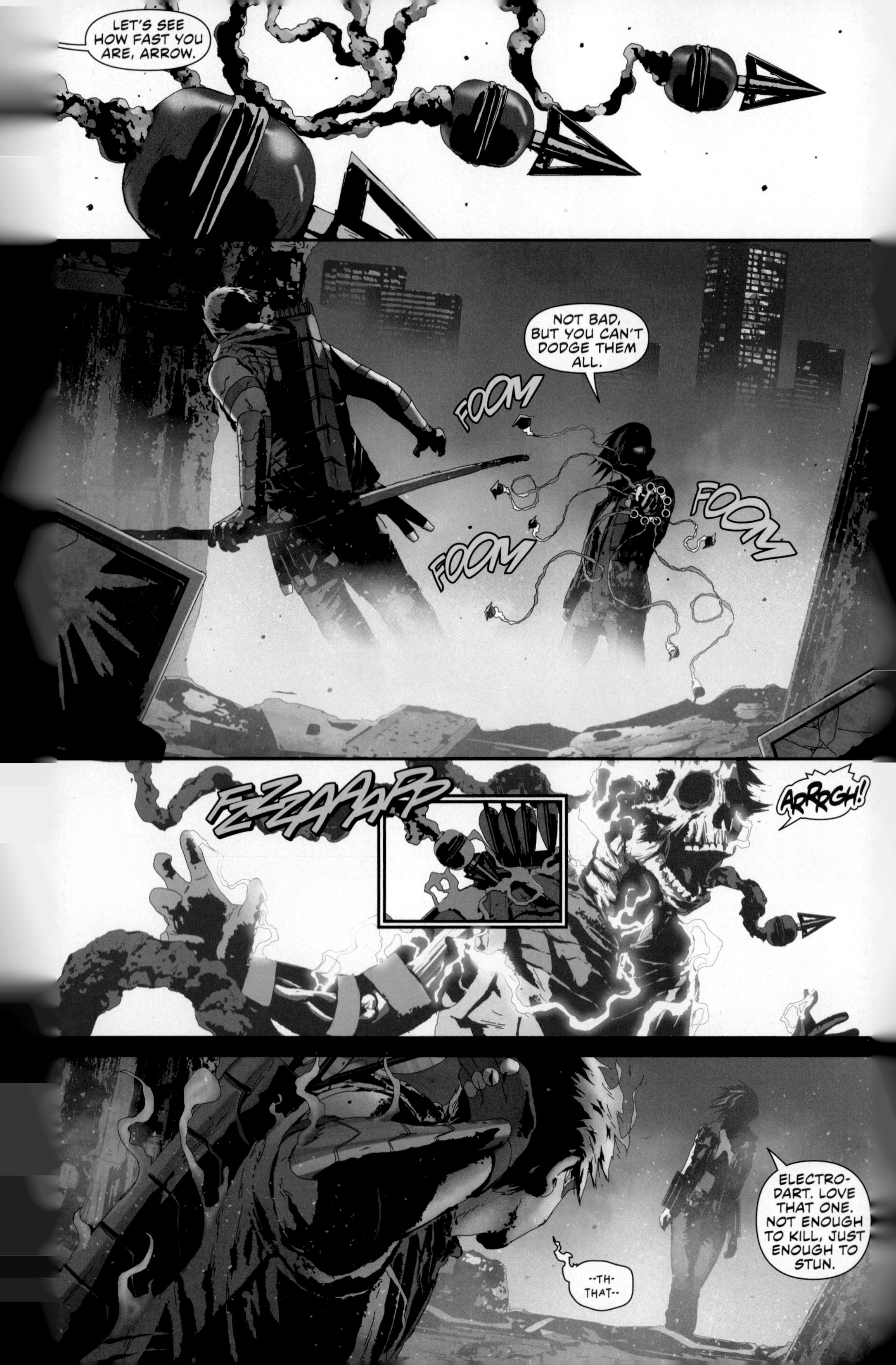
LET'S SEE HOW FAST YOU ARE, ARROW.
NOT BAD, BUT YOU CAN'T DODGE THEM ALL.
FOOM
FOOM
FOOM
FZZZAAAPP
ARRRGH!
ELECTRO-DART. LOVE THAT ONE. NOT ENOUGH TO KILL, JUST ENOUGH TO STUN.
--TH-THAT--

FWIP

THWP

THWP

THWP

UH-OH--
CLUSTER
FIRE!

RED
THU

CHOOM

CHOOM

CHOOM

LET'S TRY
THIS ONE--
FLASH-
DART!

FWOOSH

ARRGH!

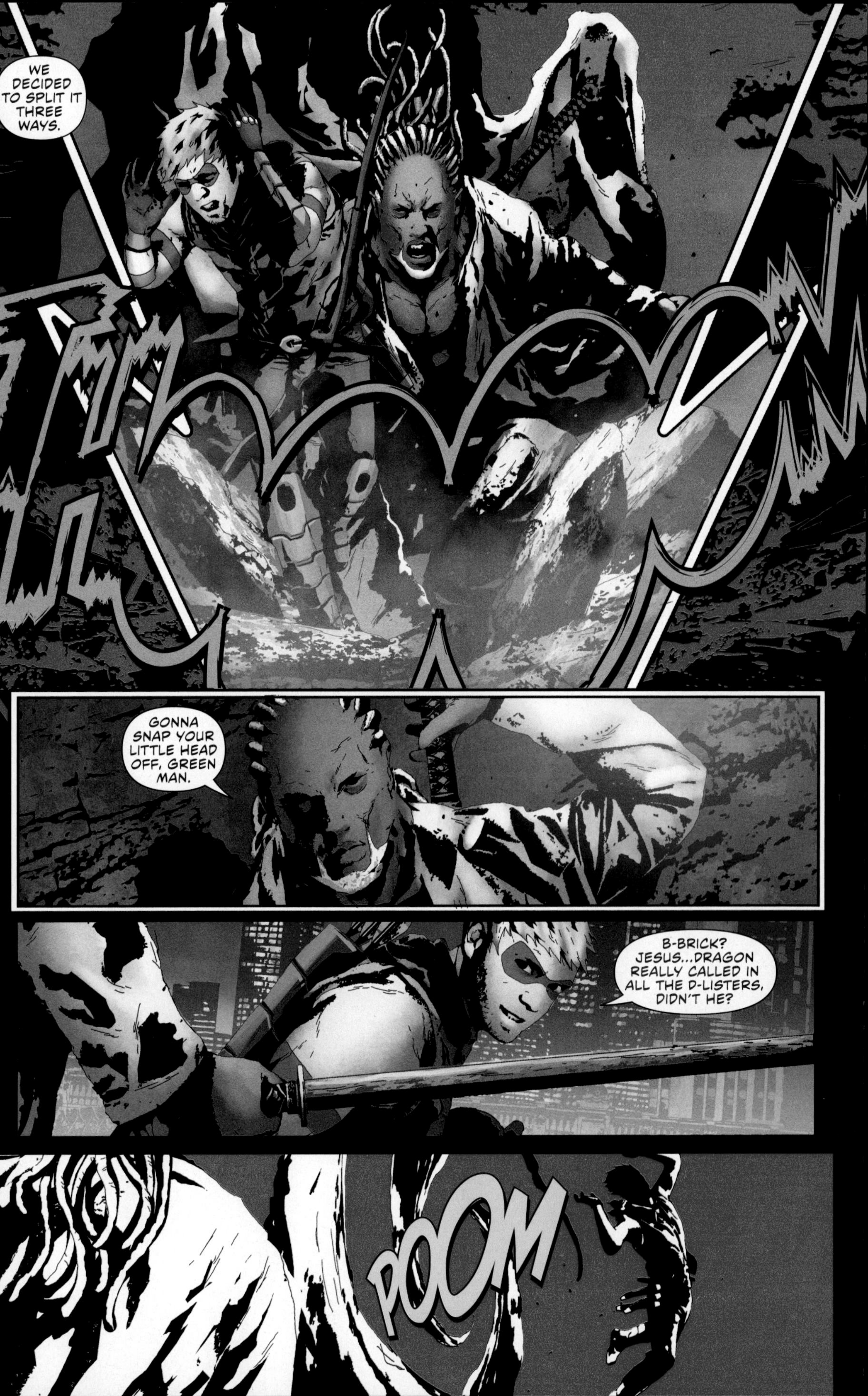

WE DECIDED TO SPLIT IT THREE WAYS.
GONNA SNAP YOUR LITTLE HEAD OFF, GREEN MAN.
B-BRICK? JESUS...DRAGON REALLY CALLED IN ALL THE D-LISTERS, DIDN'T HE?
POOM

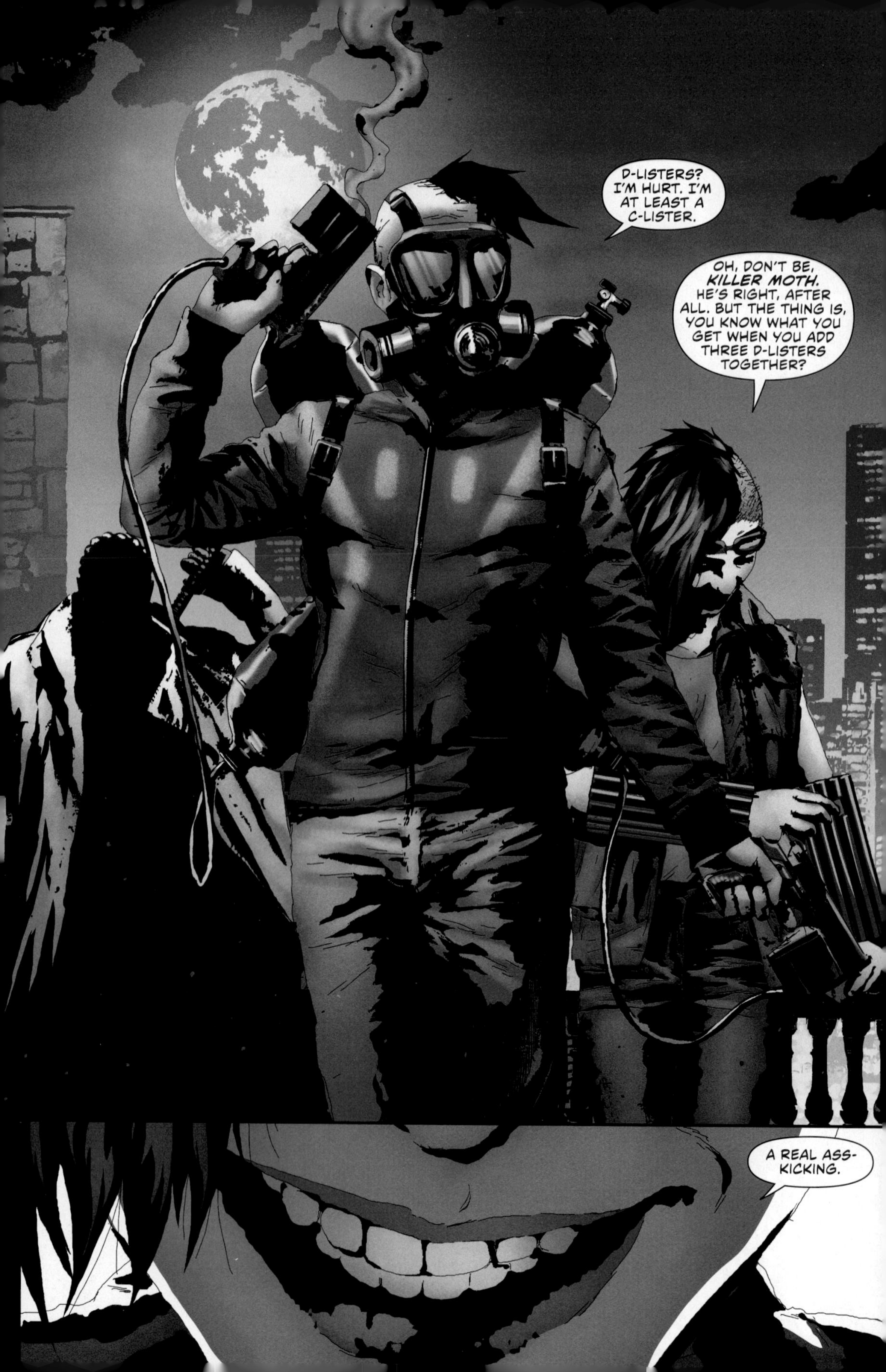
D-LISTERS? I'M HURT. I'M AT LEAST A C-LISTER.
OH, DON'T BE, KILLER MOTH. HE'S RIGHT, AFTER ALL. BUT THE THING IS, YOU KNOW WHAT YOU GET WHEN YOU ADD THREE D-LISTERS TOGETHER?
A REAL ASS-KICKING.

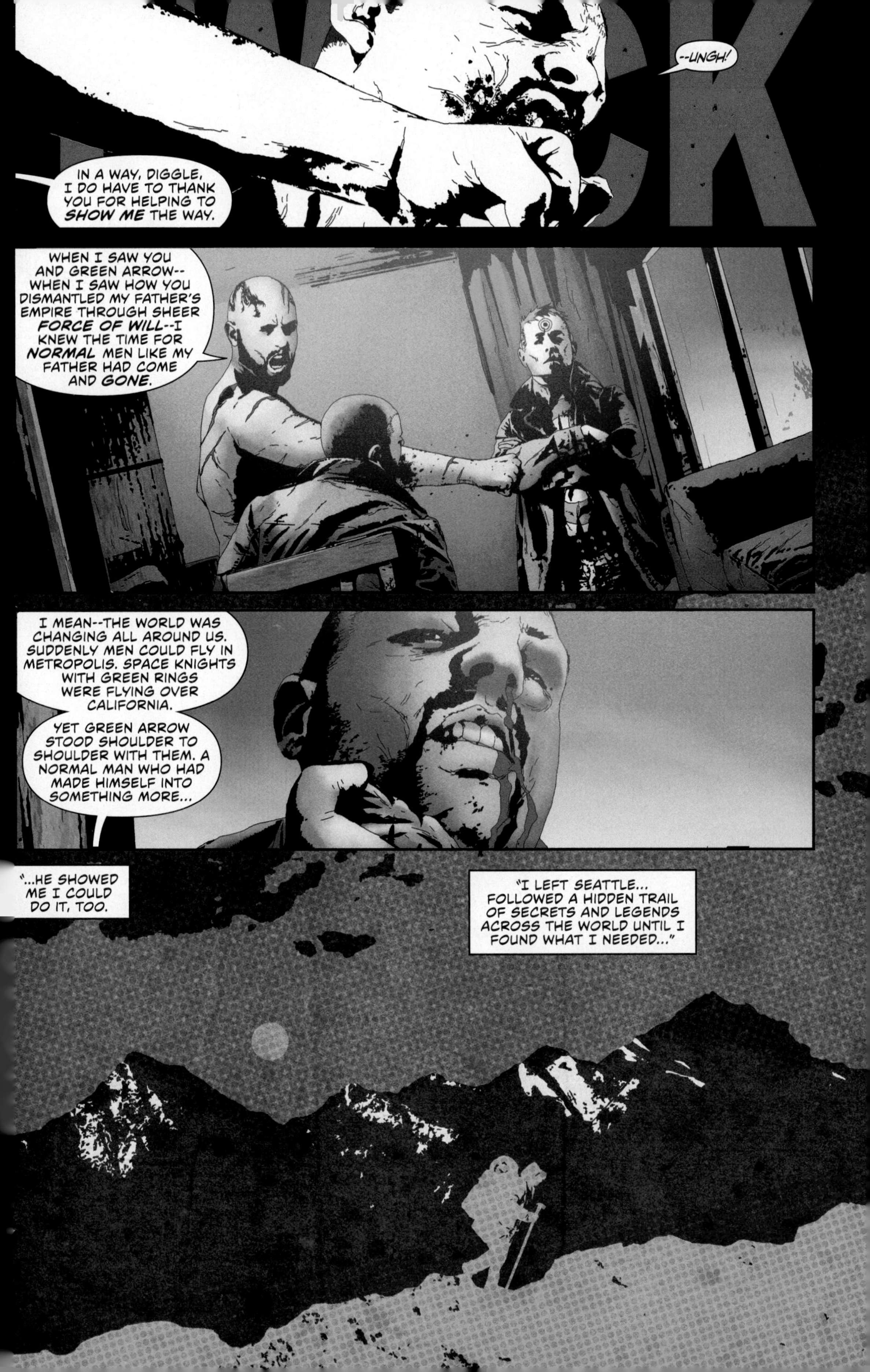
--UNGH!
IN A WAY, DIGGLE, I DO HAVE TO THANK YOU FOR HELPING TO *SHOW ME* THE WAY.
WHEN I SAW YOU AND GREEN ARROW-- WHEN I SAW HOW YOU DISMANTLED MY FATHER'S EMPIRE THROUGH SHEER *FORCE OF WILL*--I KNEW THE TIME FOR *NORMAL* MEN LIKE MY FATHER HAD COME AND *GONE*.
I MEAN--THE WORLD WAS CHANGING ALL AROUND US. SUDDENLY MEN COULD FLY IN METROPOLIS. SPACE KNIGHTS WITH GREEN RINGS WERE FLYING OVER CALIFORNIA.
YET GREEN ARROW STOOD SHOULDER TO SHOULDER WITH THEM. A NORMAL MAN WHO HAD MADE HIMSELF INTO SOMETHING MORE...
"...HE SHOWED ME I COULD DO IT, TOO.
"I LEFT SEATTLE... FOLLOWED A HIDDEN TRAIL OF SECRETS AND LEGENDS ACROSS THE WORLD UNTIL I FOUND WHAT I NEEDED..."

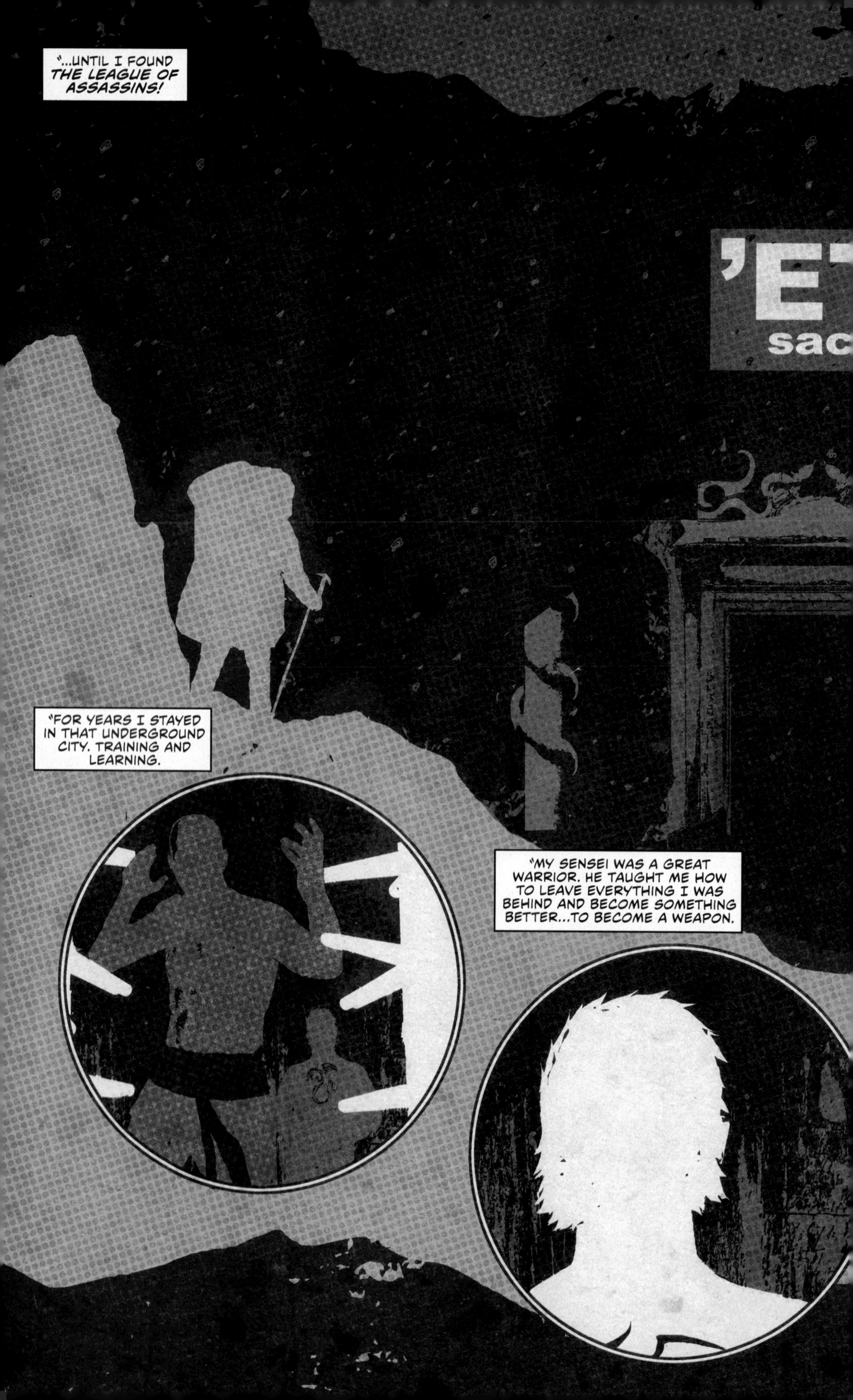
"...UNTIL I FOUND *THE LEAGUE OF ASSASSINS!*
'E
sac
"FOR YEARS I STAYED IN THAT UNDERGROUND CITY. TRAINING AND LEARNING.
"MY SENSEI WAS A GREAT WARRIOR. HE TAUGHT ME HOW TO LEAVE EVERYTHING I WAS BEHIND AND BECOME SOMETHING BETTER...TO BECOME A WEAPON.

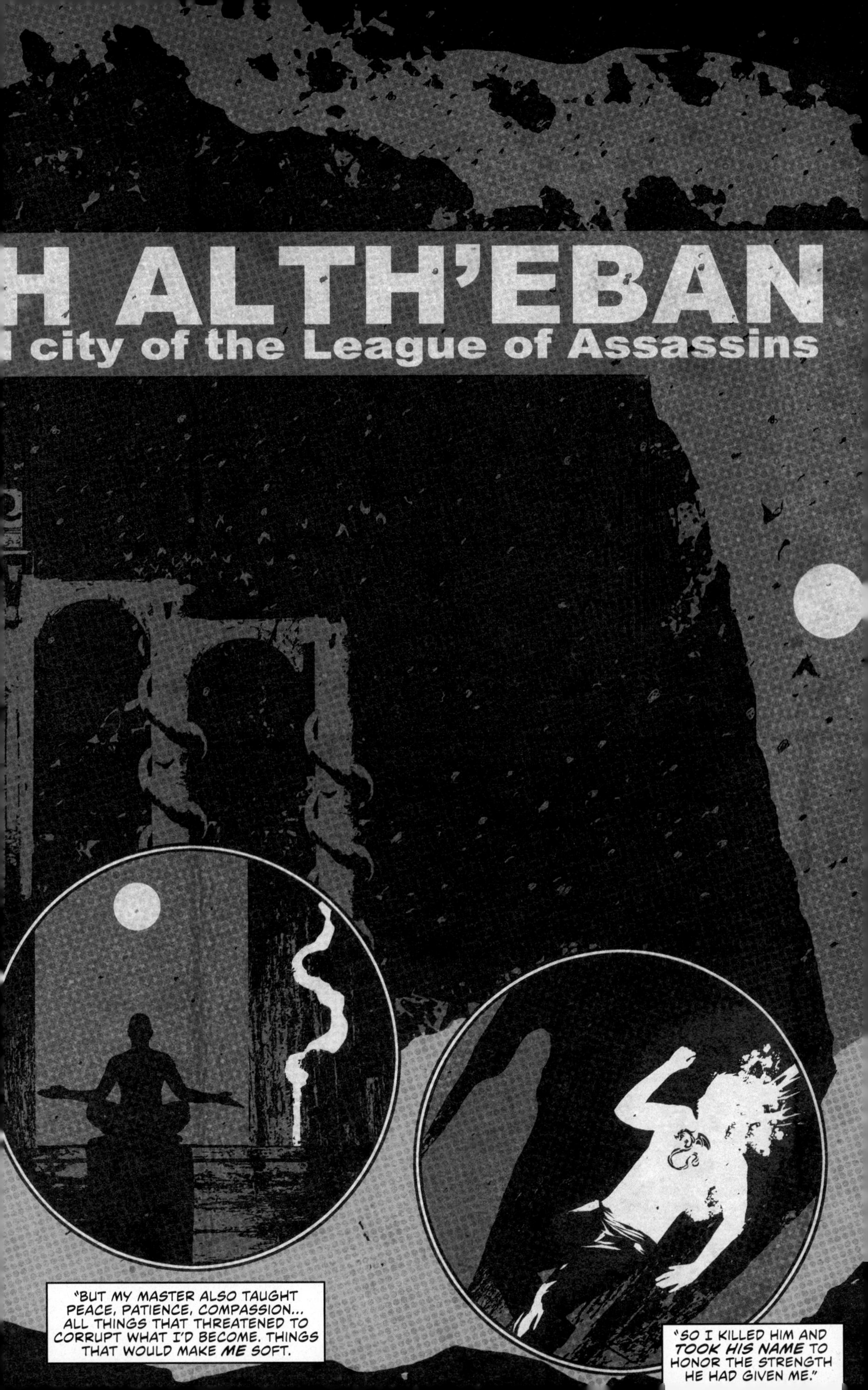

H ALTH'EBAN
city of the League of Assassins
"BUT MY MASTER ALSO TAUGHT PEACE, PATIENCE, COMPASSION... ALL THINGS THAT THREATENED TO CORRUPT WHAT I'D BECOME. THINGS THAT WOULD MAKE *ME* SOFT.
"SO I KILLED HIM AND ***TOOK HIS NAME*** TO HONOR THE STRENGTH HE HAD GIVEN ME."

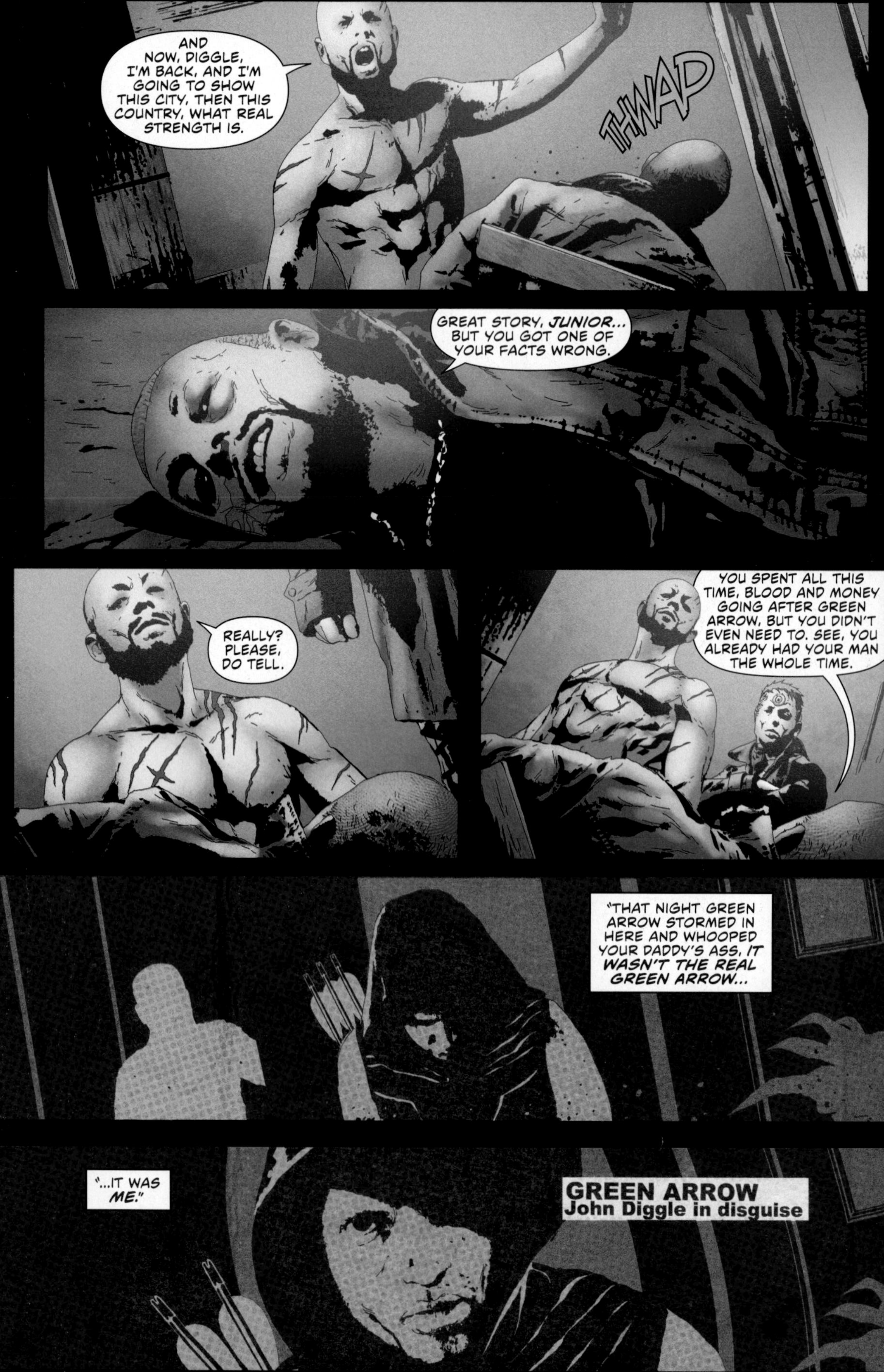

AND NOW, DIGGLE, I'M BACK, AND I'M GOING TO SHOW THIS CITY, THEN THIS COUNTRY, WHAT REAL STRENGTH IS.
THWAP
GREAT STORY, JUNIOR... BUT YOU GOT ONE OF YOUR FACTS WRONG.
REALLY? PLEASE, DO TELL.
YOU SPENT ALL THIS TIME, BLOOD AND MONEY GOING AFTER GREEN ARROW, BUT YOU DIDN'T EVEN NEED TO. SEE, YOU ALREADY HAD YOUR MAN THE WHOLE TIME.
"THAT NIGHT GREEN ARROW STORMED IN HERE AND WHOOPED YOUR DADDY'S ASS, IT WASN'T THE REAL GREEN ARROW...
"...IT WAS ME."
GREEN ARROW
John Diggle in disguise

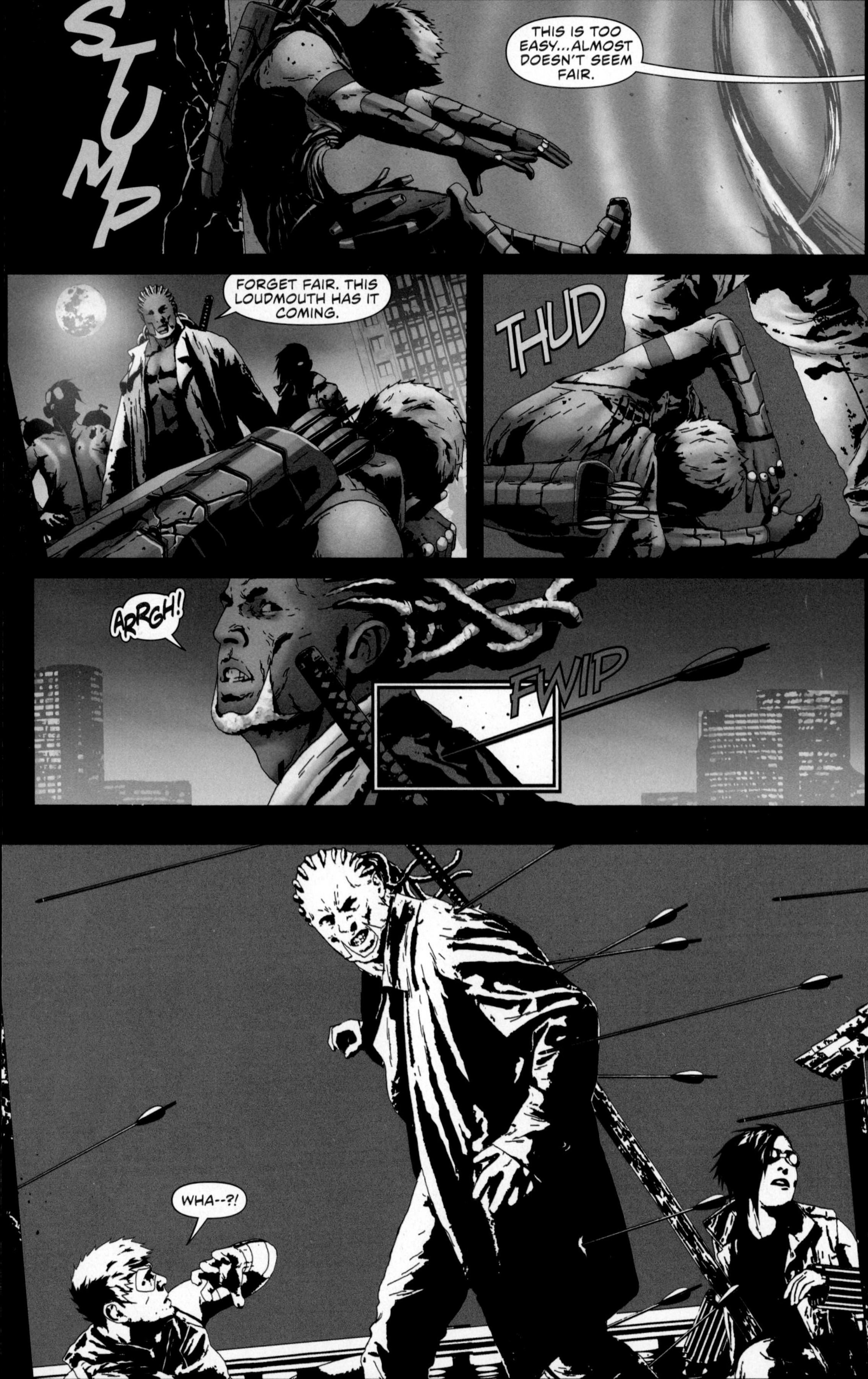
STUMP
THIS IS TOO EASY...ALMOST DOESN'T SEEM FAIR.
FORGET FAIR. THIS LOUDMOUTH HAS IT COMING.
THUD
ARRGH!
FWIP
WHA--?!

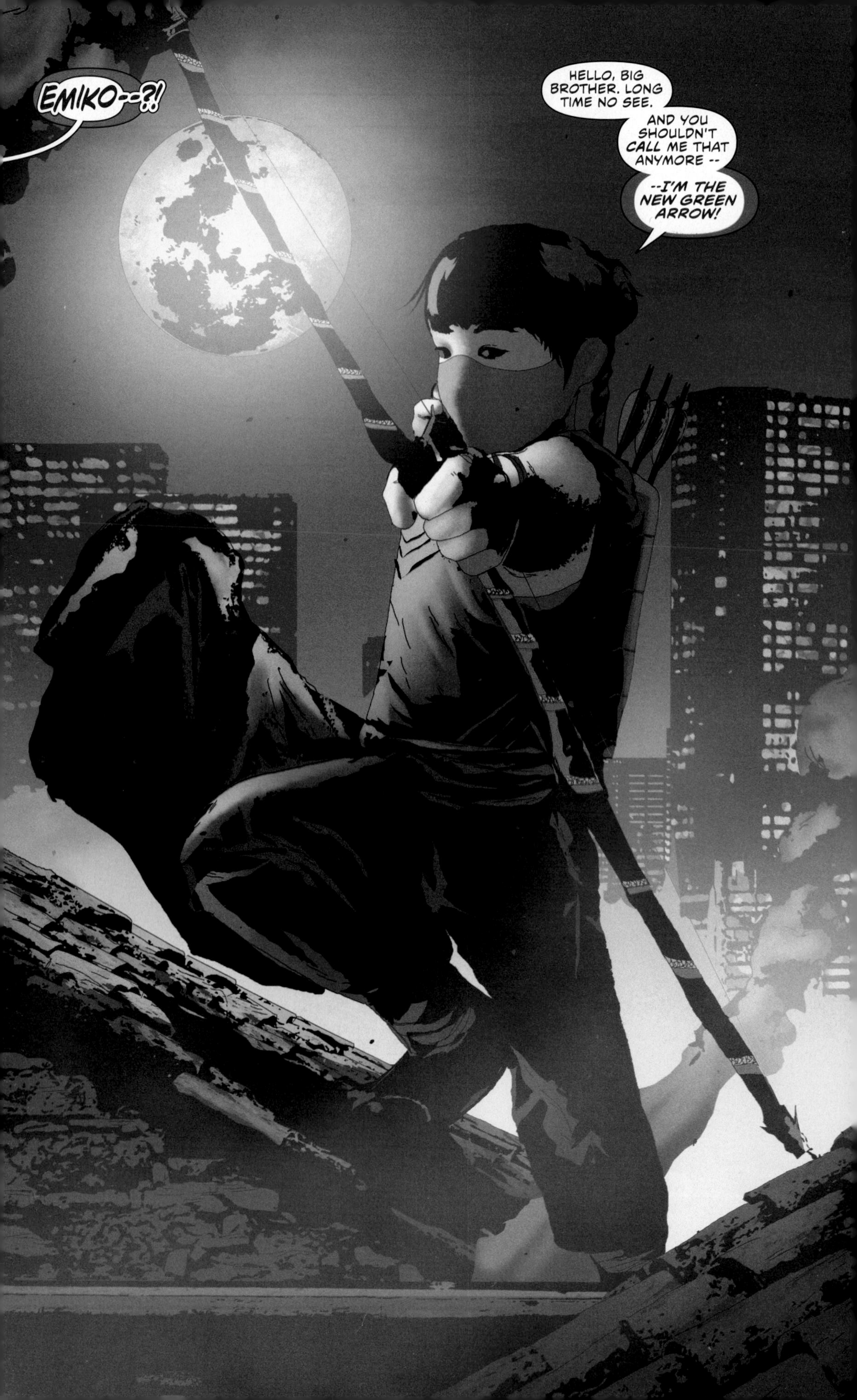
EMIKO--?!
HELLO, BIG BROTHER. LONG TIME NO SEE.
AND YOU SHOULDN'T CALL ME THAT ANYMORE --
--I'M THE NEW GREEN ARROW!

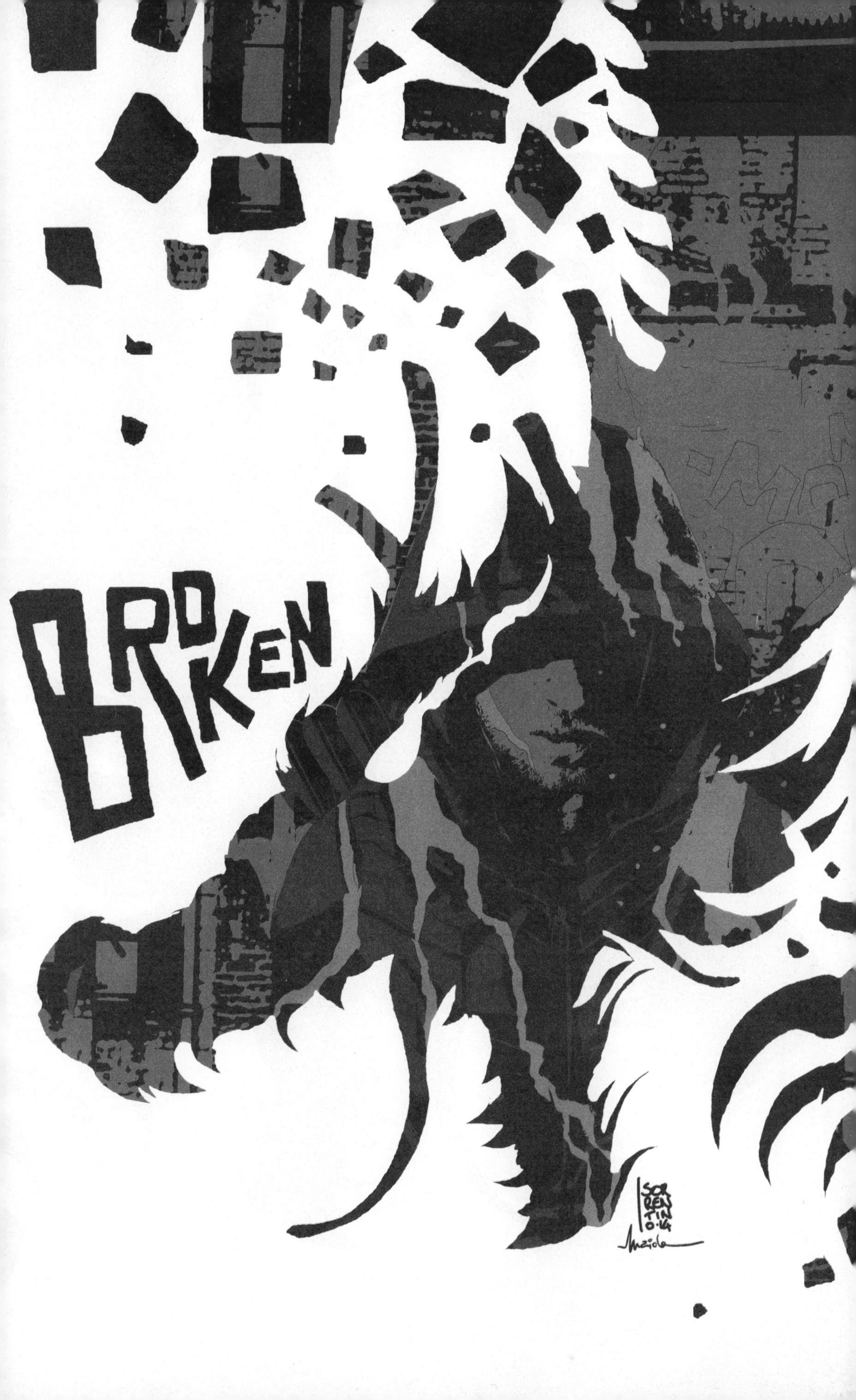
BROKEN

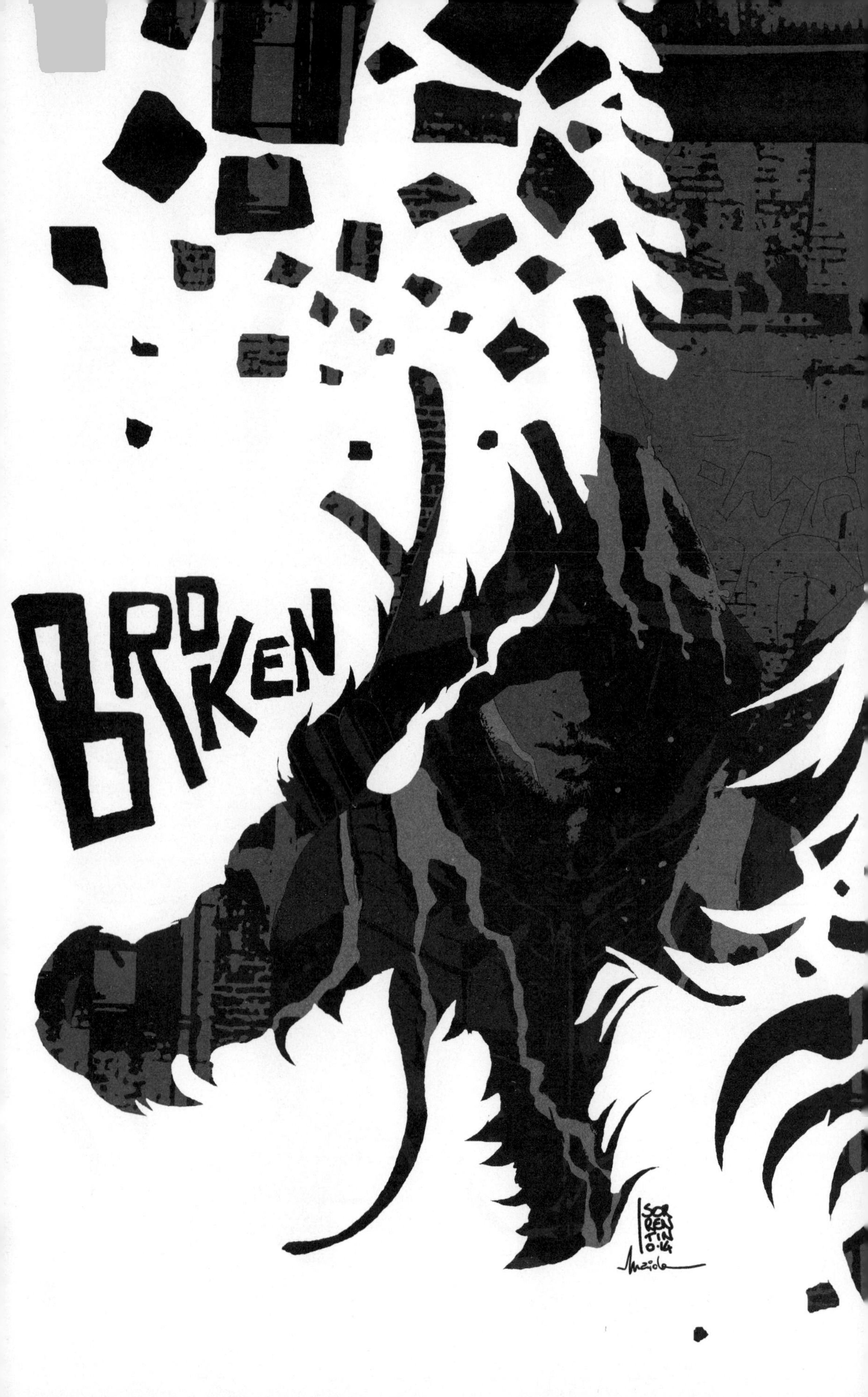
BROKEN

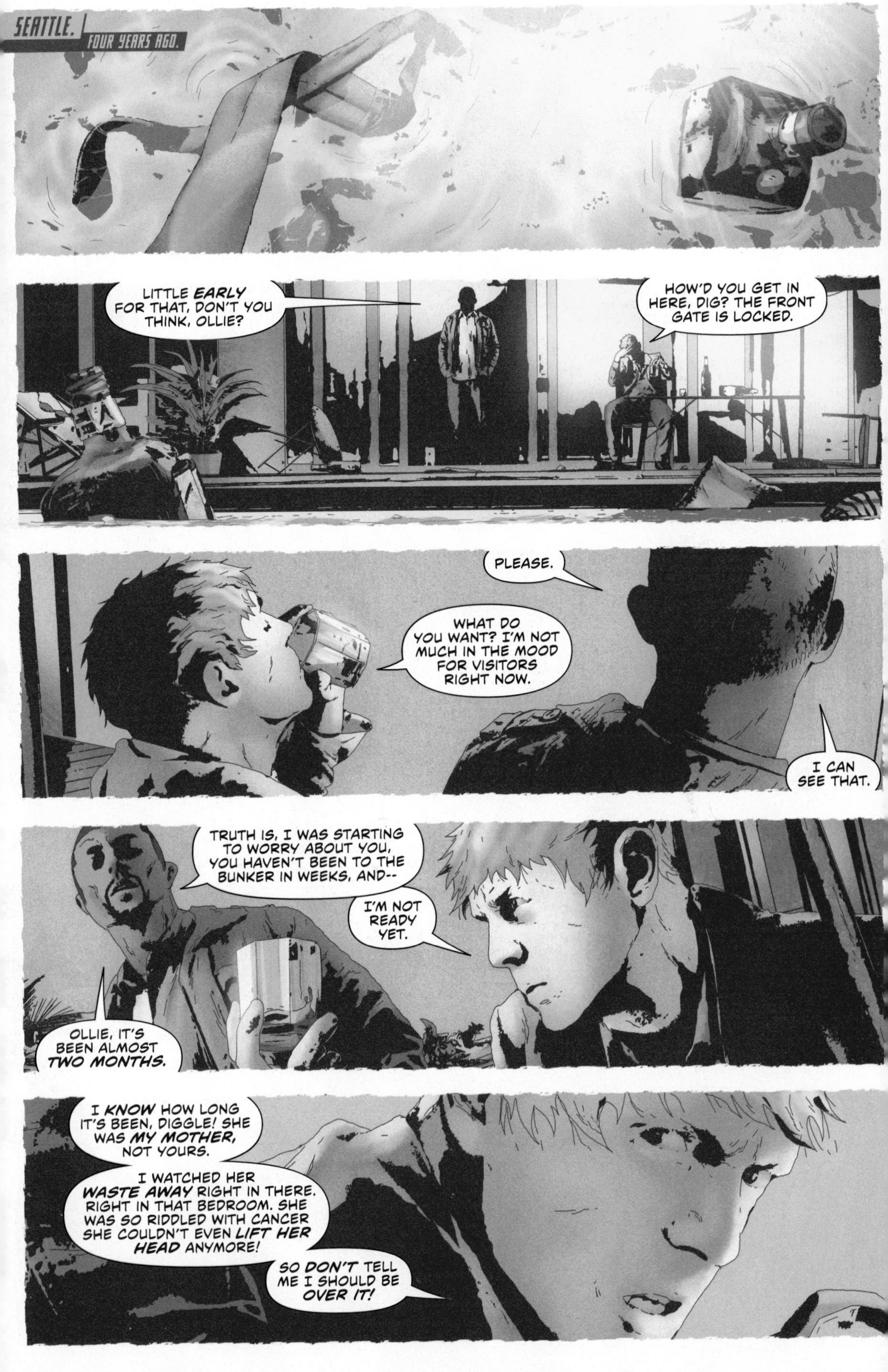
SEATTLE.
FOUR YEARS AGO.
LITTLE EARLY FOR THAT, DON'T YOU THINK, OLLIE?
HOW'D YOU GET IN HERE, DIG? THE FRONT GATE IS LOCKED.
PLEASE.
WHAT DO YOU WANT? I'M NOT MUCH IN THE MOOD FOR VISITORS RIGHT NOW.
I CAN SEE THAT.
TRUTH IS, I WAS STARTING TO WORRY ABOUT YOU, YOU HAVEN'T BEEN TO THE BUNKER IN WEEKS, AND--
I'M NOT READY YET.
OLLIE, IT'S BEEN ALMOST TWO MONTHS.
I KNOW HOW LONG IT'S BEEN, DIGGLE! SHE WAS MY MOTHER, NOT YOURS.
I WATCHED HER WASTE AWAY RIGHT IN THERE. RIGHT IN THAT BEDROOM. SHE WAS SO RIDDLED WITH CANCER SHE COULDN'T EVEN LIFT HER HEAD ANYMORE!
SO DON'T TELL ME I SHOULD BE OVER IT!

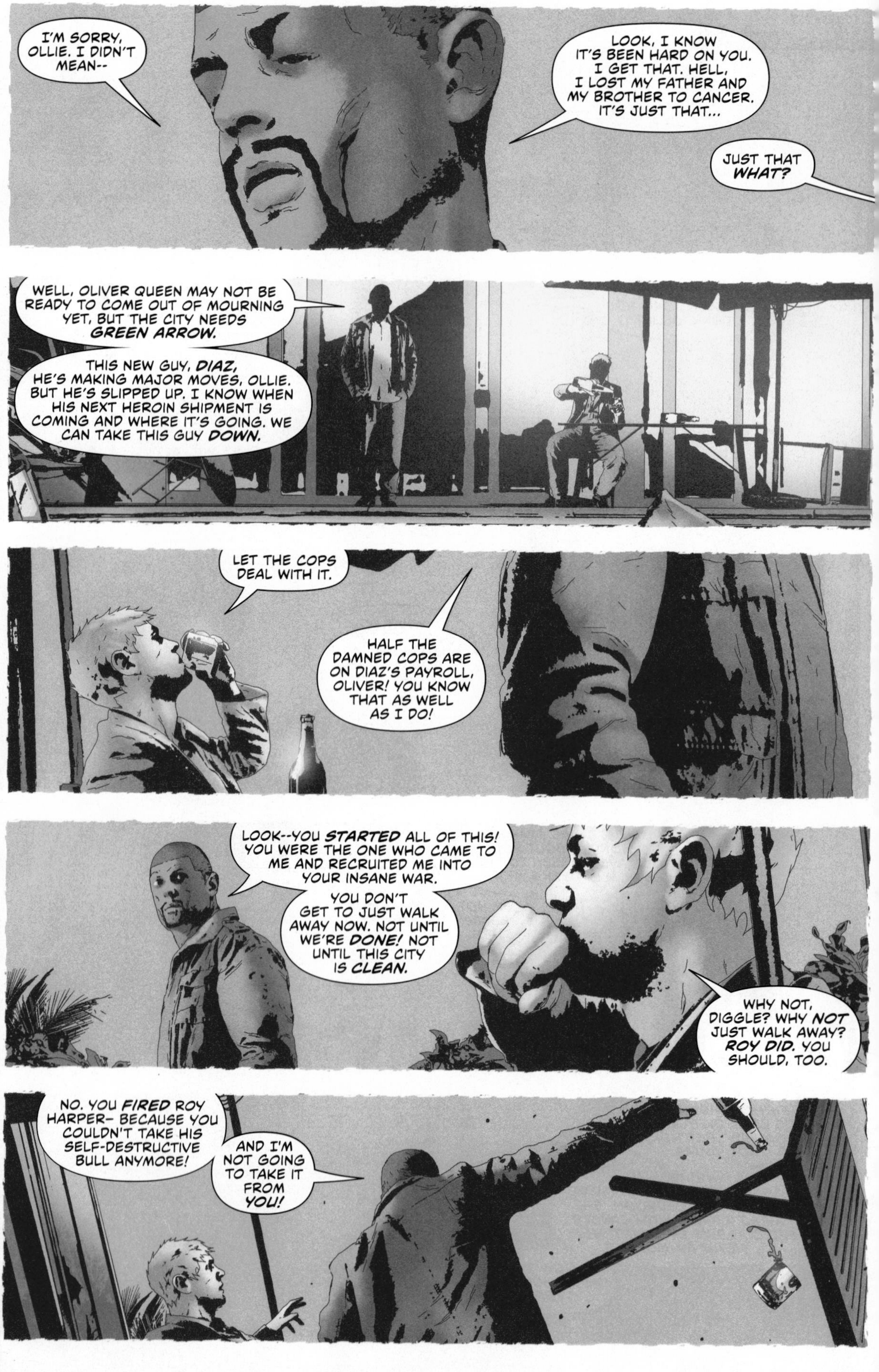
I'M SORRY, OLLIE. I DIDN'T MEAN--
LOOK, I KNOW IT'S BEEN HARD ON YOU. I GET THAT. HELL, I LOST MY FATHER AND MY BROTHER TO CANCER. IT'S JUST THAT...
JUST THAT *WHAT?*
WELL, OLIVER QUEEN MAY NOT BE READY TO COME OUT OF MOURNING YET, BUT THE CITY NEEDS *GREEN ARROW.*
THIS NEW GUY, *DIAZ,* HE'S MAKING MAJOR MOVES, OLLIE. BUT HE'S SLIPPED UP. I KNOW WHEN HIS NEXT HEROIN SHIPMENT IS COMING AND WHERE IT'S GOING. WE CAN TAKE THIS GUY *DOWN.*
LET THE COPS DEAL WITH IT.
HALF THE DAMNED COPS ARE ON DIAZ'S PAYROLL, OLIVER! YOU KNOW THAT AS WELL AS I DO!
LOOK--YOU *STARTED* ALL OF THIS! YOU WERE THE ONE WHO CAME TO ME AND RECRUITED ME INTO YOUR INSANE WAR.
YOU DON'T GET TO JUST WALK AWAY NOW. NOT UNTIL WE'RE *DONE!* NOT UNTIL THIS CITY IS *CLEAN.*
WHY NOT, DIGGLE? WHY *NOT* JUST WALK AWAY? *ROY DID.* YOU SHOULD, TOO.
NO. YOU *FIRED* ROY HARPER– BECAUSE YOU COULDN'T TAKE HIS SELF-DESTRUCTIVE BULL ANYMORE!
AND I'M NOT GOING TO TAKE IT FROM *YOU!*

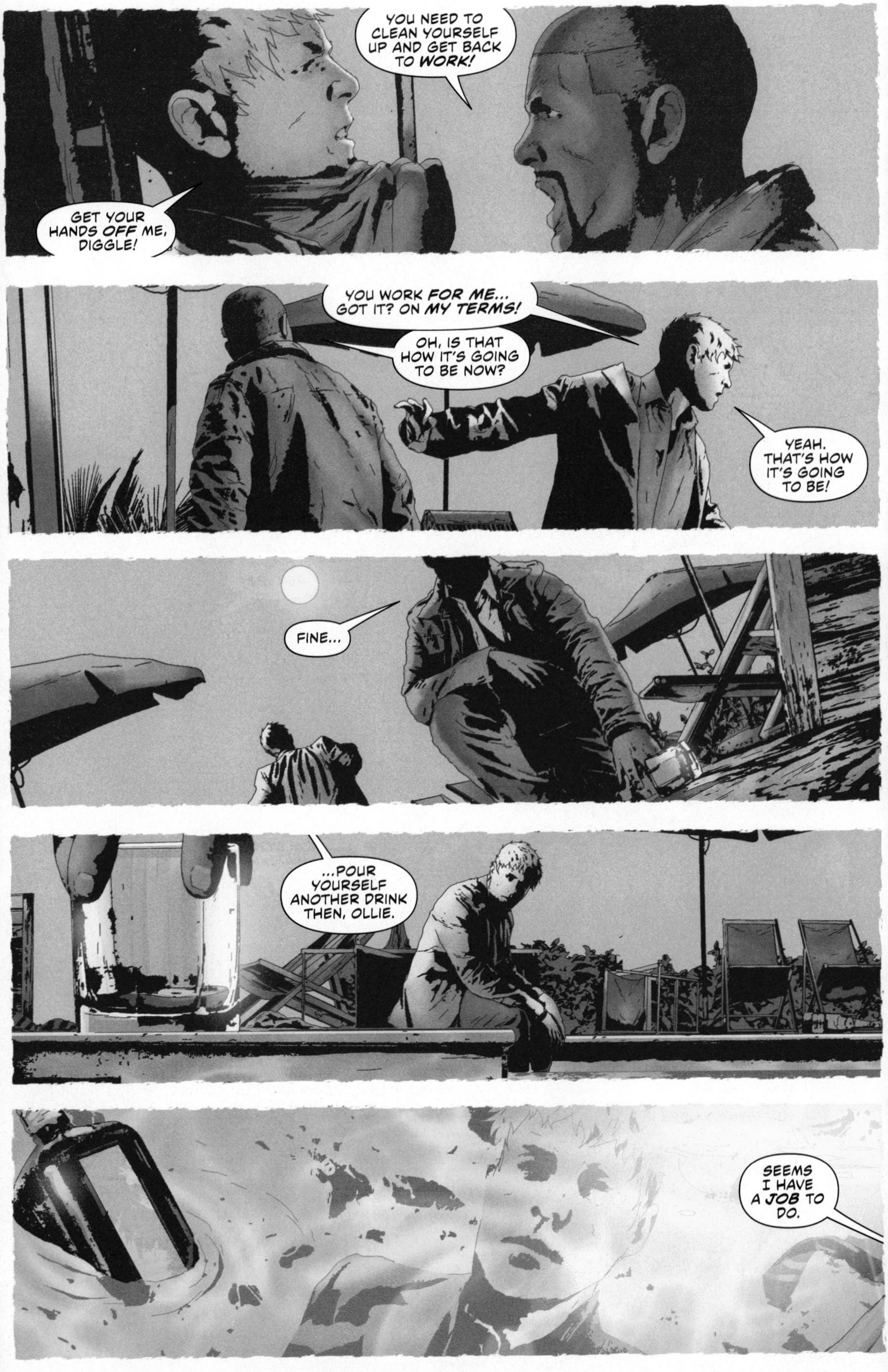
YOU NEED TO CLEAN YOURSELF UP AND GET BACK TO WORK!
GET YOUR HANDS OFF ME, DIGGLE!
YOU WORK FOR ME... GOT IT? ON MY TERMS!
OH, IS THAT HOW IT'S GOING TO BE NOW?
YEAH. THAT'S HOW IT'S GOING TO BE!
FINE...
...POUR YOURSELF ANOTHER DRINK THEN, OLLIE.
SEEMS I HAVE A JOB TO DO.

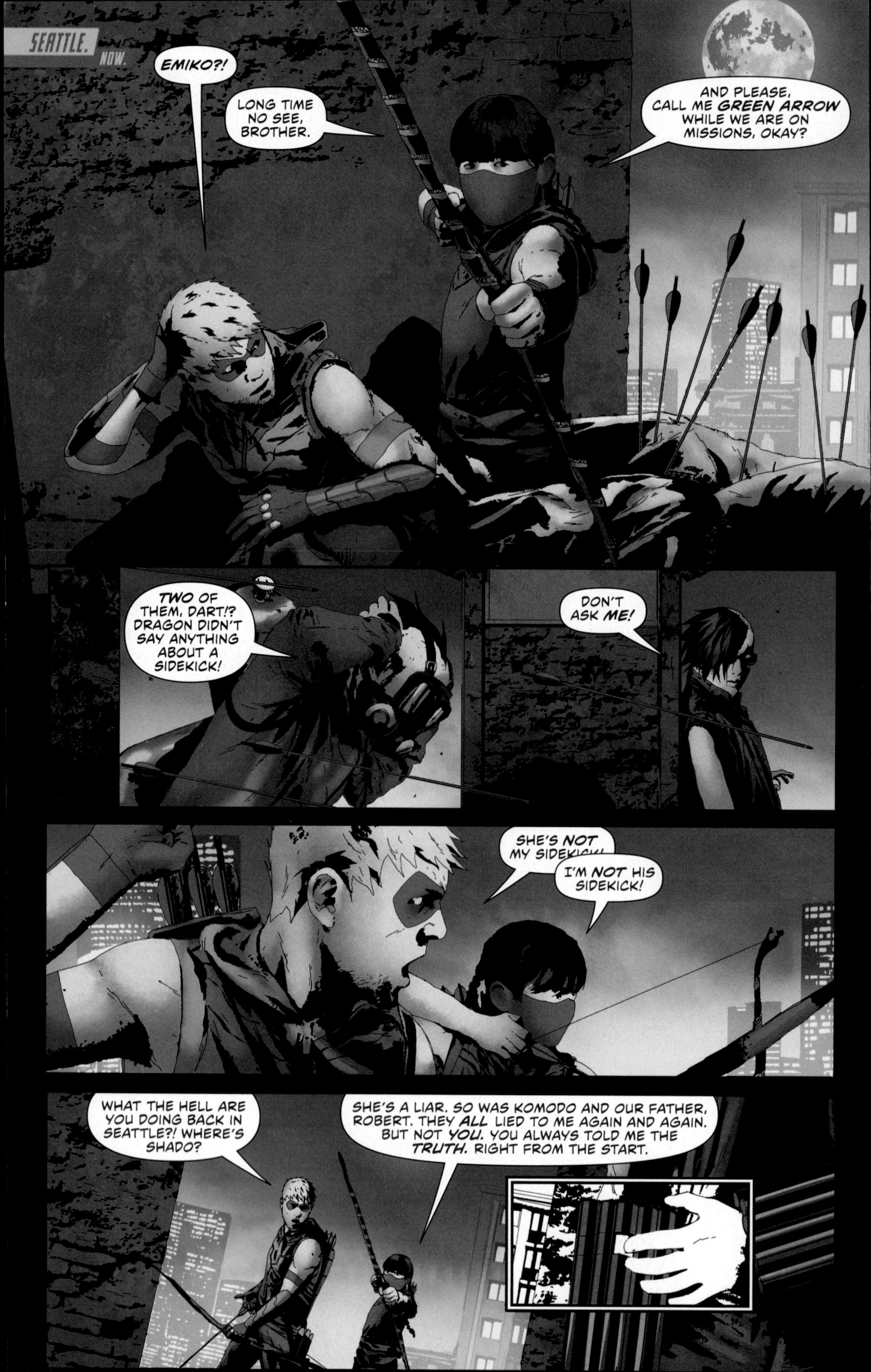
SEATTLE.
NOW.
EMIKO?!
LONG TIME NO SEE, BROTHER.
AND PLEASE, CALL ME GREEN ARROW WHILE WE ARE ON MISSIONS, OKAY?
TWO OF THEM, DART!? DRAGON DIDN'T SAY ANYTHING ABOUT A SIDEKICK!
DON'T ASK ME!
SHE'S NOT MY SIDEKICK!
I'M NOT HIS SIDEKICK!
WHAT THE HELL ARE YOU DOING BACK IN SEATTLE?! WHERE'S SHADO?
SHE'S A LIAR. SO WAS KOMODO AND OUR FATHER, ROBERT. THEY ALL LIED TO ME AGAIN AND AGAIN. BUT NOT YOU. YOU ALWAYS TOLD ME THE TRUTH. RIGHT FROM THE START.

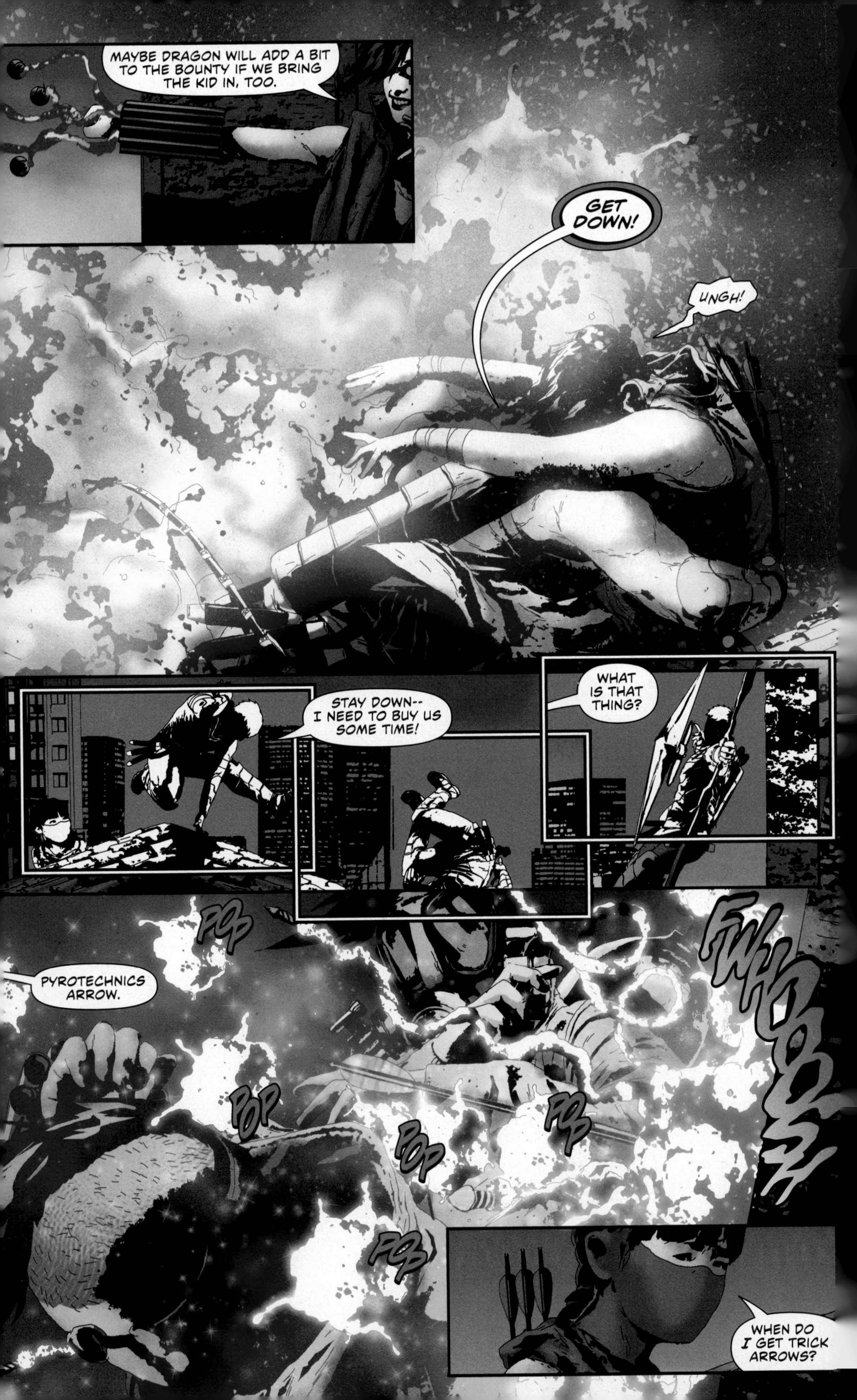
MAYBE DRAGON WILL ADD A BIT TO THE BOUNTY IF WE BRING THE KID IN, TOO.
GET DOWN!
UNGH!
STAY DOWN-- I NEED TO BUY US SOME TIME!
WHAT IS THAT THING?
POP
PYROTECHNICS ARROW.
FWHOOOOM
POP
POP
POP
POP
WHEN DO *I* GET TRICK ARROWS?

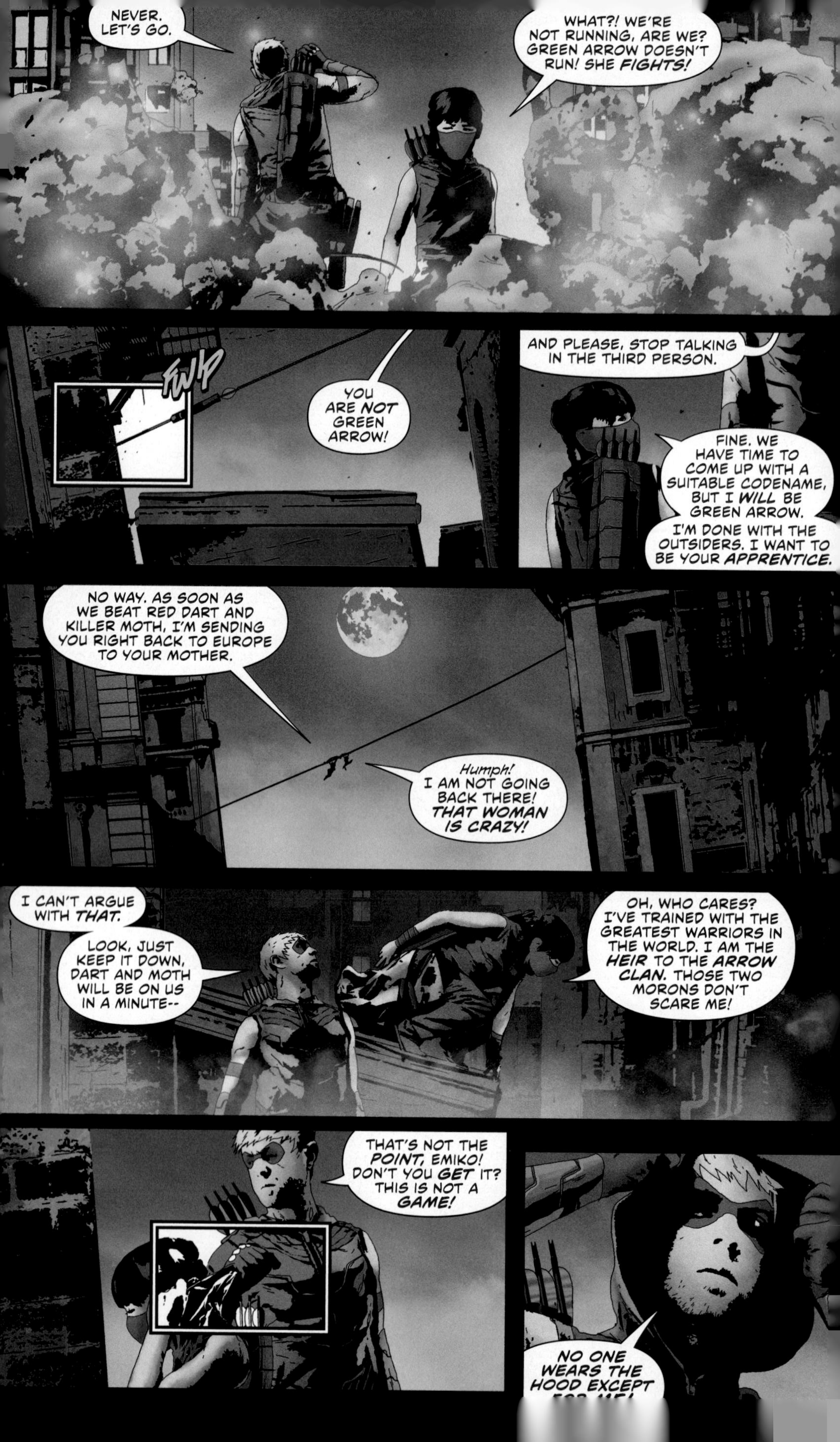
NEVER. LET'S GO.
WHAT?! WE'RE NOT RUNNING, ARE WE? GREEN ARROW DOESN'T RUN! SHE FIGHTS!
FWIP
YOU ARE NOT GREEN ARROW!
AND PLEASE, STOP TALKING IN THE THIRD PERSON.
FINE. WE HAVE TIME TO COME UP WITH A SUITABLE CODENAME, BUT I WILL BE GREEN ARROW.
I'M DONE WITH THE OUTSIDERS. I WANT TO BE YOUR APPRENTICE.
NO WAY. AS SOON AS WE BEAT RED DART AND KILLER MOTH, I'M SENDING YOU RIGHT BACK TO EUROPE TO YOUR MOTHER.
Humph! I AM NOT GOING BACK THERE! THAT WOMAN IS CRAZY!
I CAN'T ARGUE WITH THAT.
LOOK, JUST KEEP IT DOWN, DART AND MOTH WILL BE ON US IN A MINUTE--
OH, WHO CARES? I'VE TRAINED WITH THE GREATEST WARRIORS IN THE WORLD. I AM THE HEIR TO THE ARROW CLAN. THOSE TWO MORONS DON'T SCARE ME!
THAT'S NOT THE POINT, EMIKO! DON'T YOU GET IT? THIS IS NOT A GAME!
NO ONE WEARS THE HOOD EXCEPT

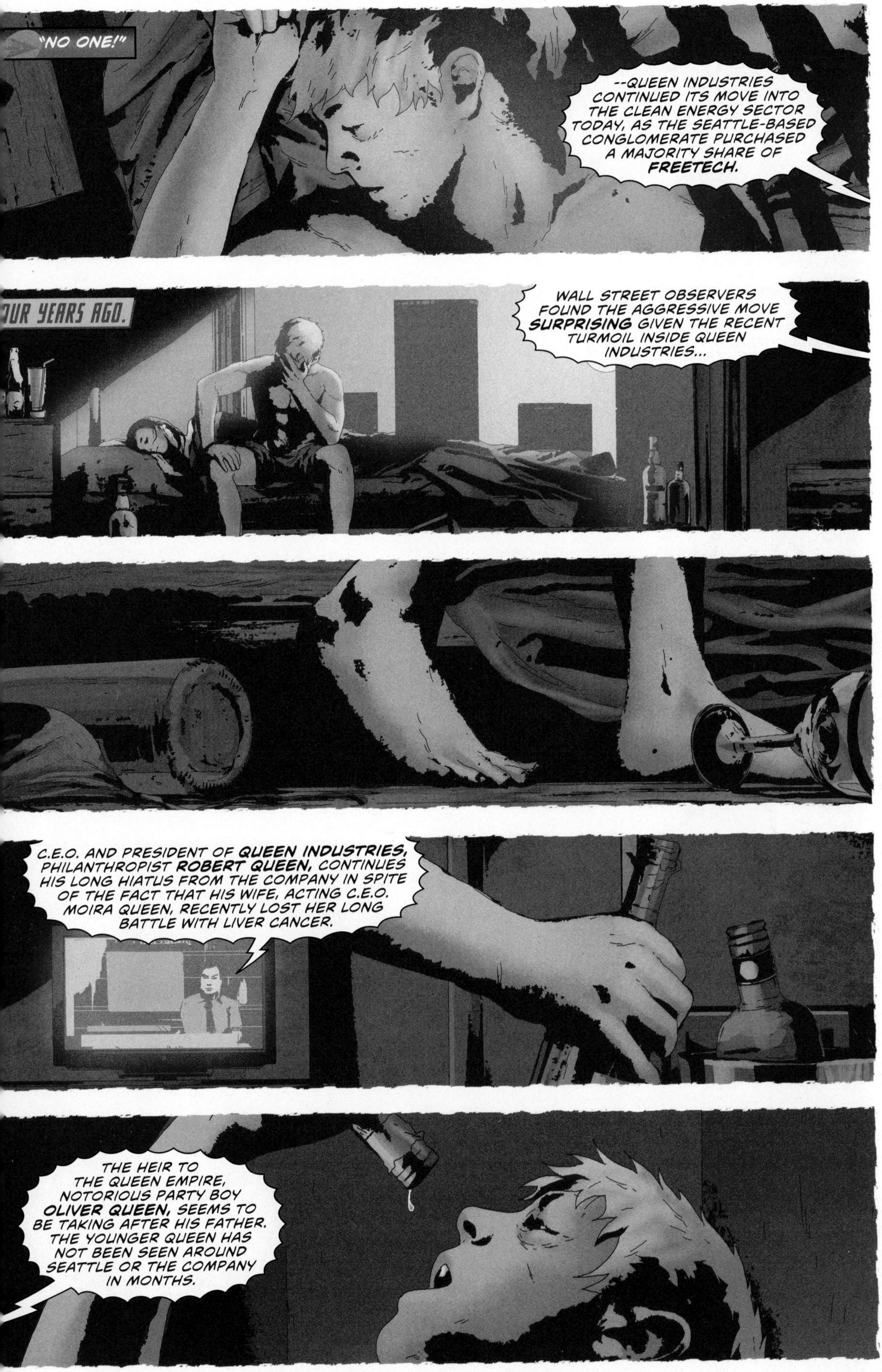
"NO ONE!"
--QUEEN INDUSTRIES CONTINUED ITS MOVE INTO THE CLEAN ENERGY SECTOR TODAY, AS THE SEATTLE-BASED CONGLOMERATE PURCHASED A MAJORITY SHARE OF FREETECH.
OUR YEARS AGO.
WALL STREET OBSERVERS FOUND THE AGGRESSIVE MOVE SURPRISING GIVEN THE RECENT TURMOIL INSIDE QUEEN INDUSTRIES...
C.E.O. AND PRESIDENT OF QUEEN INDUSTRIES, PHILANTHROPIST ROBERT QUEEN, CONTINUES HIS LONG HIATUS FROM THE COMPANY IN SPITE OF THE FACT THAT HIS WIFE, ACTING C.E.O. MOIRA QUEEN, RECENTLY LOST HER LONG BATTLE WITH LIVER CANCER.
THE HEIR TO THE QUEEN EMPIRE, NOTORIOUS PARTY BOY OLIVER QUEEN, SEEMS TO BE TAKING AFTER HIS FATHER. THE YOUNGER QUEEN HAS NOT BEEN SEEN AROUND SEATTLE OR THE COMPANY IN MONTHS.

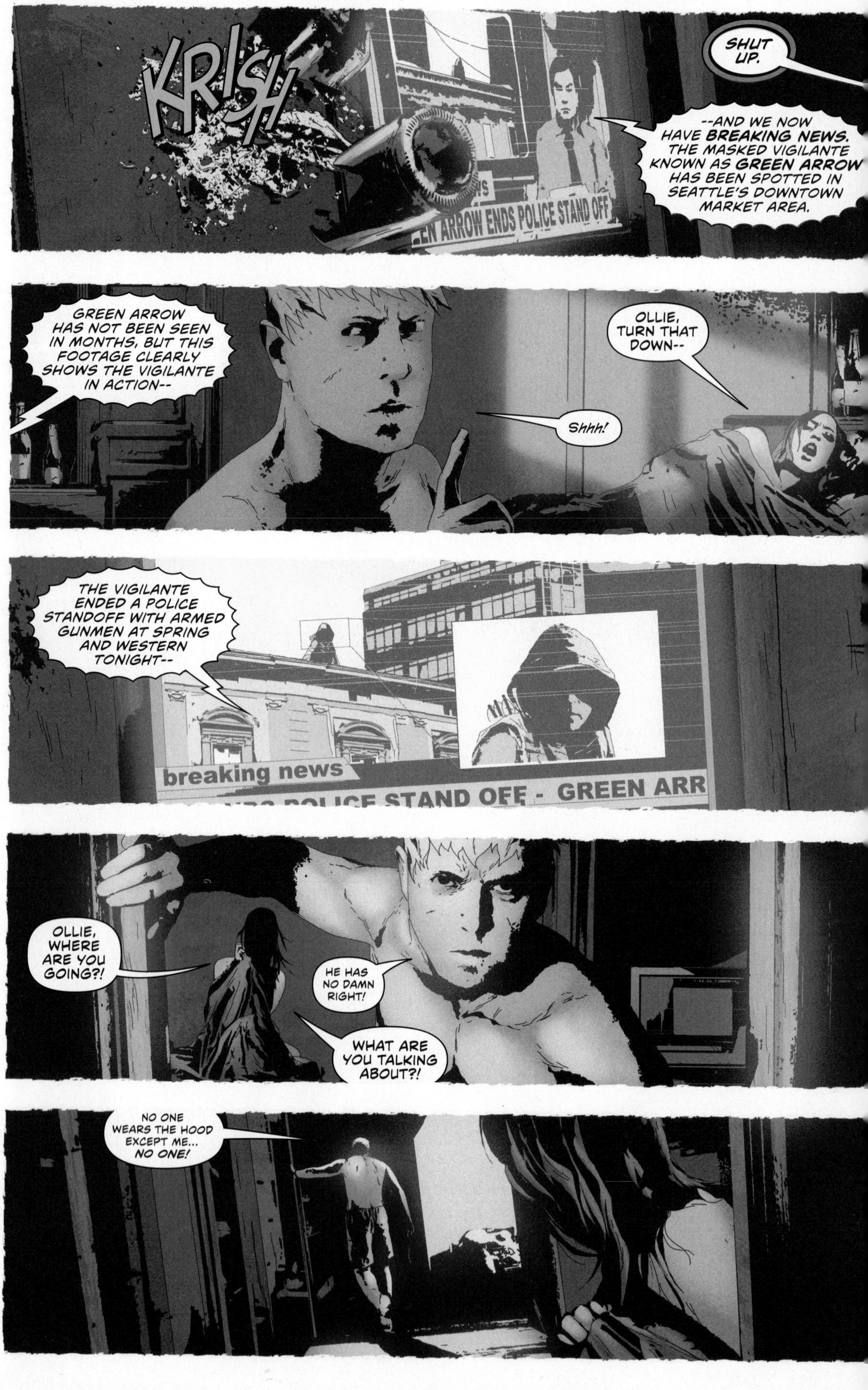
KRISH
SHUT UP.
--AND WE NOW HAVE BREAKING NEWS. THE MASKED VIGILANTE KNOWN AS GREEN ARROW HAS BEEN SPOTTED IN SEATTLE'S DOWNTOWN MARKET AREA.
EN ARROW ENDS POLICE STAND OFF
GREEN ARROW HAS NOT BEEN SEEN IN MONTHS, BUT THIS FOOTAGE CLEARLY SHOWS THE VIGILANTE IN ACTION--
OLLIE, TURN THAT DOWN--
Shhh!
THE VIGILANTE ENDED A POLICE STANDOFF WITH ARMED GUNMEN AT SPRING AND WESTERN TONIGHT--
breaking news
POLICE STAND OFF - GREEN ARR
OLLIE, WHERE ARE YOU GOING?!
HE HAS NO DAMN RIGHT!
WHAT ARE YOU TALKING ABOUT?!
NO ONE WEARS THE HOOD EXCEPT ME... NO ONE!

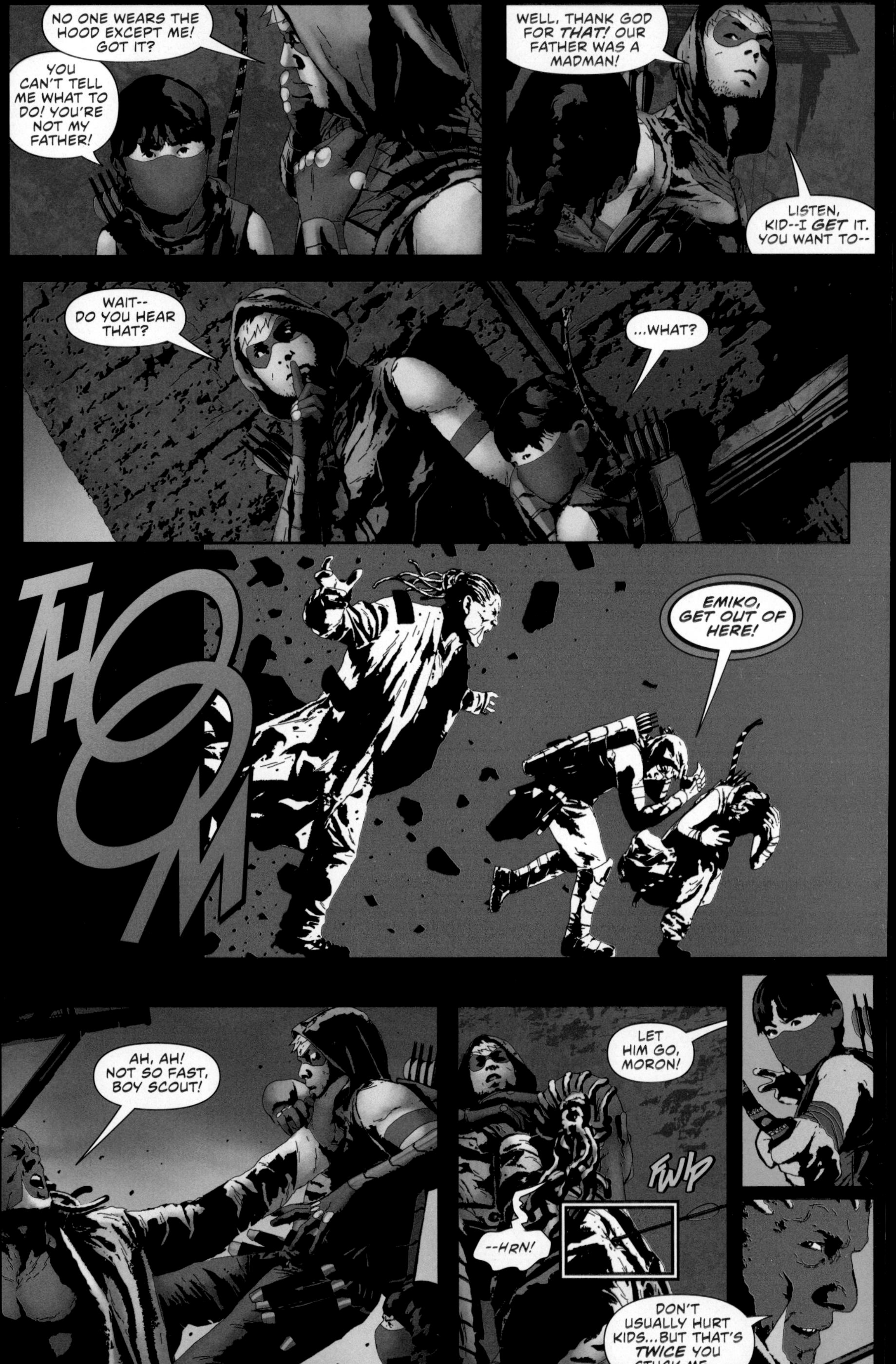
NO ONE WEARS THE HOOD EXCEPT ME! GOT IT?
YOU CAN'T TELL ME WHAT TO DO! YOU'RE NOT MY FATHER!
WELL, THANK GOD FOR THAT! OUR FATHER WAS A MADMAN!
LISTEN, KID--I GET IT. YOU WANT TO--
WAIT-- DO YOU HEAR THAT?
...WHAT?
THOOM
EMIKO, GET OUT OF HERE!
AH, AH! NOT SO FAST, BOY SCOUT!
LET HIM GO, MORON!
FWIP
--HRN!
DON'T USUALLY HURT KIDS...BUT THAT'S TWICE YOU STUCK ME...

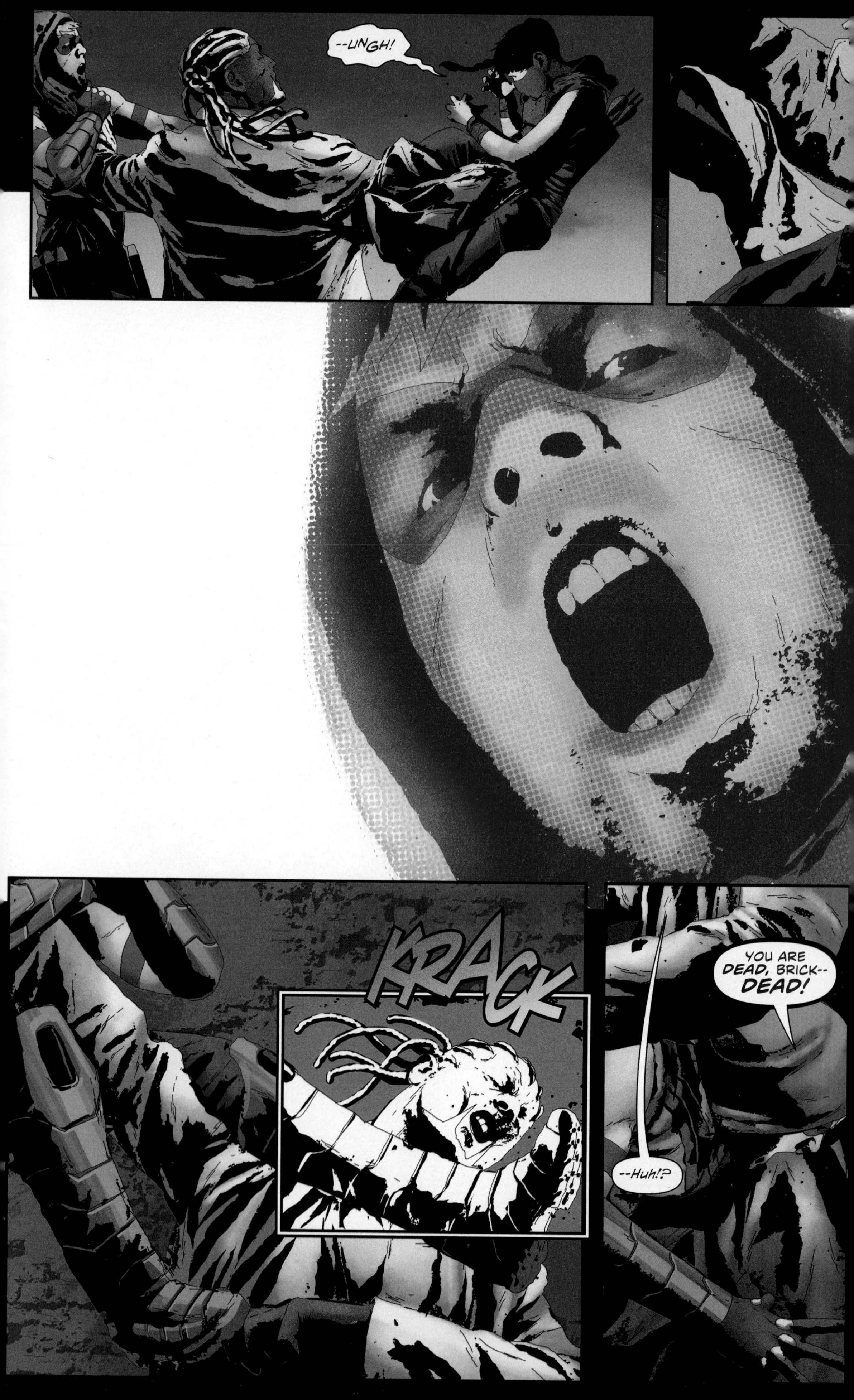
--UNGH!
KRACK
YOU ARE DEAD, BRICK-- DEAD!
--Huh!?

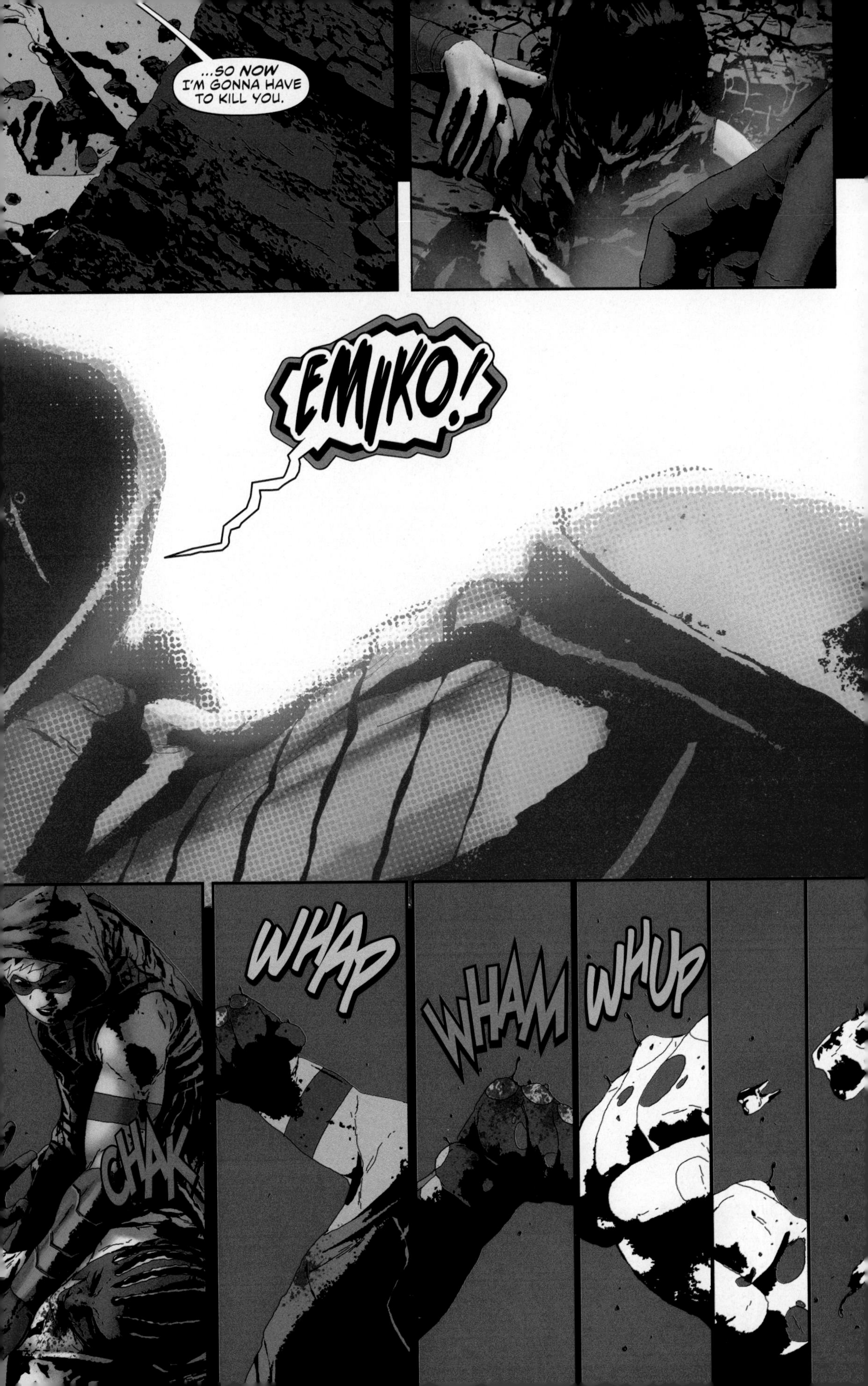
...SO NOW I'M GONNA HAVE TO KILL YOU.
EMIKO!
CHAK
WHAP
WHAM
WHUP

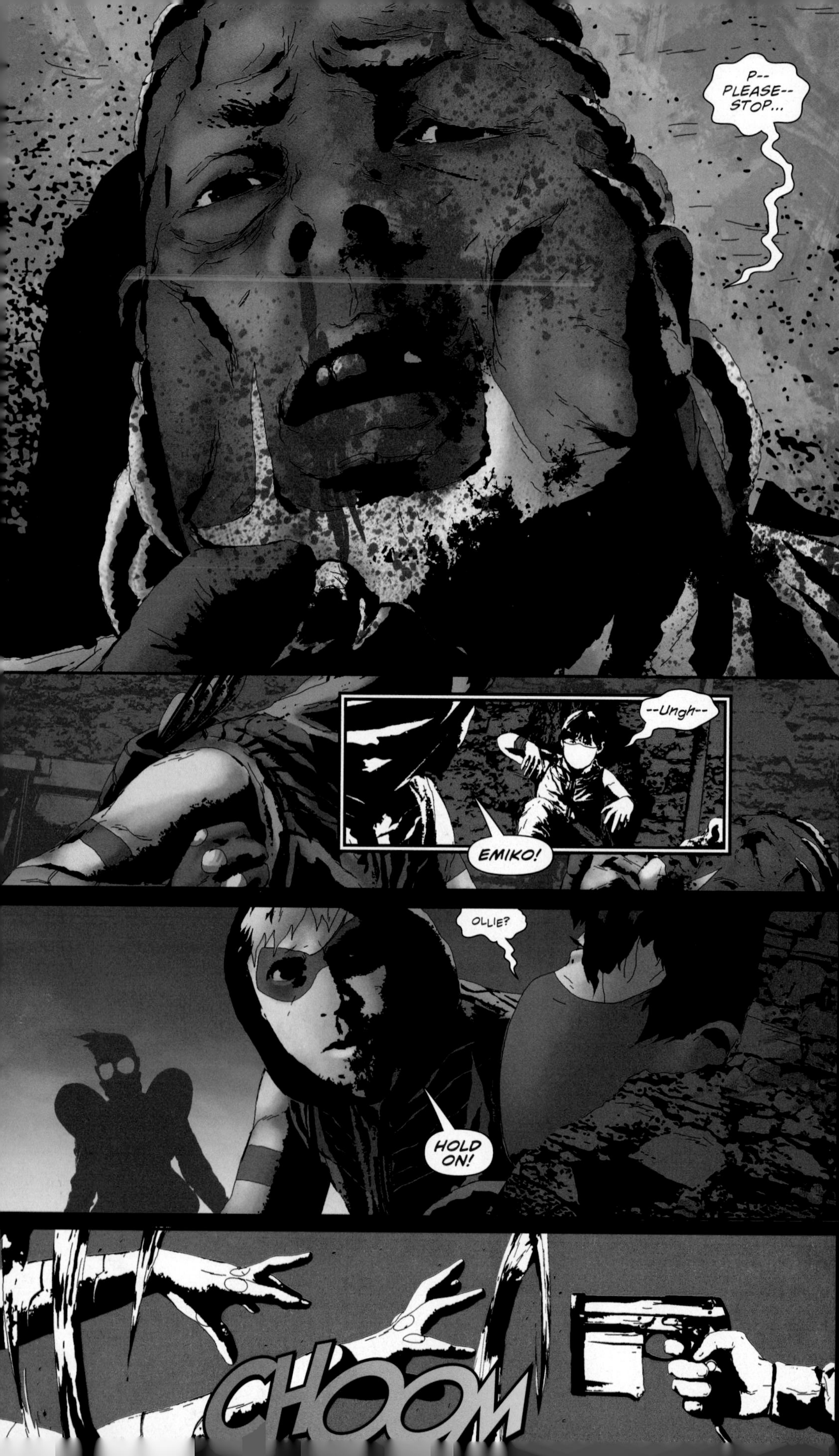
P-- PLEASE-- STOP...
--Ungh--
EMIKO!
OLLIE?
HOLD ON!
CHOOM

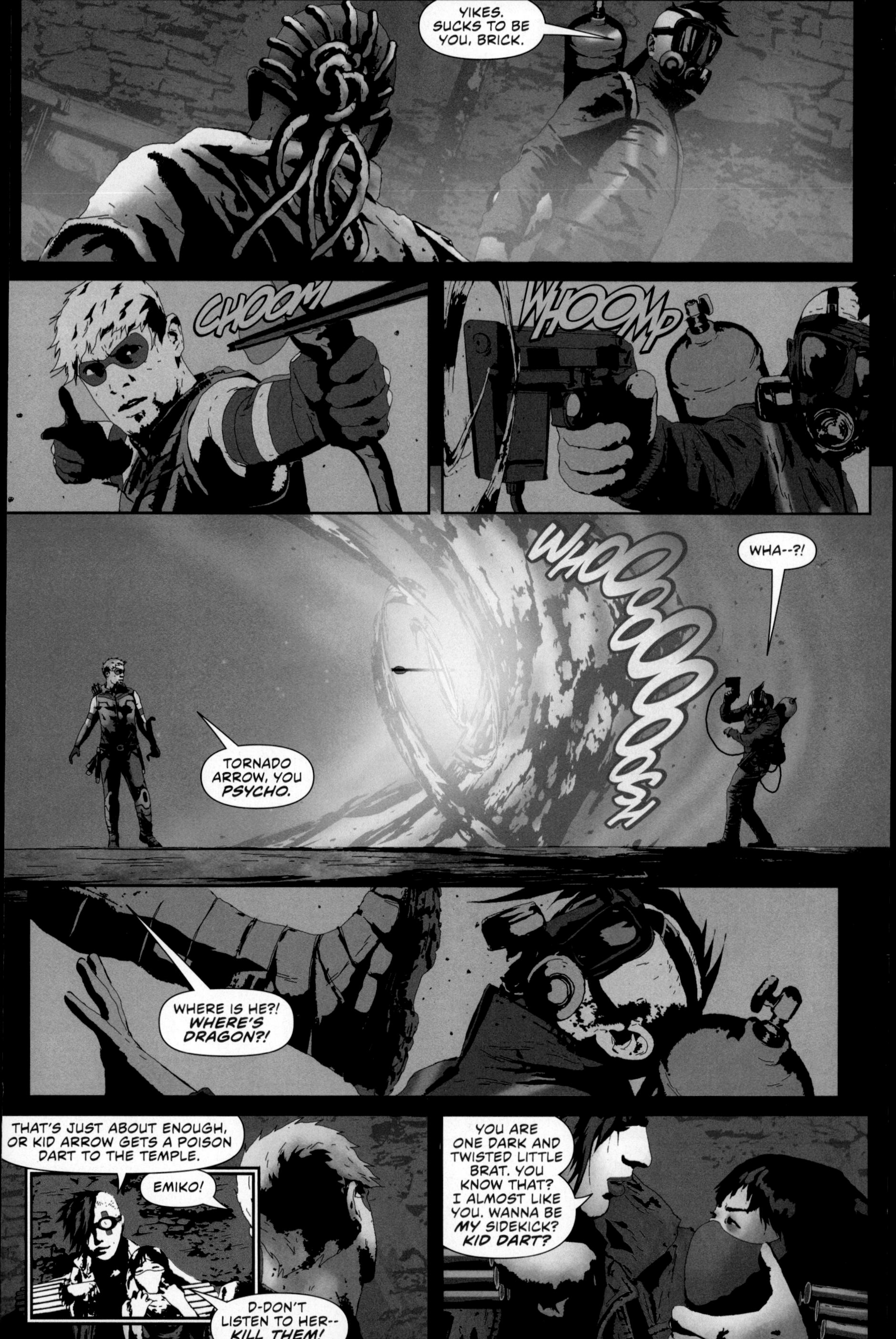
YIKES. SUCKS TO BE YOU, BRICK.
CHOOM
WHOOMP
WHOOOOOOOOOOM
WHA--?!
TORNADO ARROW, YOU *PSYCHO.*
WHERE IS HE?! *WHERE'S DRAGON?!*
THAT'S JUST ABOUT ENOUGH, OR KID ARROW GETS A POISON DART TO THE TEMPLE.
EMIKO!
D-DON'T LISTEN TO HER-- *KILL THEM!*
YOU ARE ONE DARK AND TWISTED LITTLE BRAT. YOU KNOW THAT? I ALMOST LIKE YOU. WANNA BE *MY* SIDEKICK? *KID DART?*

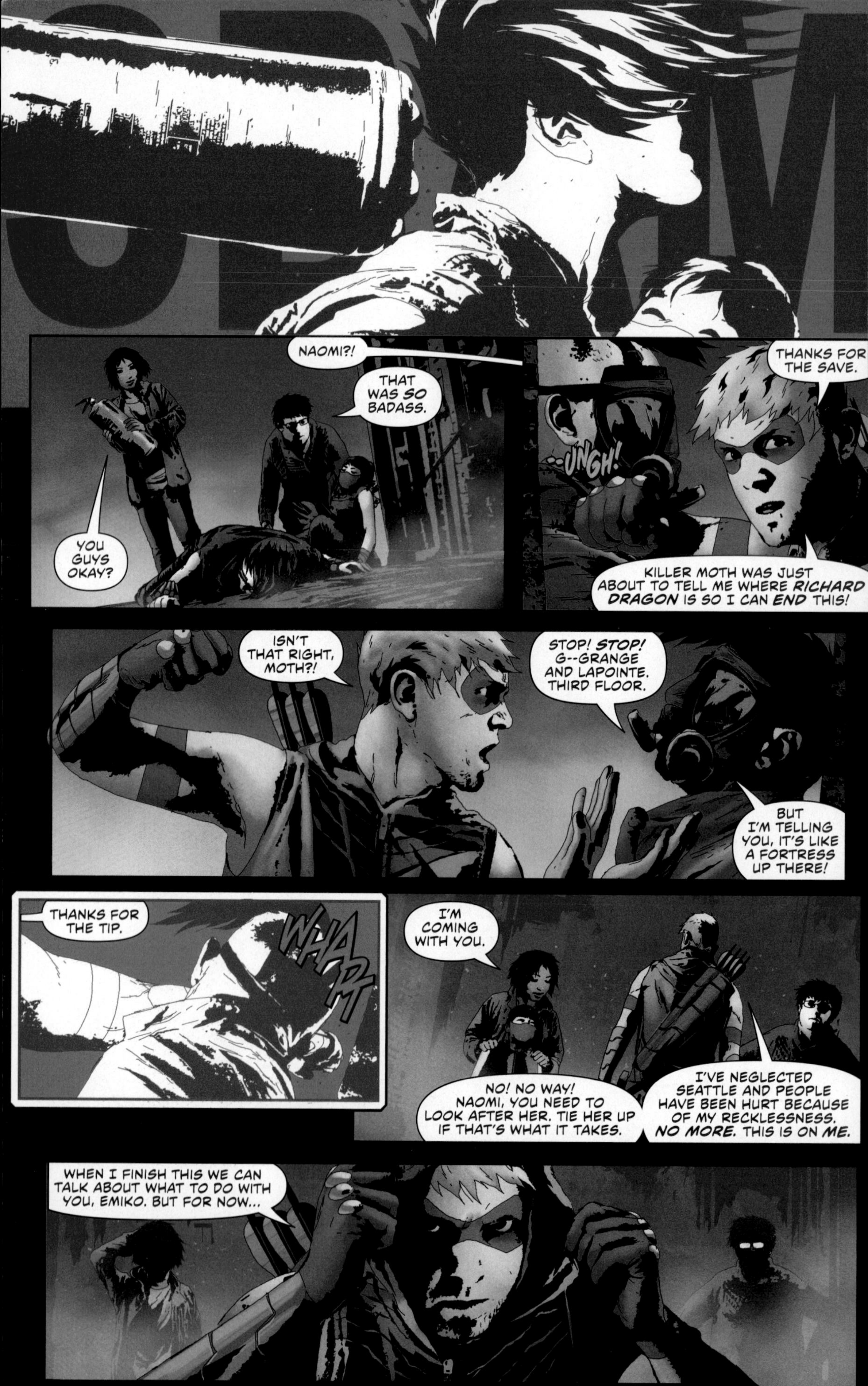
NAOMI?!
THAT WAS SO BADASS.
YOU GUYS OKAY?
THANKS FOR THE SAVE.
UNGH!
KILLER MOTH WAS JUST ABOUT TO TELL ME WHERE RICHARD DRAGON IS SO I CAN END THIS!
ISN'T THAT RIGHT, MOTH?!
STOP! STOP! G--GRANGE AND LAPOINTE. THIRD FLOOR.
BUT I'M TELLING YOU, IT'S LIKE A FORTRESS UP THERE!
THANKS FOR THE TIP.
WHAPP
I'M COMING WITH YOU.
NO! NO WAY! NAOMI, YOU NEED TO LOOK AFTER HER. TIE HER UP IF THAT'S WHAT IT TAKES.
I'VE NEGLECTED SEATTLE AND PEOPLE HAVE BEEN HURT BECAUSE OF MY RECKLESSNESS. NO MORE. THIS IS ON ME.
WHEN I FINISH THIS WE CAN TALK ABOUT WHAT TO DO WITH YOU, EMIKO. BUT FOR NOW...

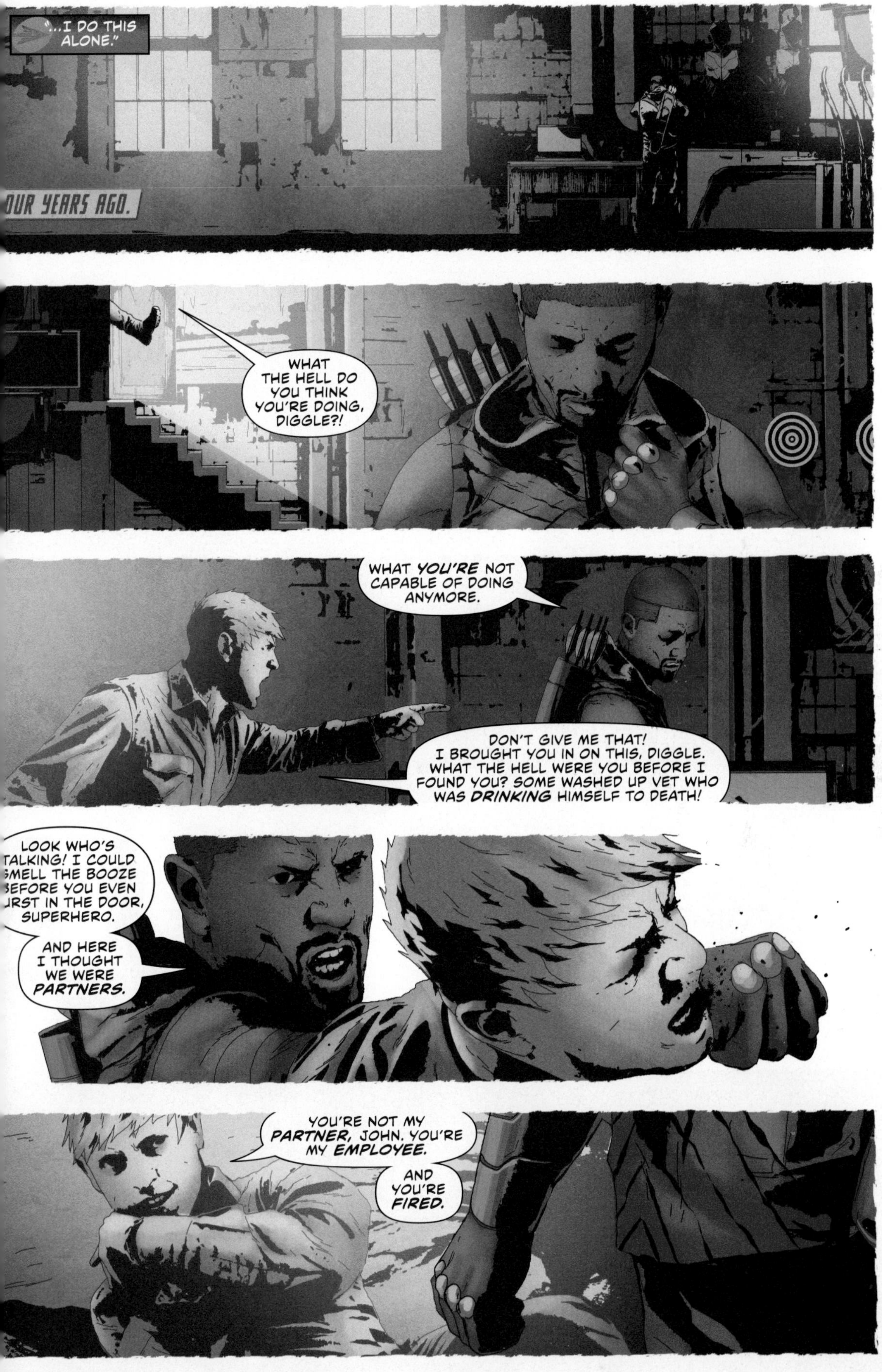
"...I DO THIS ALONE."
OUR YEARS AGO.
WHAT THE HELL DO YOU THINK YOU'RE DOING, DIGGLE?!
WHAT YOU'RE NOT CAPABLE OF DOING ANYMORE.
DON'T GIVE ME THAT! I BROUGHT YOU IN ON THIS, DIGGLE. WHAT THE HELL WERE YOU BEFORE I FOUND YOU? SOME WASHED UP VET WHO WAS DRINKING HIMSELF TO DEATH!
LOOK WHO'S TALKING! I COULD SMELL THE BOOZE BEFORE YOU EVEN URST IN THE DOOR, SUPERHERO.
AND HERE I THOUGHT WE WERE PARTNERS.
YOU'RE NOT MY PARTNER, JOHN. YOU'RE MY EMPLOYEE.
AND YOU'RE FIRED.

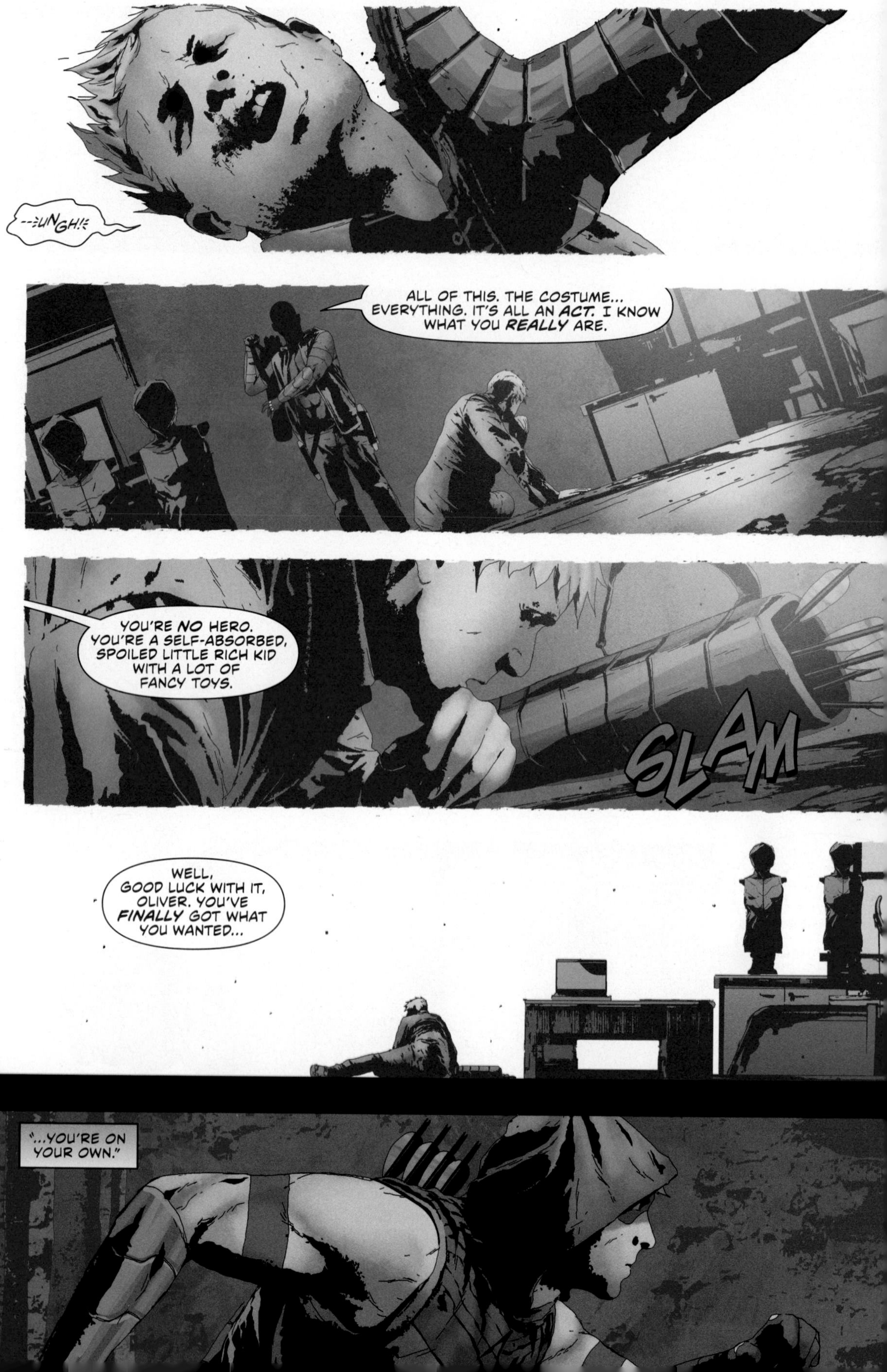
--UNGH!--
ALL OF THIS. THE COSTUME... EVERYTHING. IT'S ALL AN ACT. I KNOW WHAT YOU REALLY ARE.
YOU'RE NO HERO. YOU'RE A SELF-ABSORBED, SPOILED LITTLE RICH KID WITH A LOT OF FANCY TOYS.
SLAM
WELL, GOOD LUCK WITH IT, OLIVER. YOU'VE FINALLY GOT WHAT YOU WANTED...
"...YOU'RE ON YOUR OWN."

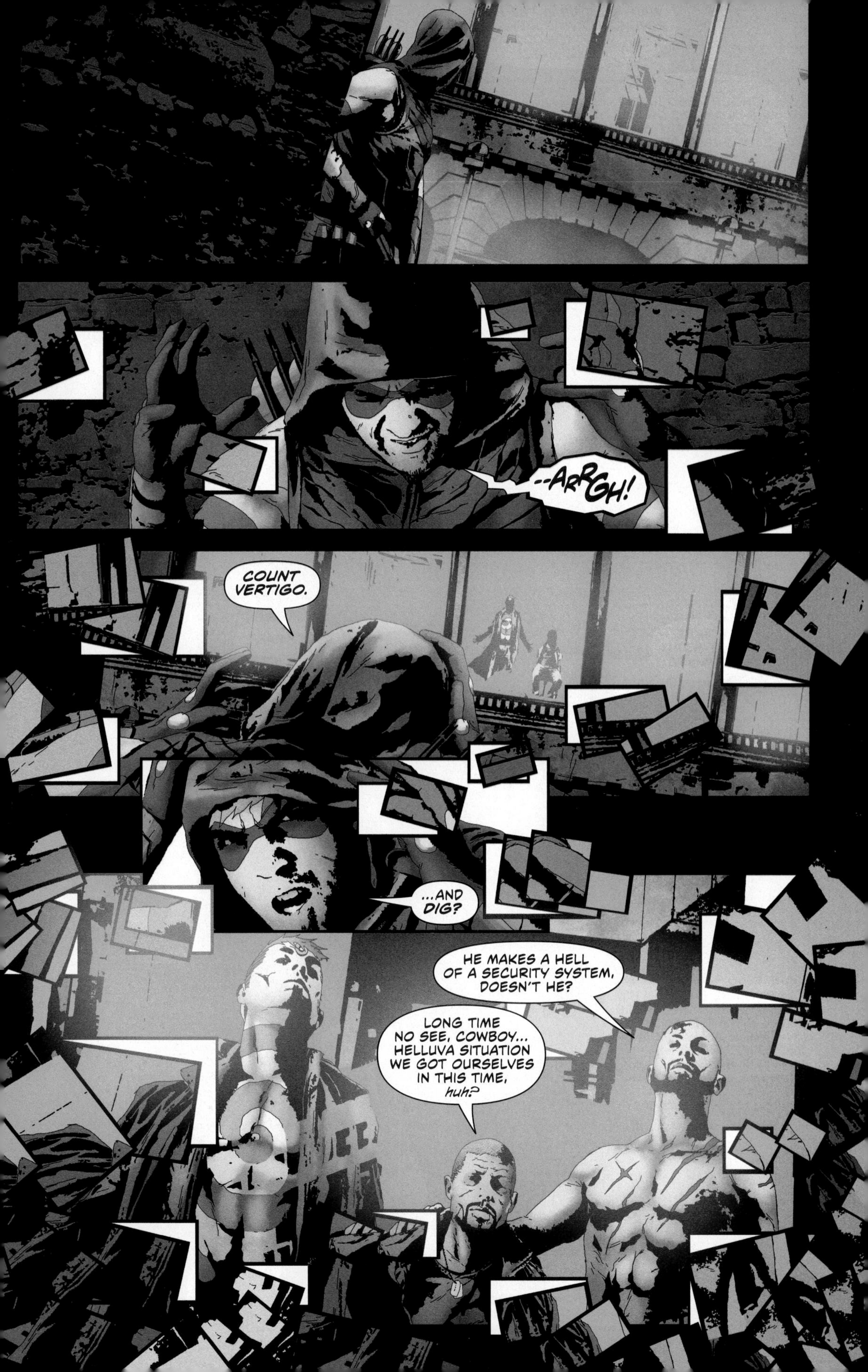
--ARRRGH!
COUNT VERTIGO.
...AND DIG?
HE MAKES A HELL OF A SECURITY SYSTEM, DOESN'T HE?
LONG TIME NO SEE, COWBOY... HELLUVA SITUATION WE GOT OURSELVES IN THIS TIME, huh?

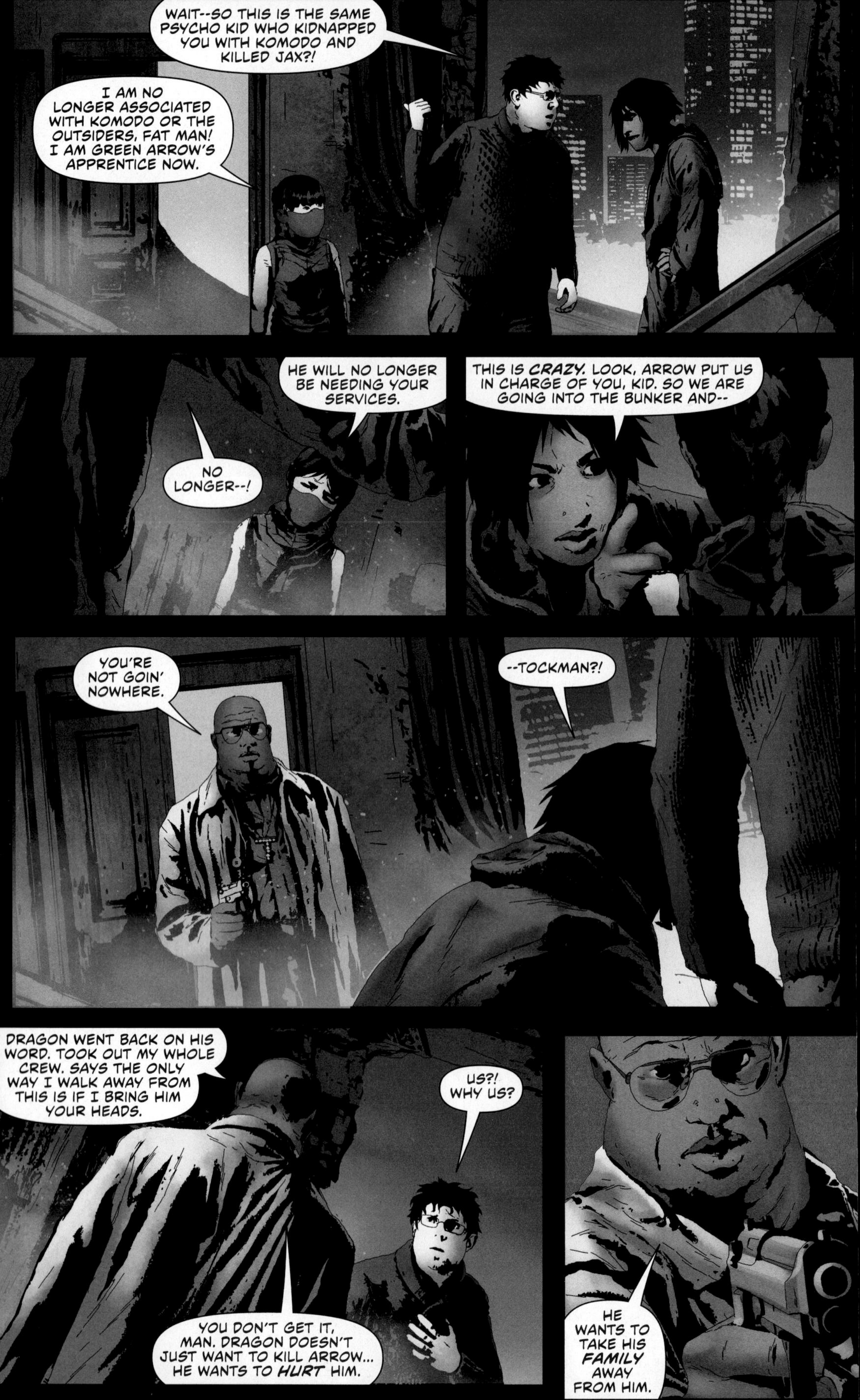

WAIT--SO THIS IS THE SAME PSYCHO KID WHO KIDNAPPED YOU WITH KOMODO AND KILLED JAX?!
I AM NO LONGER ASSOCIATED WITH KOMODO OR THE OUTSIDERS, FAT MAN! I AM GREEN ARROW'S APPRENTICE NOW.
HE WILL NO LONGER BE NEEDING YOUR SERVICES.
NO LONGER--!
THIS IS *CRAZY.* LOOK, ARROW PUT US IN CHARGE OF YOU, KID. SO WE ARE GOING INTO THE BUNKER AND--
YOU'RE NOT GOIN' NOWHERE.
--TOCKMAN?!
DRAGON WENT BACK ON HIS WORD. TOOK OUT MY WHOLE CREW. SAYS THE ONLY WAY I WALK AWAY FROM THIS IS IF I BRING HIM YOUR HEADS.
US?! WHY US?
YOU DON'T GET IT, MAN. DRAGON DOESN'T JUST WANT TO KILL ARROW... HE WANTS TO *HURT* HIM.
HE WANTS TO TAKE HIS *FAMILY* AWAY FROM HIM.

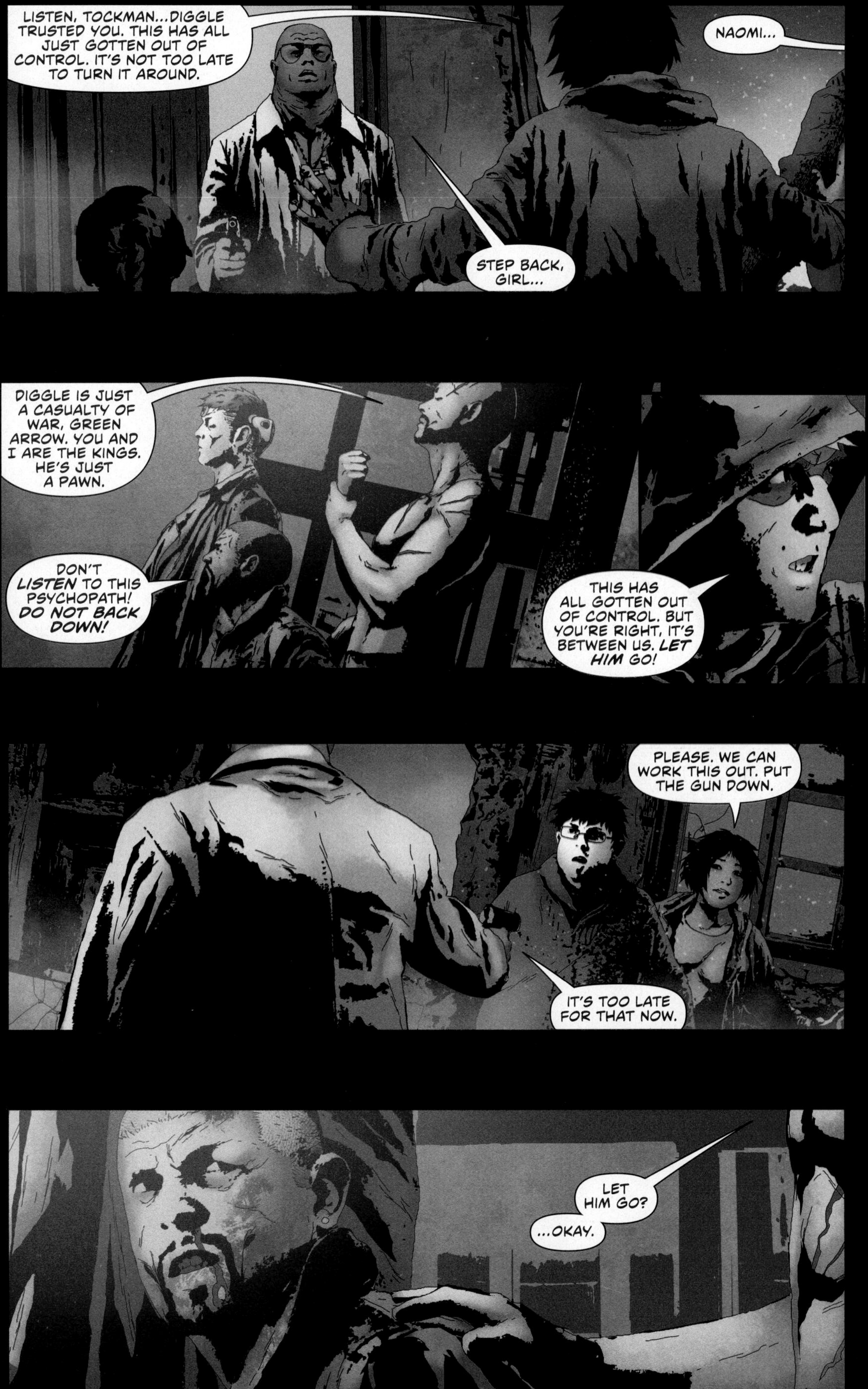
LISTEN, TOCKMAN...DIGGLE TRUSTED YOU. THIS HAS ALL JUST GOTTEN OUT OF CONTROL. IT'S NOT TOO LATE TO TURN IT AROUND.
NAOMI...
STEP BACK, GIRL...
DIGGLE IS JUST A CASUALTY OF WAR, GREEN ARROW. YOU AND I ARE THE KINGS. HE'S JUST A PAWN.
DON'T *LISTEN* TO THIS PSYCHOPATH! *DO NOT BACK DOWN!*
THIS HAS ALL GOTTEN OUT OF CONTROL. BUT YOU'RE RIGHT, IT'S BETWEEN US. *LET HIM* GO!
PLEASE. WE CAN WORK THIS OUT. PUT THE GUN DOWN.
IT'S TOO LATE FOR THAT NOW.
LET HIM GO?
...OKAY.

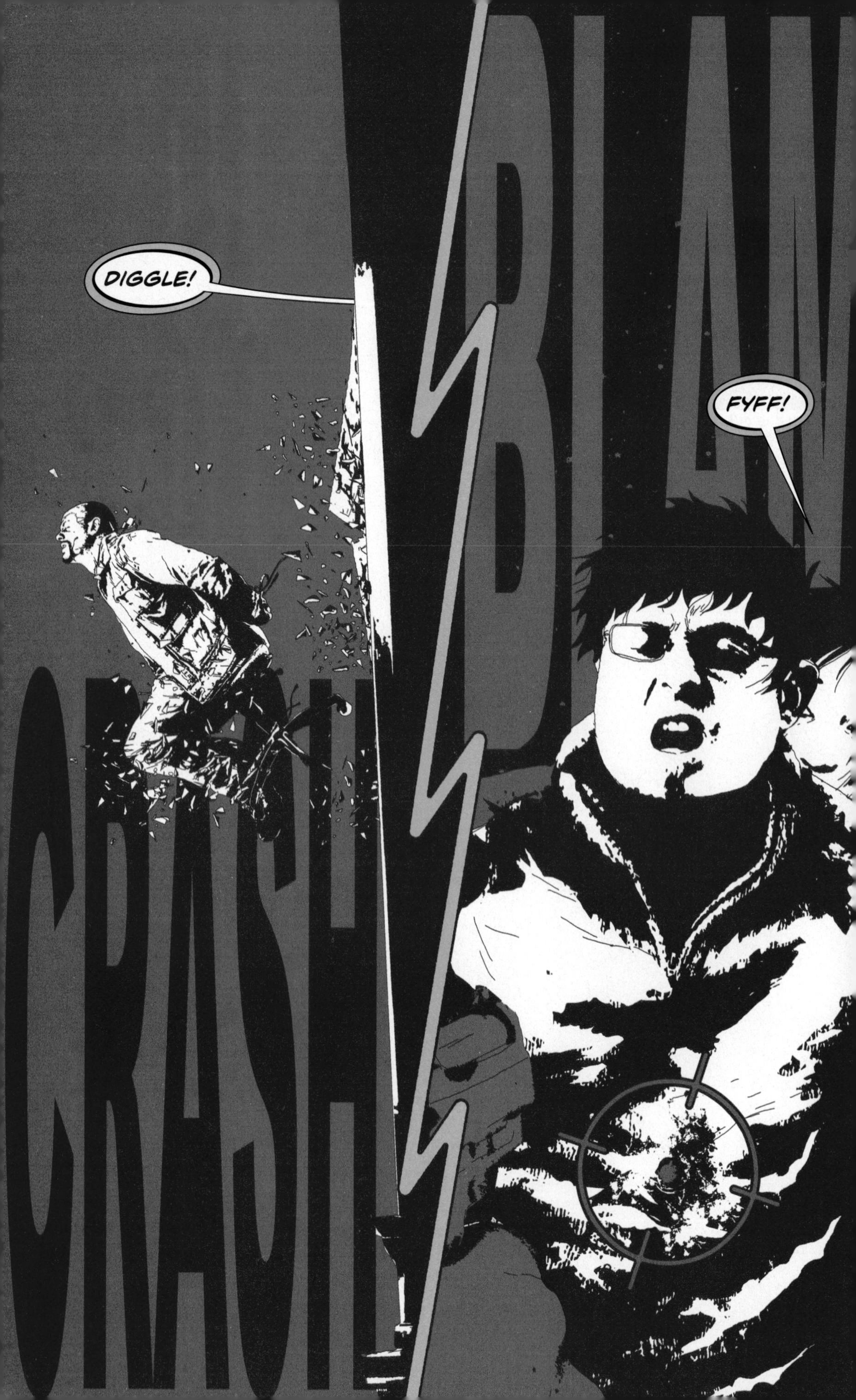
DIGGLE!
CRASH!
BLAM
FYFF!

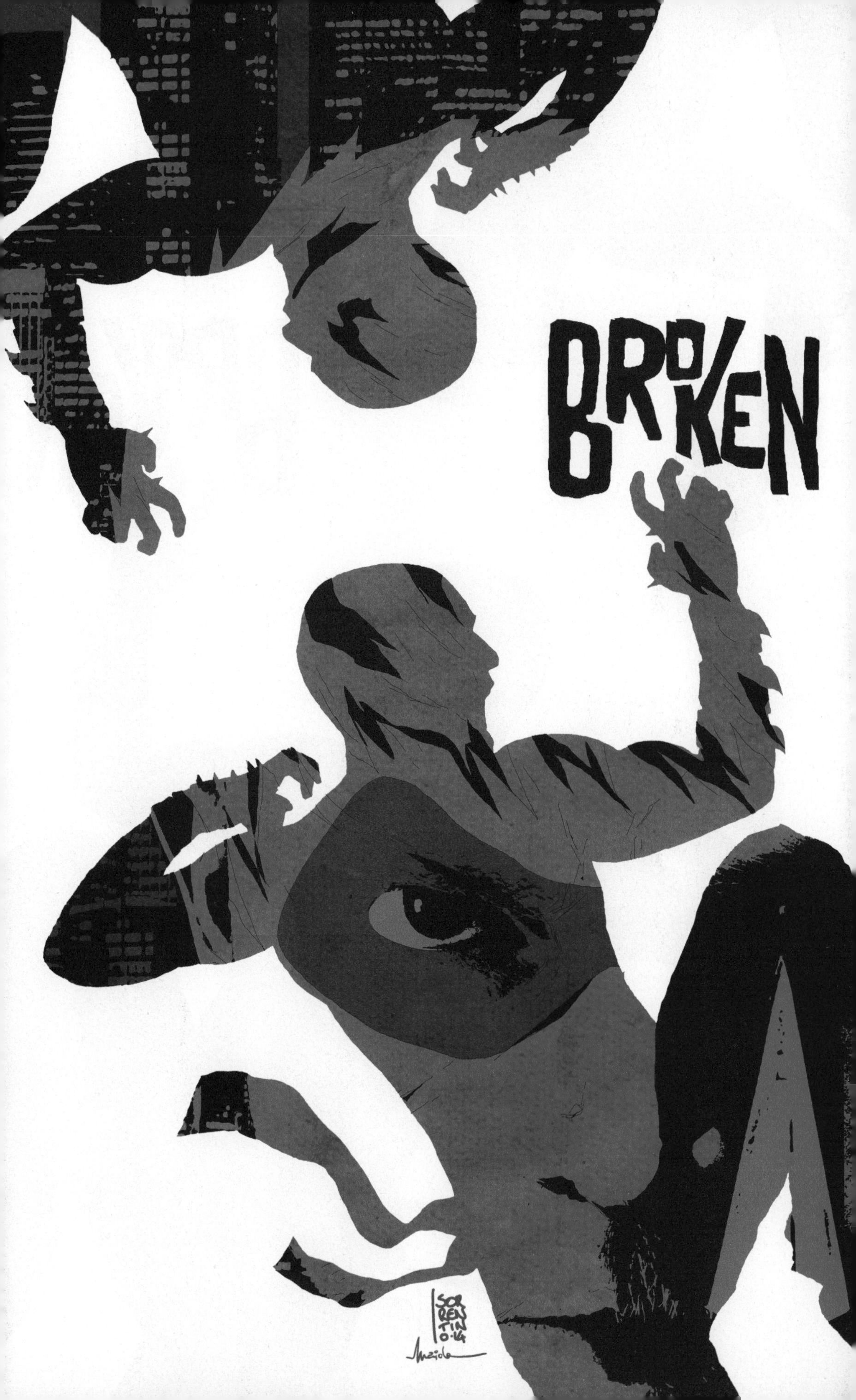
BROKEN
SORRENTINO 14

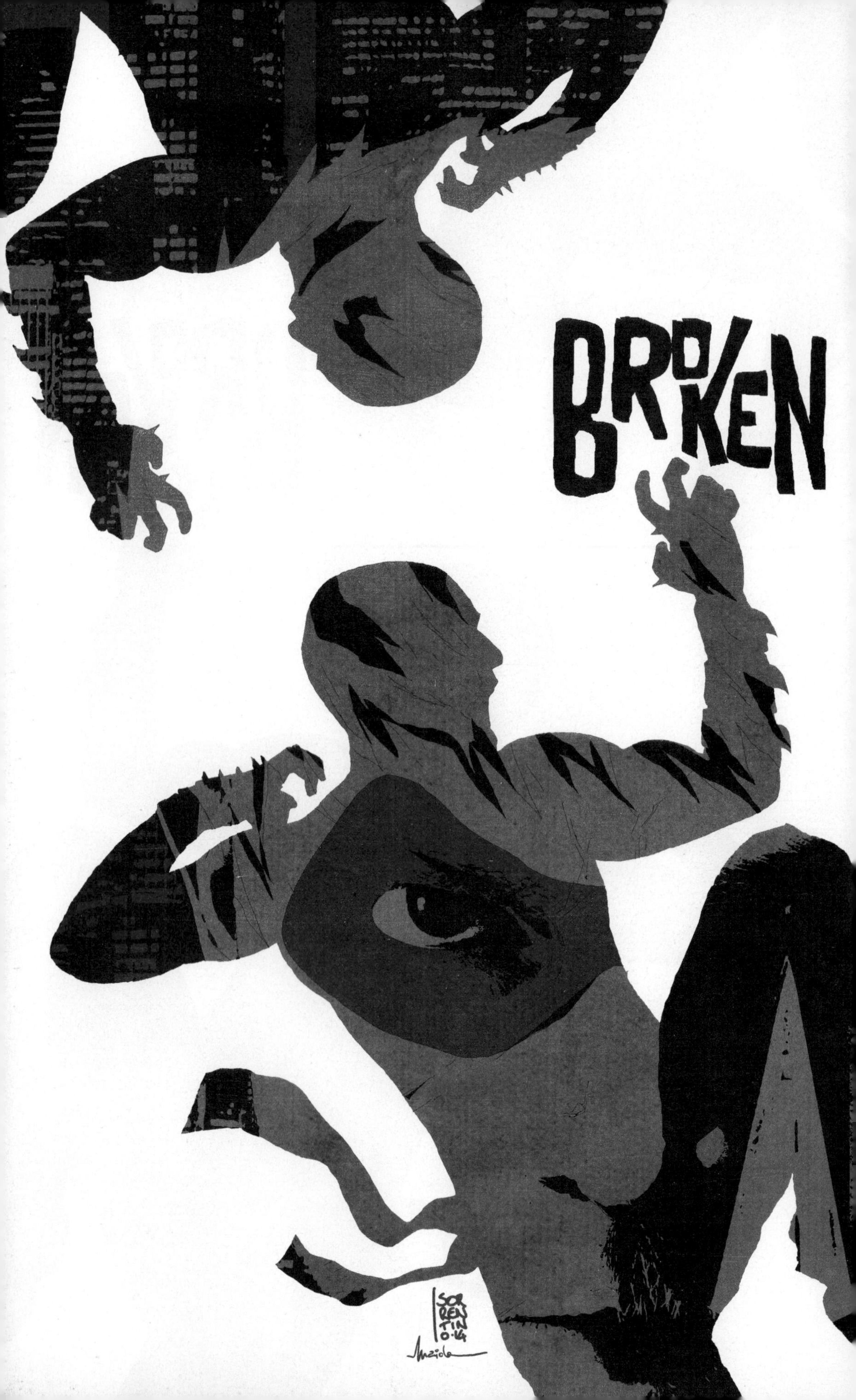
BROKEN
SORRENTINO·14

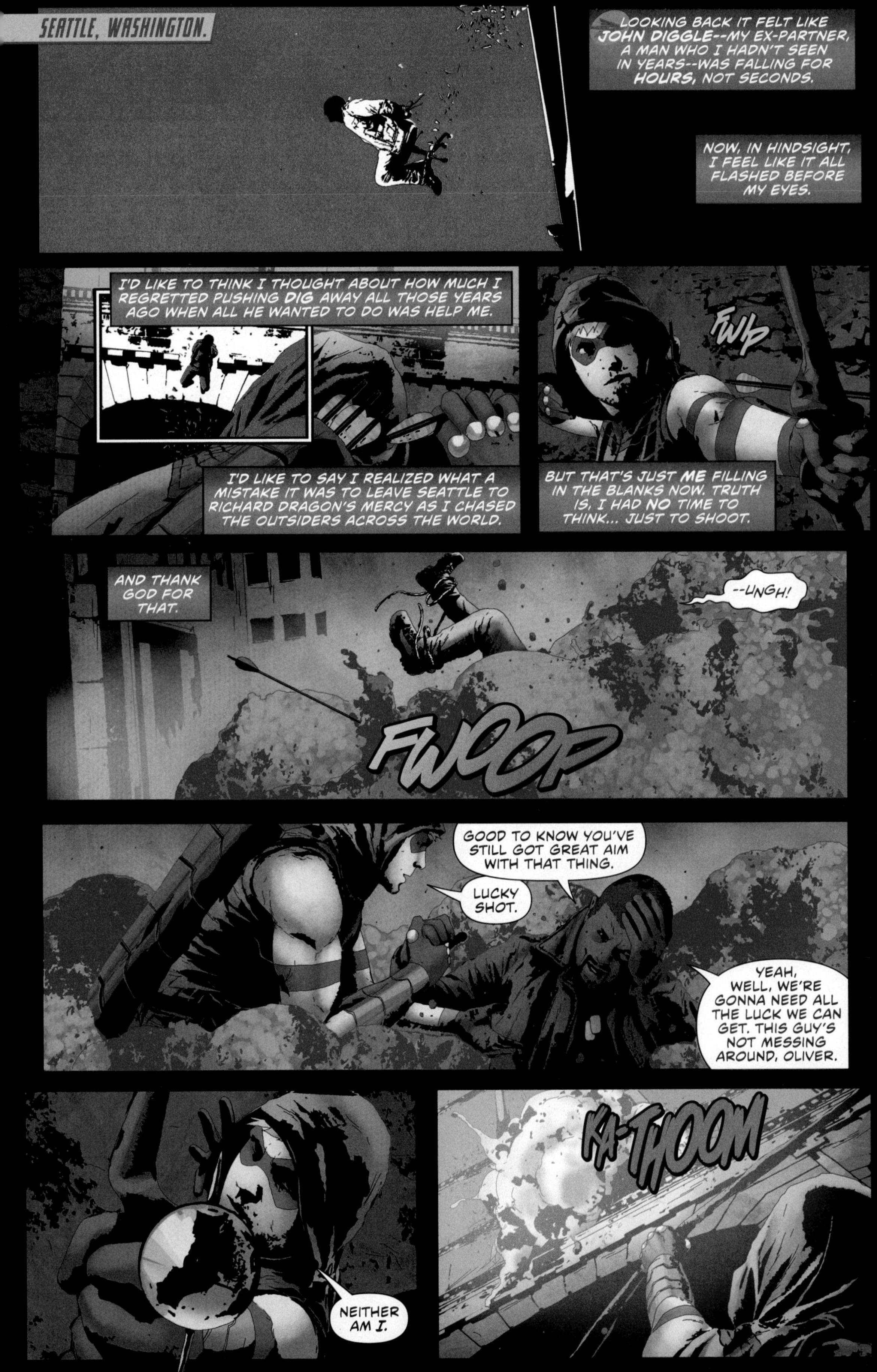
SEATTLE, WASHINGTON.
LOOKING BACK IT FELT LIKE JOHN DIGGLE--MY EX-PARTNER, A MAN WHO I HADN'T SEEN IN YEARS--WAS FALLING FOR HOURS, NOT SECONDS.
NOW, IN HINDSIGHT, I FEEL LIKE IT ALL FLASHED BEFORE MY EYES.
I'D LIKE TO THINK I THOUGHT ABOUT HOW MUCH I REGRETTED PUSHING DIG AWAY ALL THOSE YEARS AGO WHEN ALL HE WANTED TO DO WAS HELP ME.
I'D LIKE TO SAY I REALIZED WHAT A MISTAKE IT WAS TO LEAVE SEATTLE TO RICHARD DRAGON'S MERCY AS I CHASED THE OUTSIDERS ACROSS THE WORLD.
FWIP
BUT THAT'S JUST ME FILLING IN THE BLANKS NOW. TRUTH IS, I HAD NO TIME TO THINK... JUST TO SHOOT.
AND THANK GOD FOR THAT.
--UNGH!
FWOOP
GOOD TO KNOW YOU'VE STILL GOT GREAT AIM WITH THAT THING.
LUCKY SHOT.
YEAH, WELL, WE'RE GONNA NEED ALL THE LUCK WE CAN GET. THIS GUY'S NOT MESSING AROUND, OLIVER.
NEITHER AM I.
KA-THOOM

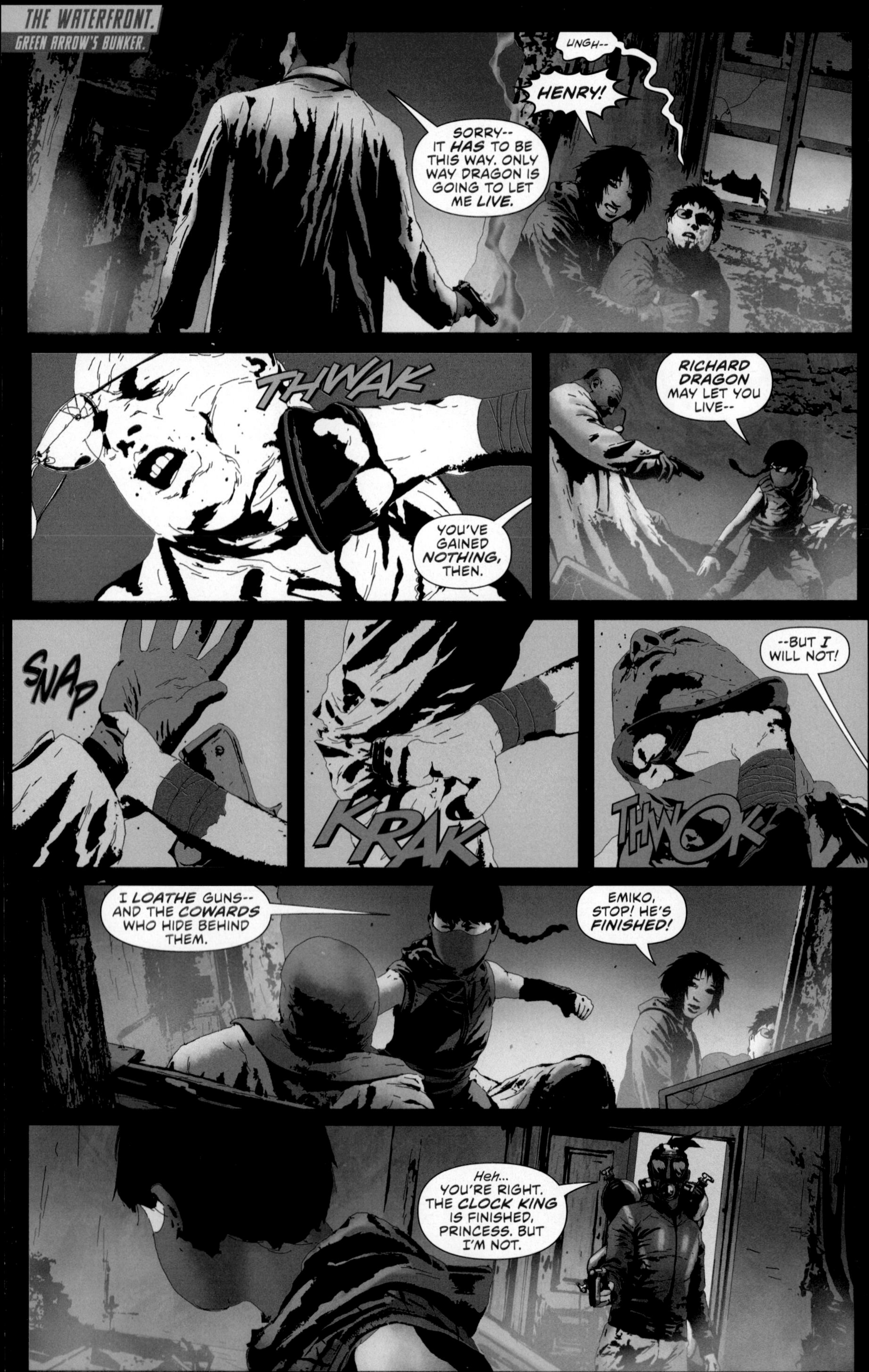

THE WATERFRONT.
GREEN ARROW'S BUNKER.
UNGH--
HENRY!
SORRY-- IT HAS TO BE THIS WAY. ONLY WAY DRAGON IS GOING TO LET ME LIVE.
THWAK
YOU'VE GAINED NOTHING, THEN.
RICHARD DRAGON MAY LET YOU LIVE--
SNAP
KRAK
--BUT I WILL NOT!
THWOK
I LOATHE GUNS-- AND THE COWARDS WHO HIDE BEHIND THEM.
EMIKO, STOP! HE'S FINISHED!
Heh... YOU'RE RIGHT. THE CLOCK KING IS FINISHED, PRINCESS. BUT I'M NOT.

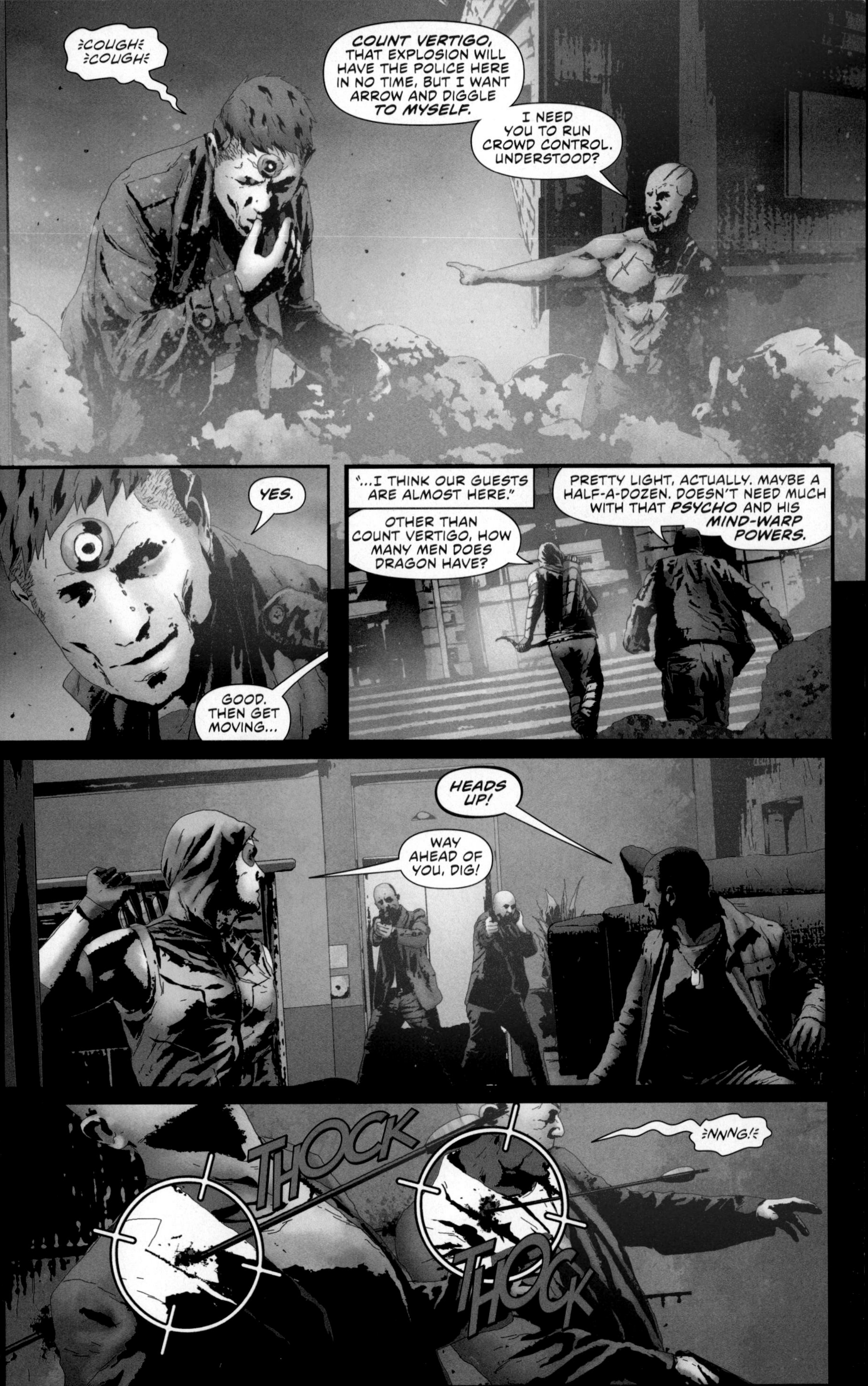
COUNT VERTIGO, THAT EXPLOSION WILL HAVE THE POLICE HERE IN NO TIME, BUT I WANT ARROW AND DIGGLE TO MYSELF.
COUGH COUGH
I NEED YOU TO RUN CROWD CONTROL. UNDERSTOOD?
YES.
GOOD. THEN GET MOVING...
"...I THINK OUR GUESTS ARE ALMOST HERE."
OTHER THAN COUNT VERTIGO, HOW MANY MEN DOES DRAGON HAVE?
PRETTY LIGHT, ACTUALLY. MAYBE A HALF-A-DOZEN. DOESN'T NEED MUCH WITH THAT PSYCHO AND HIS MIND-WARP POWERS.
HEADS UP!
WAY AHEAD OF YOU, DIG!
THOCK
NNNG!
THOCK

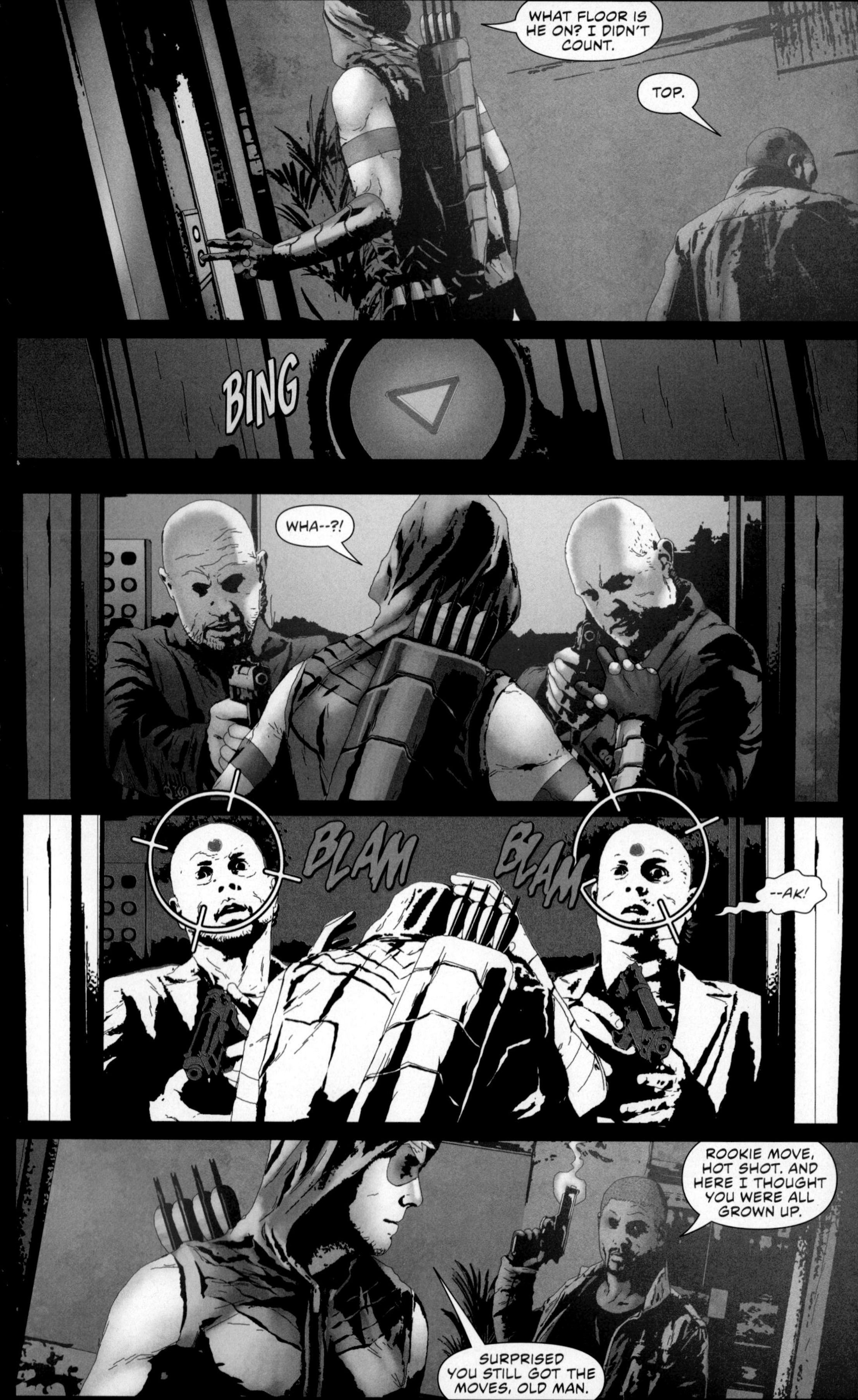
WHAT FLOOR IS HE ON? I DIDN'T COUNT.
TOP.
BING
WHA--?!
BLAM
BLAM
--AK!
ROOKIE MOVE, HOT SHOT. AND HERE I THOUGHT YOU WERE ALL GROWN UP.
SURPRISED YOU STILL GOT THE MOVES, OLD MAN.

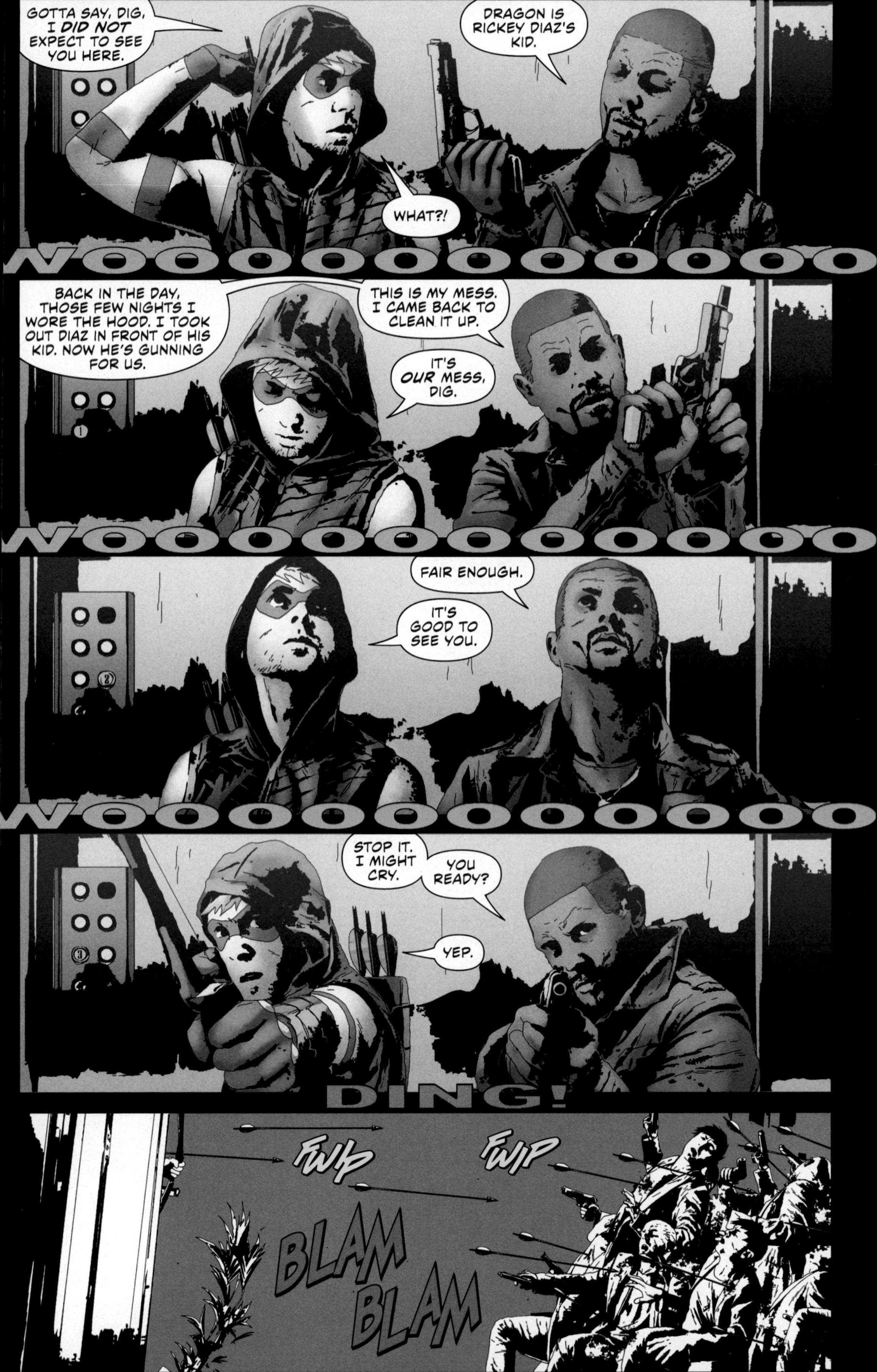
GOTTA SAY, DIG, I DID NOT EXPECT TO SEE YOU HERE.
DRAGON IS RICKEY DIAZ'S KID.
WHAT?!
WOOOOOOOOOOOOO
BACK IN THE DAY, THOSE FEW NIGHTS I WORE THE HOOD. I TOOK OUT DIAZ IN FRONT OF HIS KID. NOW HE'S GUNNING FOR US.
THIS IS MY MESS. I CAME BACK TO CLEAN IT UP.
IT'S OUR MESS, DIG.
WOOOOOOOOOOOOO
FAIR ENOUGH.
IT'S GOOD TO SEE YOU.
WOOOOOOOOOOOOO
STOP IT. I MIGHT CRY.
YOU READY?
YEP.
DING!
FWIP
FWIP
BLAM
BLAM

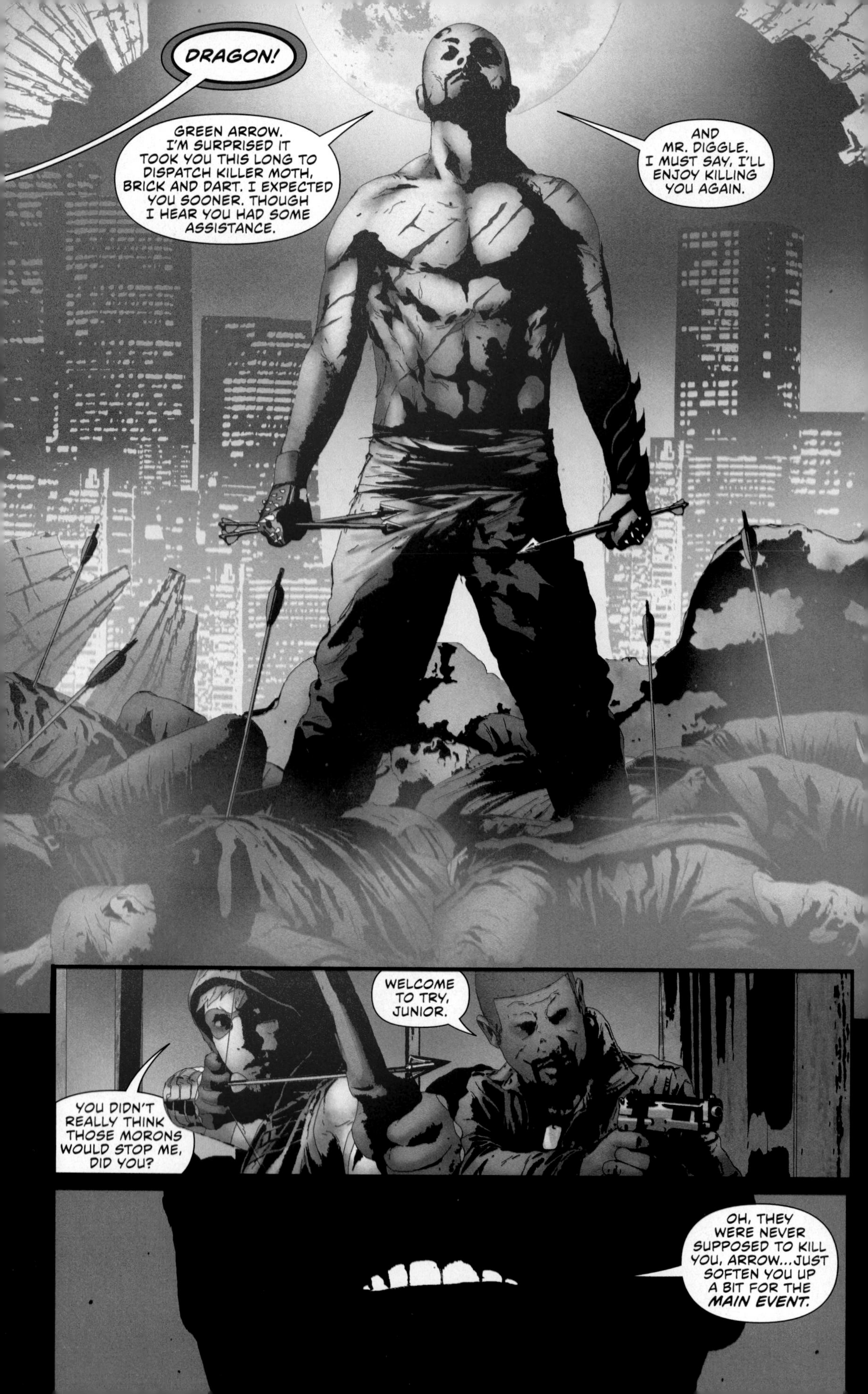
DRAGON!
GREEN ARROW. I'M SURPRISED IT TOOK YOU THIS LONG TO DISPATCH KILLER MOTH, BRICK AND DART. I EXPECTED YOU SOONER. THOUGH I HEAR YOU HAD SOME ASSISTANCE.
AND MR. DIGGLE. I MUST SAY, I'LL ENJOY KILLING YOU AGAIN.
WELCOME TO TRY, JUNIOR.
YOU DIDN'T REALLY THINK THOSE MORONS WOULD STOP ME, DID YOU?
OH, THEY WERE NEVER SUPPOSED TO KILL YOU, ARROW...JUST SOFTEN YOU UP A BIT FOR THE *MAIN EVENT.*

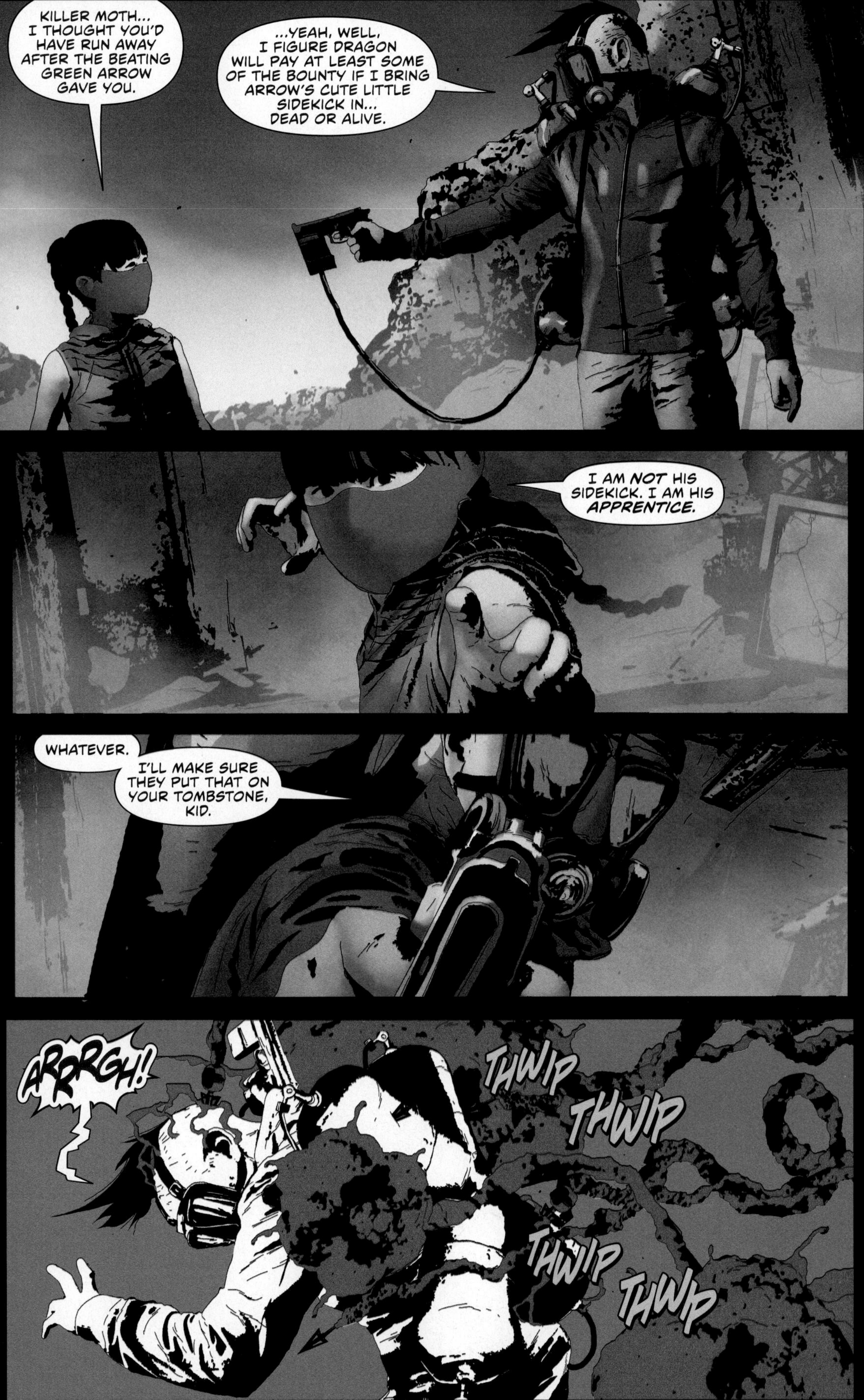
KILLER MOTH... I THOUGHT YOU'D HAVE RUN AWAY AFTER THE BEATING GREEN ARROW GAVE YOU.
...YEAH, WELL, I FIGURE DRAGON WILL PAY AT LEAST SOME OF THE BOUNTY IF I BRING ARROW'S CUTE LITTLE SIDEKICK IN... DEAD OR ALIVE.
I AM NOT HIS SIDEKICK. I AM HIS APPRENTICE.
WHATEVER.
I'LL MAKE SURE THEY PUT THAT ON YOUR TOMBSTONE, KID.
ARRRGH!
THWIP
THWIP
THWIP
THWIP

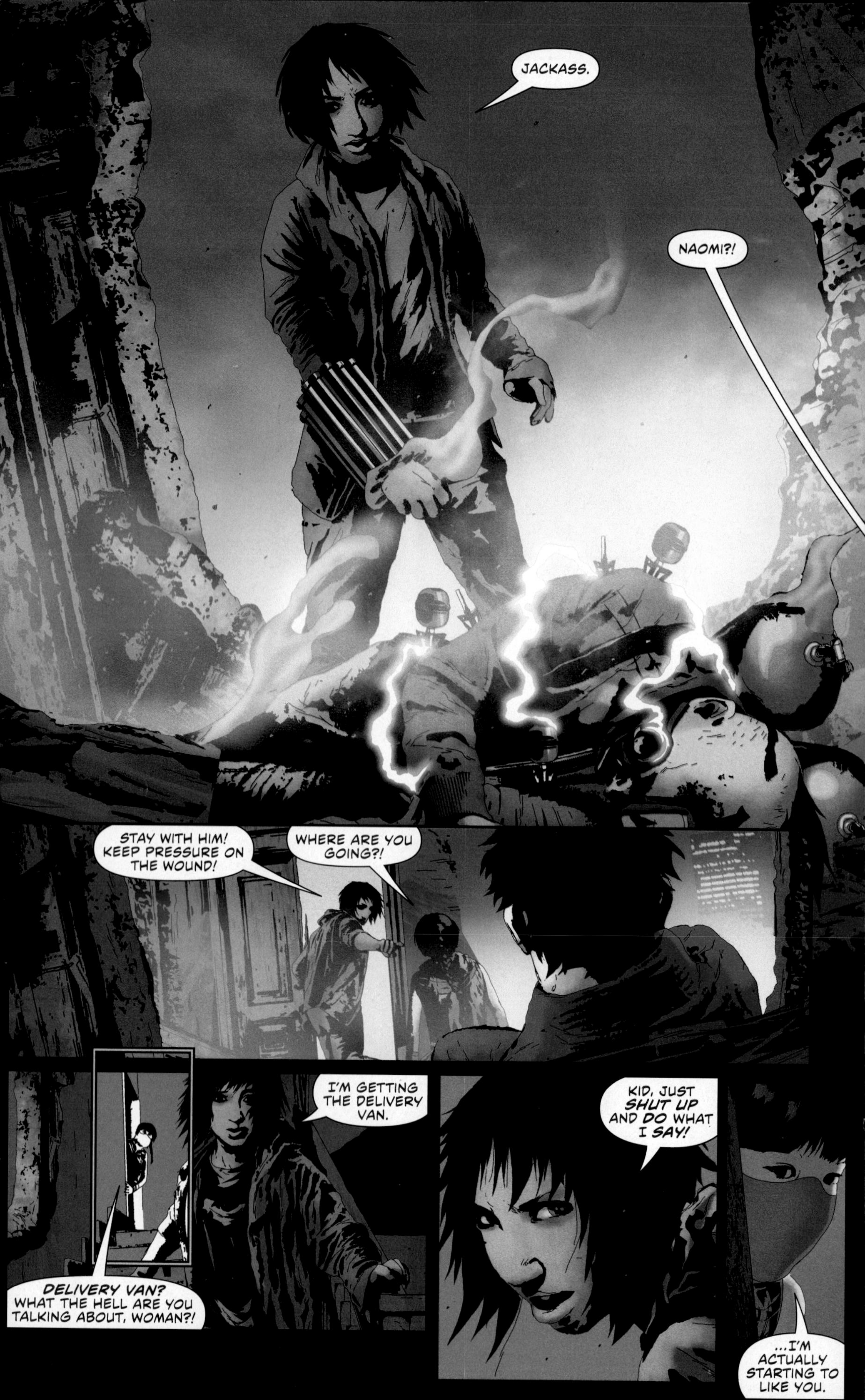
JACKASS.
NAOMI?!
STAY WITH HIM! KEEP PRESSURE ON THE WOUND!
WHERE ARE YOU GOING?!
I'M GETTING THE DELIVERY VAN.
DELIVERY VAN? WHAT THE HELL ARE YOU TALKING ABOUT, WOMAN?!
KID, JUST SHUT UP AND DO WHAT I SAY!
...I'M ACTUALLY STARTING TO LIKE YOU.

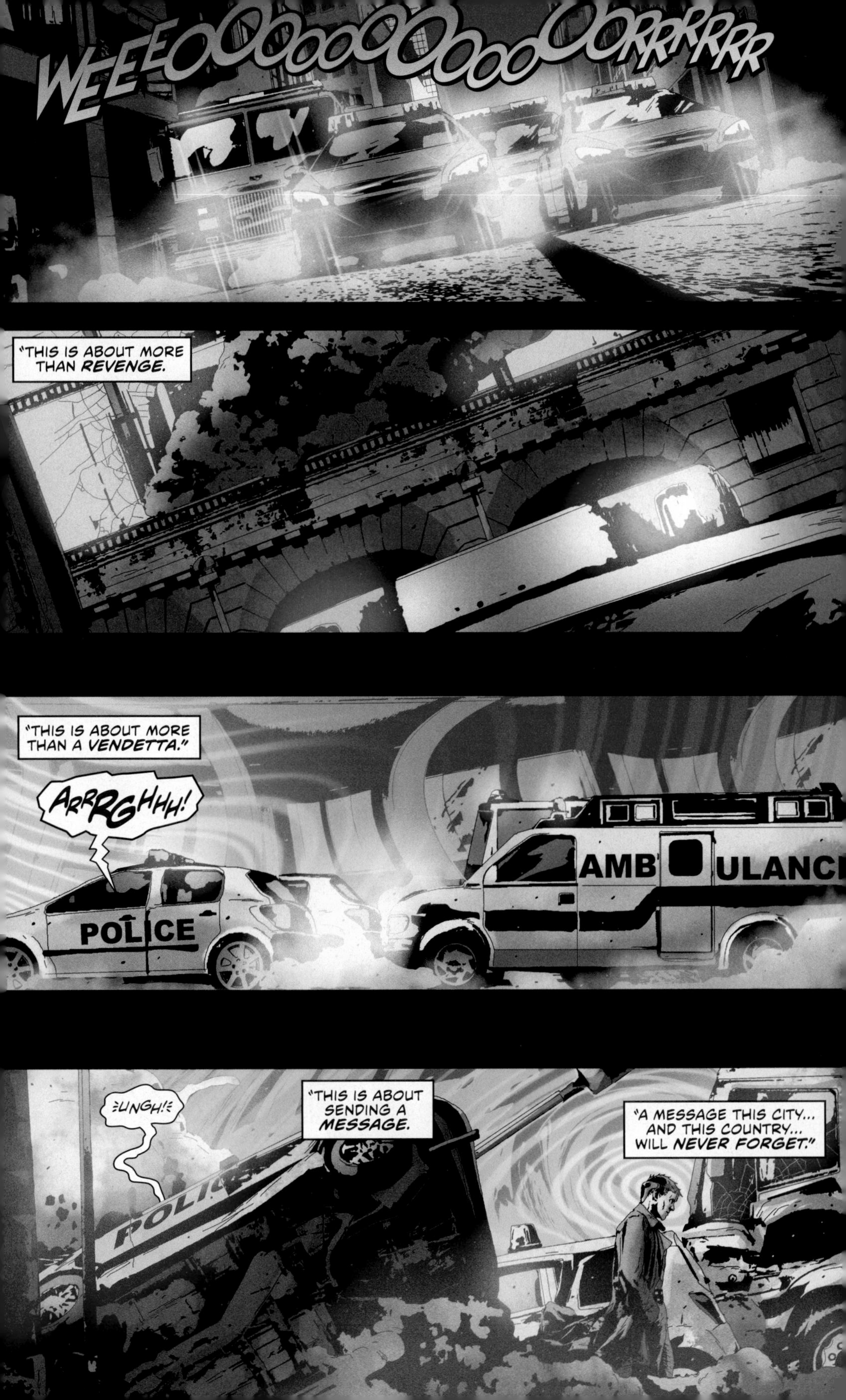
WEEEOOOOOOOOOOOOOORRRRRR
"THIS IS ABOUT MORE THAN REVENGE.
"THIS IS ABOUT MORE THAN A VENDETTA."
ARRRGHHH!
POLICE
AMBULANCE
UNGH!
"THIS IS ABOUT SENDING A MESSAGE.
"A MESSAGE THIS CITY... AND THIS COUNTRY... WILL NEVER FORGET."

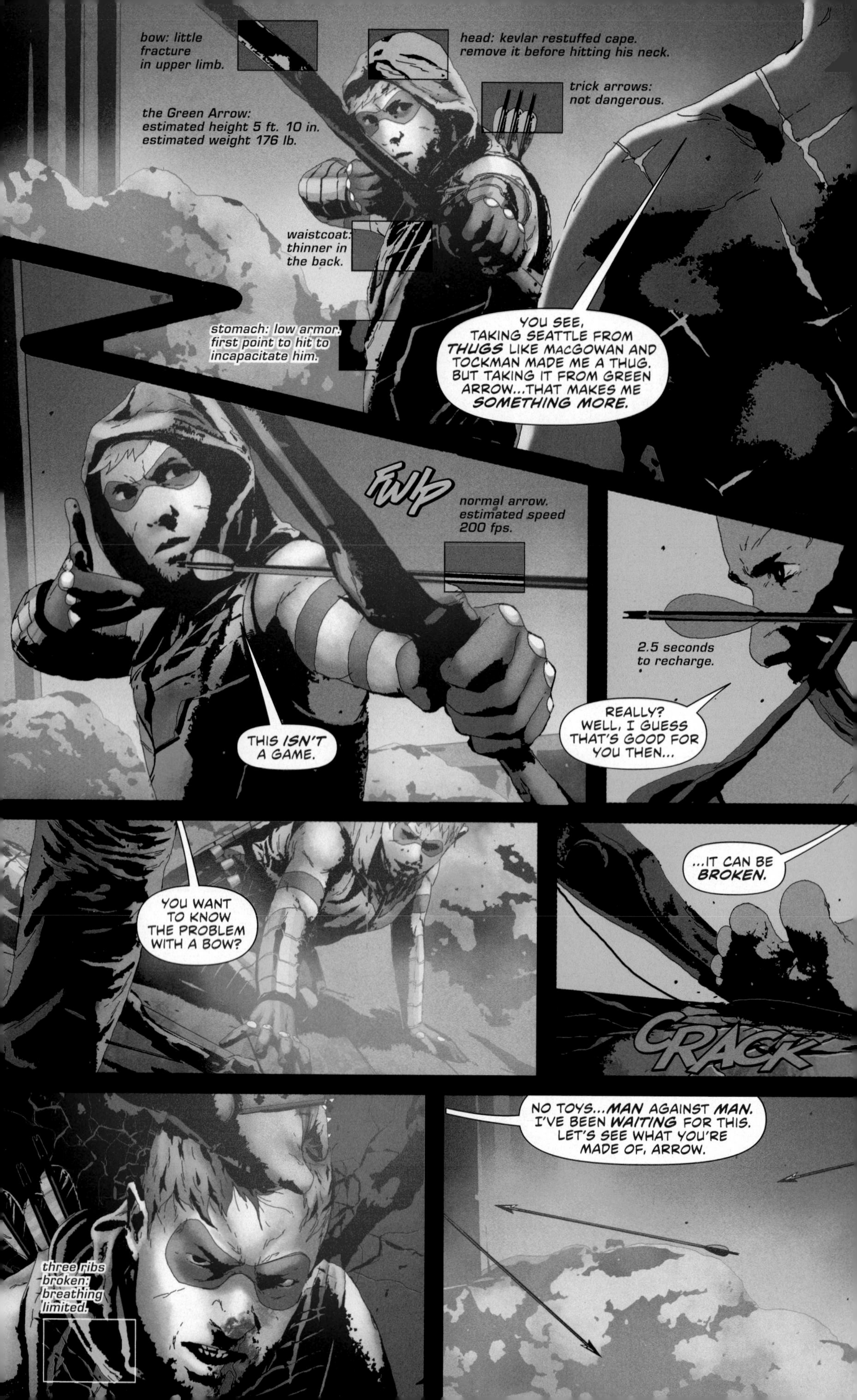

bow: little fracture in upper limb.
head: kevlar restuffed cape. remove it before hitting his neck.
trick arrows: not dangerous.
the Green Arrow: estimated height 5 ft. 10 in. estimated weight 176 lb.
waistcoat: thinner in the back.
stomach: low armor. first point to hit to incapacitate him.
YOU SEE, TAKING SEATTLE FROM THUGS LIKE MACGOWAN AND TOCKMAN MADE ME A THUG. BUT TAKING IT FROM GREEN ARROW...THAT MAKES ME SOMETHING MORE.
FWIP
normal arrow. estimated speed 200 fps.
THIS ISN'T A GAME.
2.5 seconds to recharge.
REALLY? WELL, I GUESS THAT'S GOOD FOR YOU THEN...
YOU WANT TO KNOW THE PROBLEM WITH A BOW?
...IT CAN BE BROKEN.
CRACK
three ribs broken: breathing limited.
NO TOYS...MAN AGAINST MAN. I'VE BEEN WAITING FOR THIS. LET'S SEE WHAT YOU'RE MADE OF, ARROW.

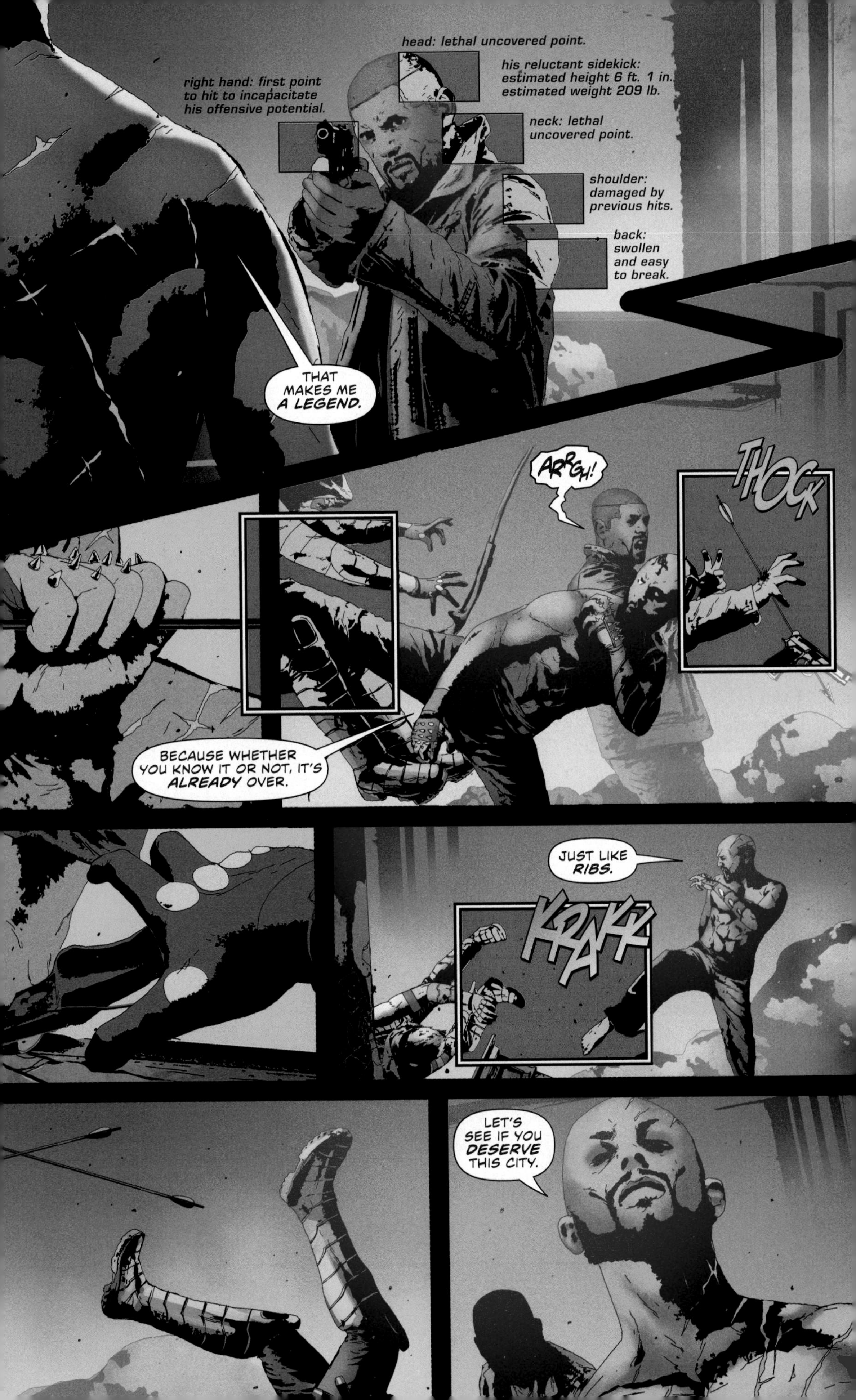

head: lethal uncovered point.
right hand: first point to hit to incapacitate his offensive potential.
his reluctant sidekick: estimated height 6 ft. 1 in. estimated weight 209 lb.
neck: lethal uncovered point.
shoulder: damaged by previous hits.
back: swollen and easy to break.
THAT MAKES ME A LEGEND.
ARRGH!
THOCK
BECAUSE WHETHER YOU KNOW IT OR NOT, IT'S ALREADY OVER.
JUST LIKE RIBS.
KRAKK
LET'S SEE IF YOU DESERVE THIS CITY.

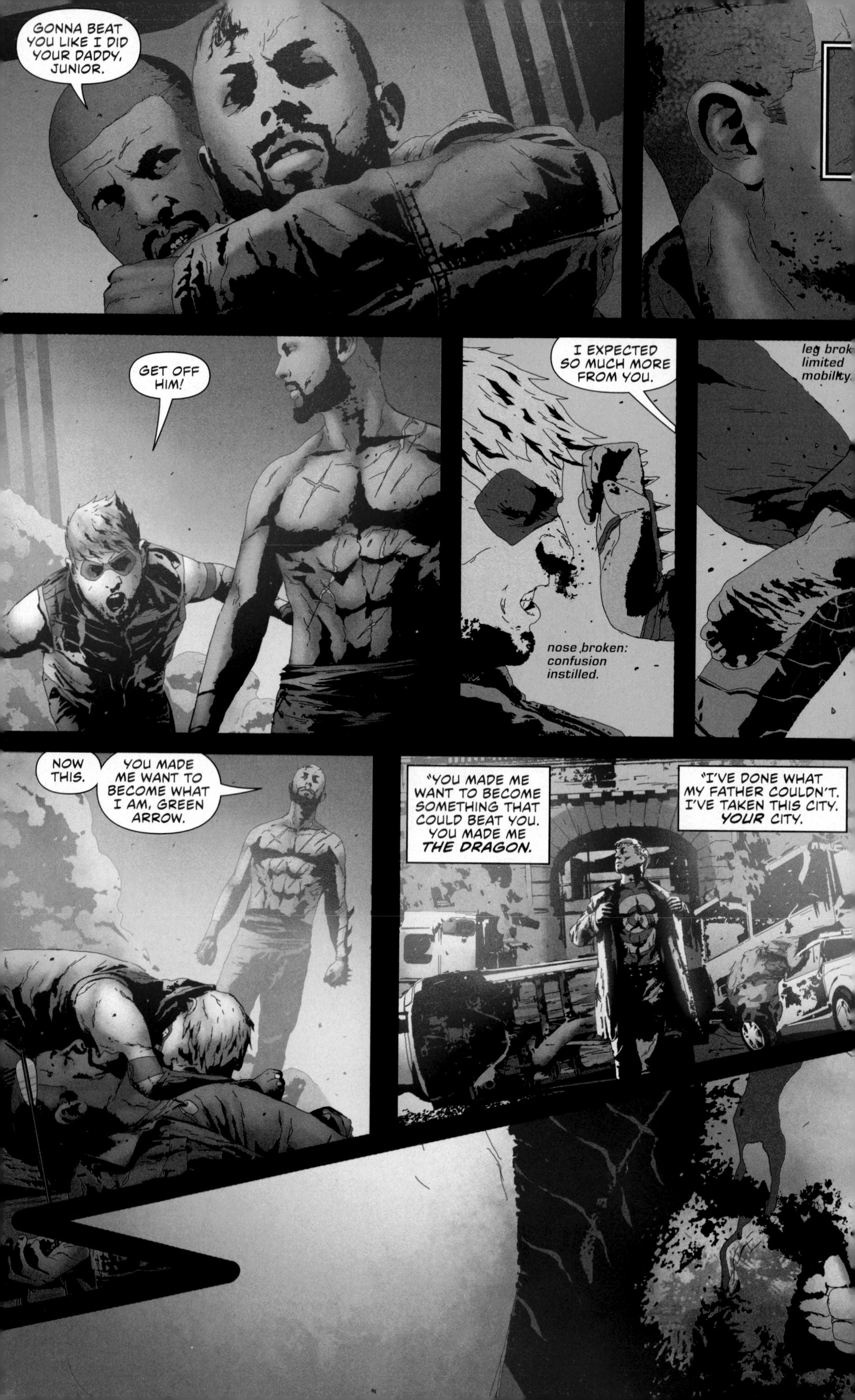
GONNA BEAT YOU LIKE I DID YOUR DADDY, JUNIOR.
GET OFF HIM!
I EXPECTED SO MUCH MORE FROM YOU.
nose broken: confusion instilled.
leg brok limited mobility.
NOW THIS.
YOU MADE ME WANT TO BECOME WHAT I AM, GREEN ARROW.
"YOU MADE ME WANT TO BECOME SOMETHING THAT COULD BEAT YOU. YOU MADE ME THE DRAGON.
"I'VE DONE WHAT MY FATHER COULDN'T. I'VE TAKEN THIS CITY. YOUR CITY.

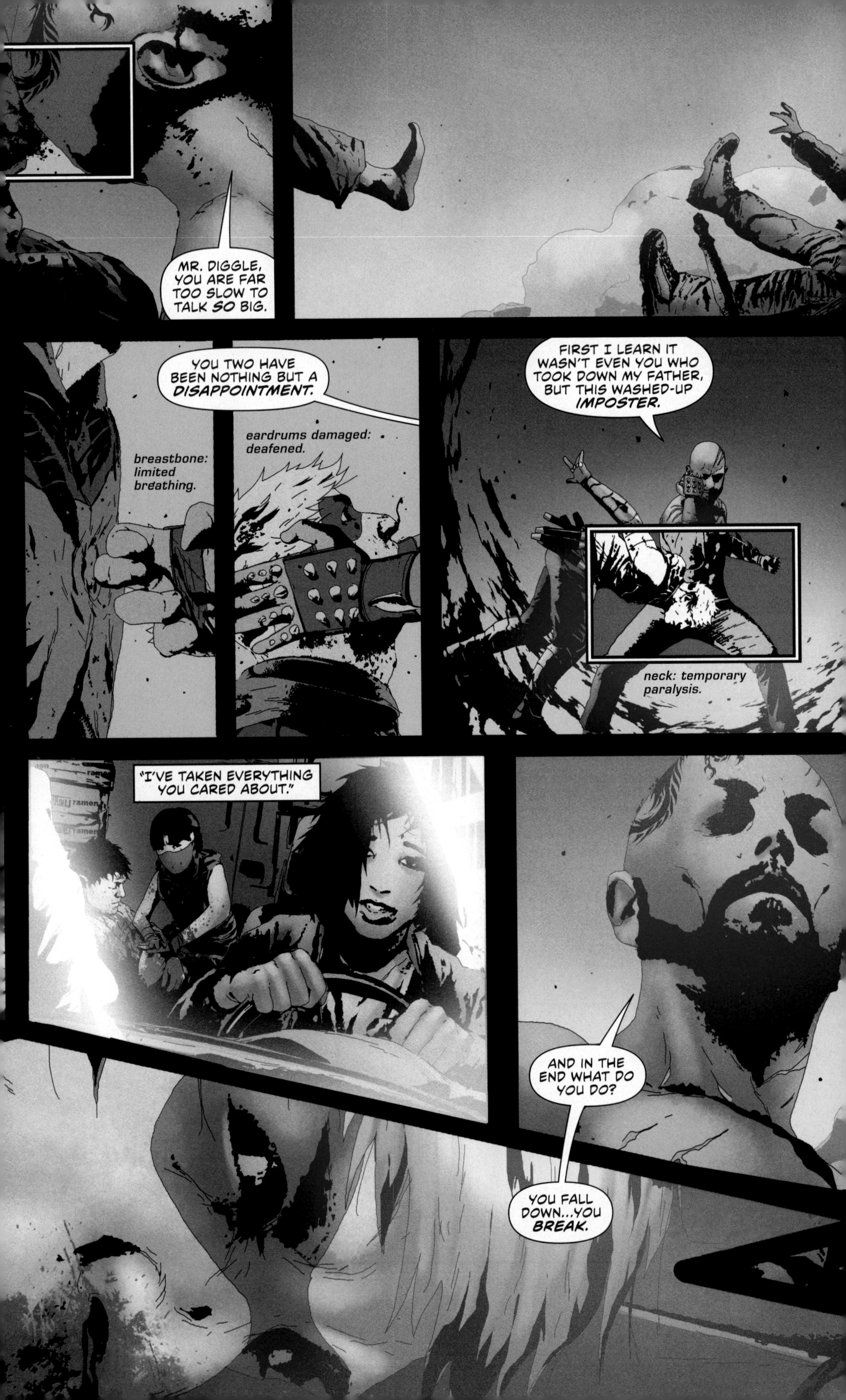

MR. DIGGLE, YOU ARE FAR TOO SLOW TO TALK SO BIG.
YOU TWO HAVE BEEN NOTHING BUT A DISAPPOINTMENT.
breastbone: limited breathing.
eardrums damaged: deafened.
FIRST I LEARN IT WASN'T EVEN YOU WHO TOOK DOWN MY FATHER, BUT THIS WASHED-UP IMPOSTER.
neck: temporary paralysis.
"I'VE TAKEN EVERYTHING YOU CARED ABOUT."
AND IN THE END WHAT DO YOU DO?
YOU FALL DOWN...YOU BREAK.

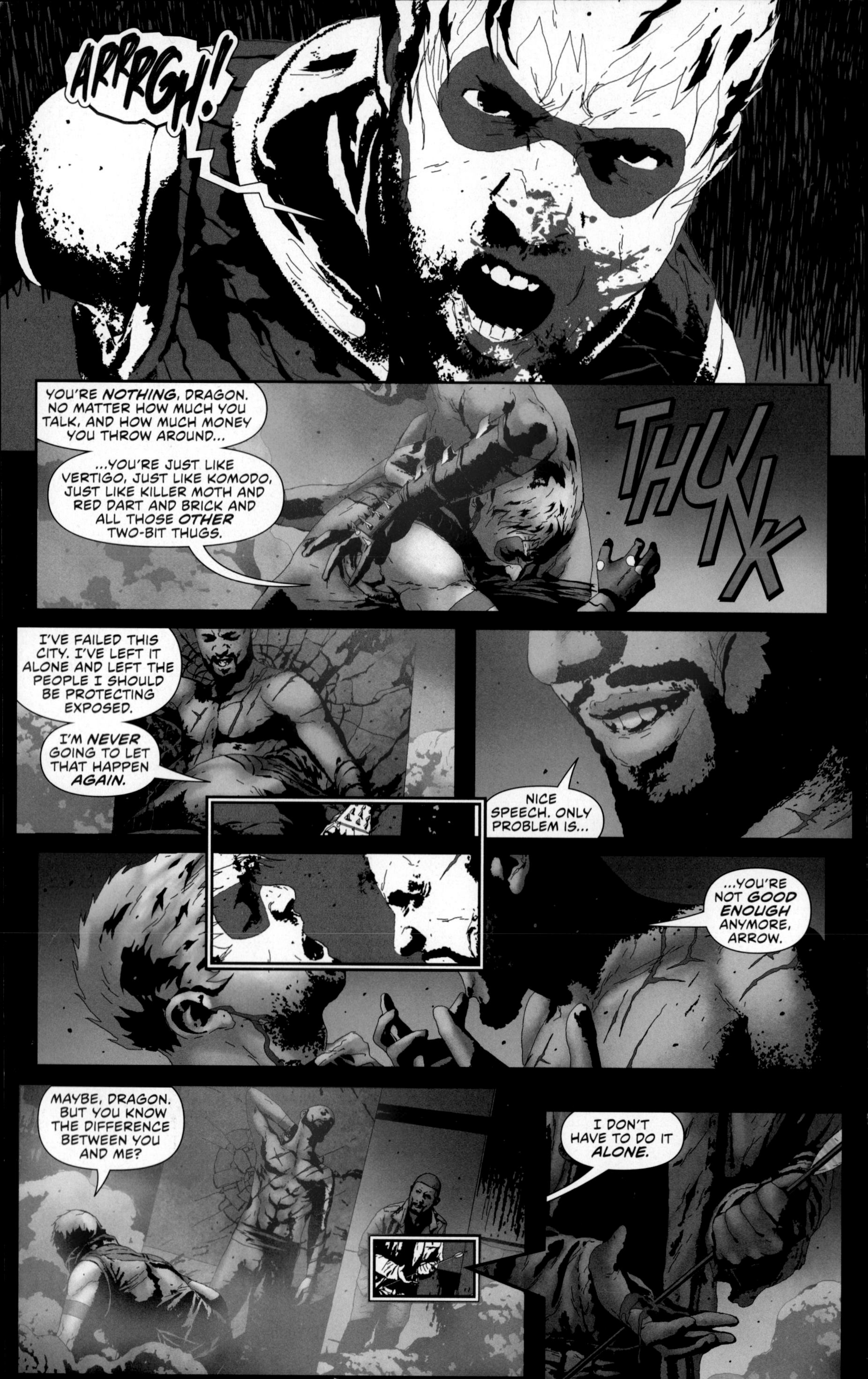
ARRRGH!
YOU'RE NOTHING, DRAGON. NO MATTER HOW MUCH YOU TALK, AND HOW MUCH MONEY YOU THROW AROUND...
...YOU'RE JUST LIKE VERTIGO, JUST LIKE KOMODO, JUST LIKE KILLER MOTH AND RED DART AND BRICK AND ALL THOSE OTHER TWO-BIT THUGS.
THUNK
I'VE FAILED THIS CITY. I'VE LEFT IT ALONE AND LEFT THE PEOPLE I SHOULD BE PROTECTING EXPOSED.
I'M NEVER GOING TO LET THAT HAPPEN AGAIN.
NICE SPEECH. ONLY PROBLEM IS...
...YOU'RE NOT GOOD ENOUGH ANYMORE, ARROW.
MAYBE, DRAGON. BUT YOU KNOW THE DIFFERENCE BETWEEN YOU AND ME?
I DON'T HAVE TO DO IT ALONE.

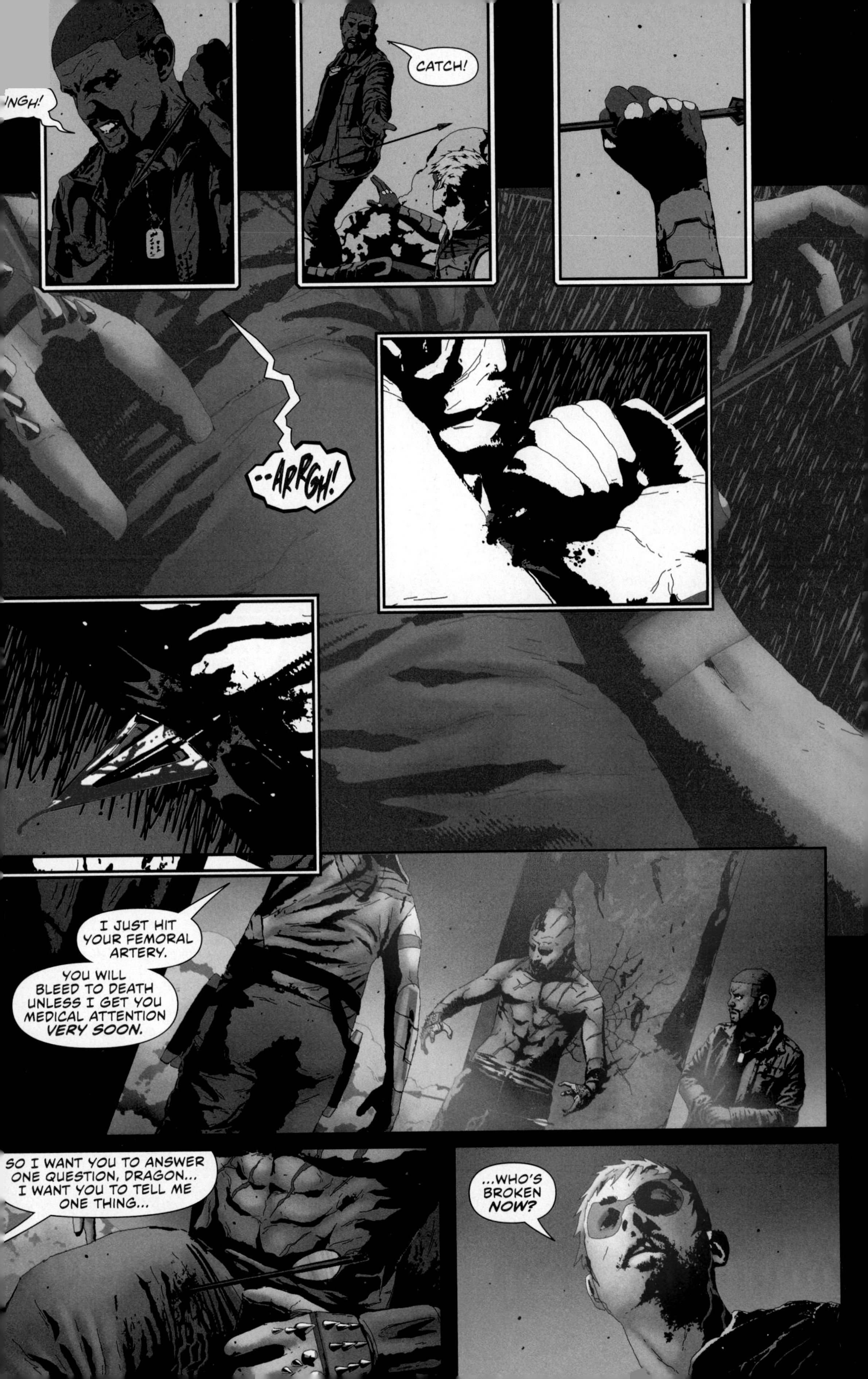

NGH!
CATCH!
--ARRGH!
I JUST HIT YOUR FEMORAL ARTERY.
YOU WILL BLEED TO DEATH UNLESS I GET YOU MEDICAL ATTENTION VERY SOON.
SO I WANT YOU TO ANSWER ONE QUESTION, DRAGON... I WANT YOU TO TELL ME ONE THING...
...WHO'S BROKEN NOW?

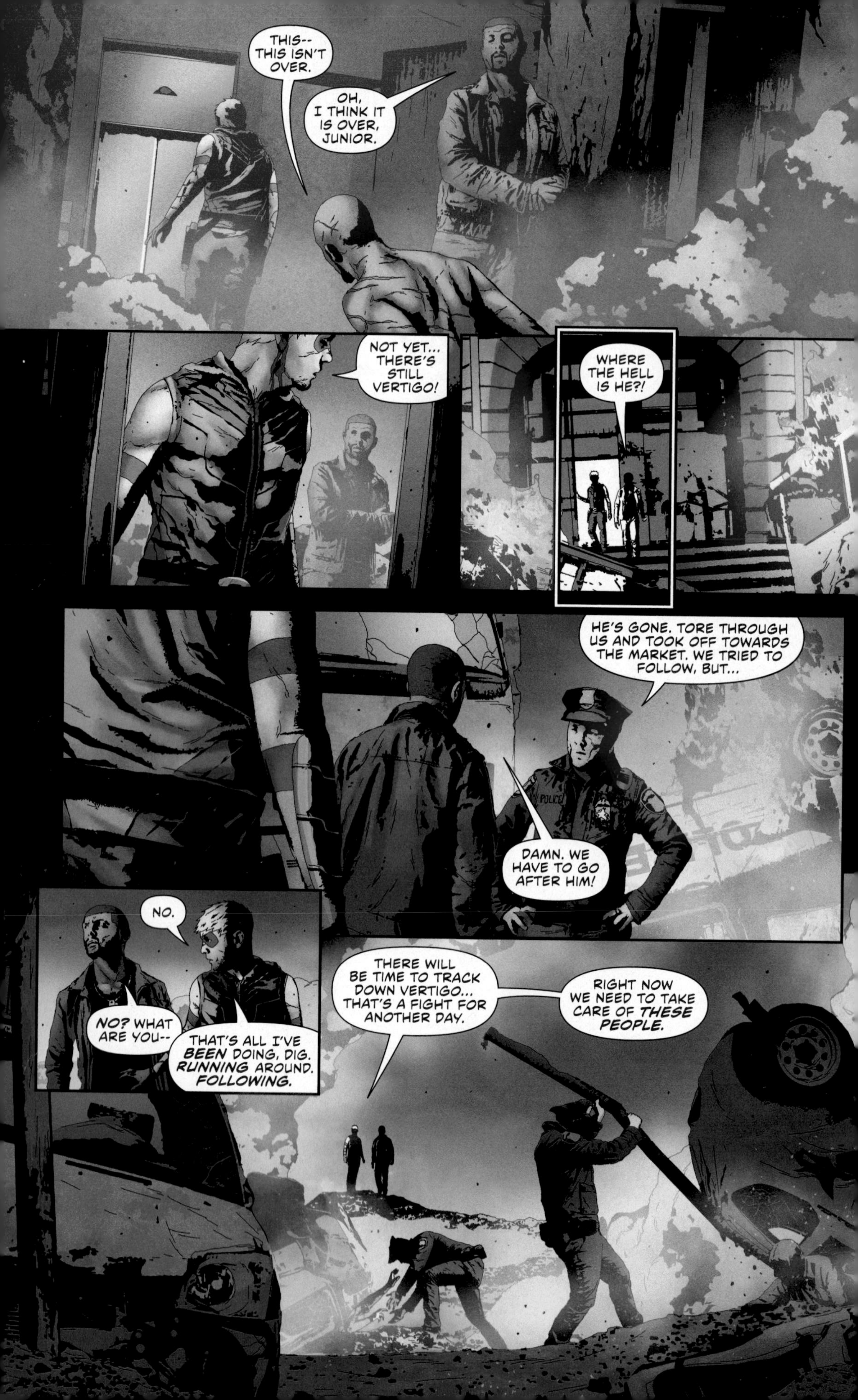
THIS-- THIS ISN'T OVER.
OH, I THINK IT IS OVER, JUNIOR.
NOT YET... THERE'S STILL VERTIGO!
WHERE THE HELL IS HE?!
HE'S GONE. TORE THROUGH US AND TOOK OFF TOWARDS THE MARKET. WE TRIED TO FOLLOW, BUT...
DAMN. WE HAVE TO GO AFTER HIM!
NO.
NO? WHAT ARE YOU--
THAT'S ALL I'VE BEEN DOING, DIG. RUNNING AROUND. FOLLOWING.
THERE WILL BE TIME TO TRACK DOWN VERTIGO... THAT'S A FIGHT FOR ANOTHER DAY.
RIGHT NOW WE NEED TO TAKE CARE OF THESE PEOPLE.
POLICE

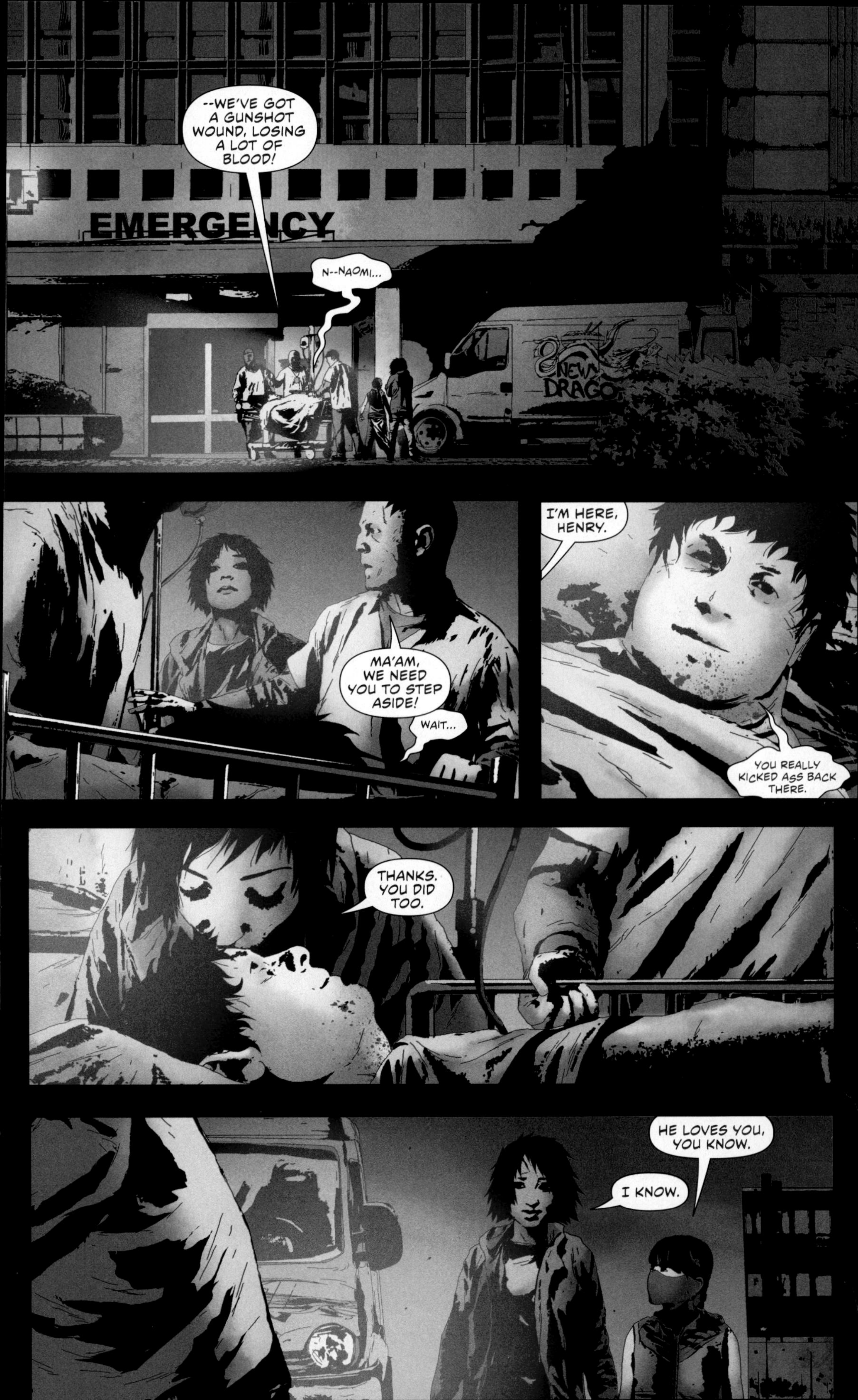
--WE'VE GOT A GUNSHOT WOUND, LOSING A LOT OF BLOOD!
EMERGENCY
N--NAOMI...
NEW DRAGO
MA'AM, WE NEED YOU TO STEP ASIDE!
WAIT...
I'M HERE, HENRY.
YOU REALLY KICKED ASS BACK THERE.
THANKS. YOU DID TOO.
HE LOVES YOU, YOU KNOW.
I KNOW.

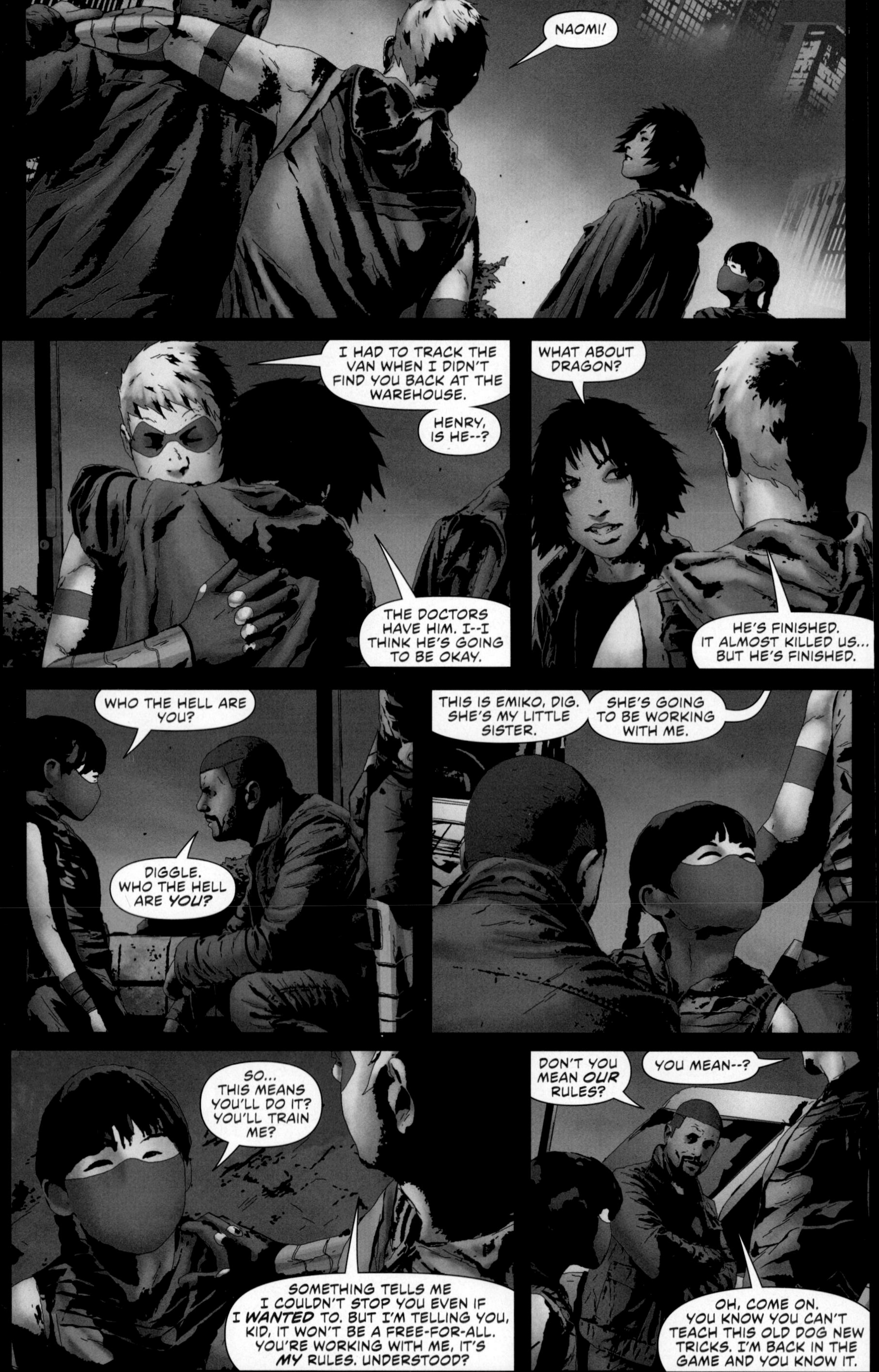
NAOMI!
I HAD TO TRACK THE VAN WHEN I DIDN'T FIND YOU BACK AT THE WAREHOUSE.
HENRY, IS HE--?
THE DOCTORS HAVE HIM. I--I THINK HE'S GOING TO BE OKAY.
WHAT ABOUT DRAGON?
HE'S FINISHED. IT ALMOST KILLED US... BUT HE'S FINISHED.
WHO THE HELL ARE YOU?
DIGGLE. WHO THE HELL ARE *YOU?*
THIS IS EMIKO, DIG. SHE'S MY LITTLE SISTER.
SHE'S GOING TO BE WORKING WITH ME.
SO... THIS MEANS YOU'LL DO IT? YOU'LL TRAIN ME?
SOMETHING TELLS ME I COULDN'T STOP YOU EVEN IF I ***WANTED*** TO. BUT I'M TELLING YOU, KID, IT WON'T BE A FREE-FOR-ALL. YOU'RE WORKING WITH ME, IT'S ***MY*** RULES. UNDERSTOOD?
DON'T YOU MEAN ***OUR*** RULES?
YOU MEAN--?
OH, COME ON. YOU KNOW YOU CAN'T TEACH THIS OLD DOG NEW TRICKS. I'M BACK IN THE GAME AND YOU KNOW IT.

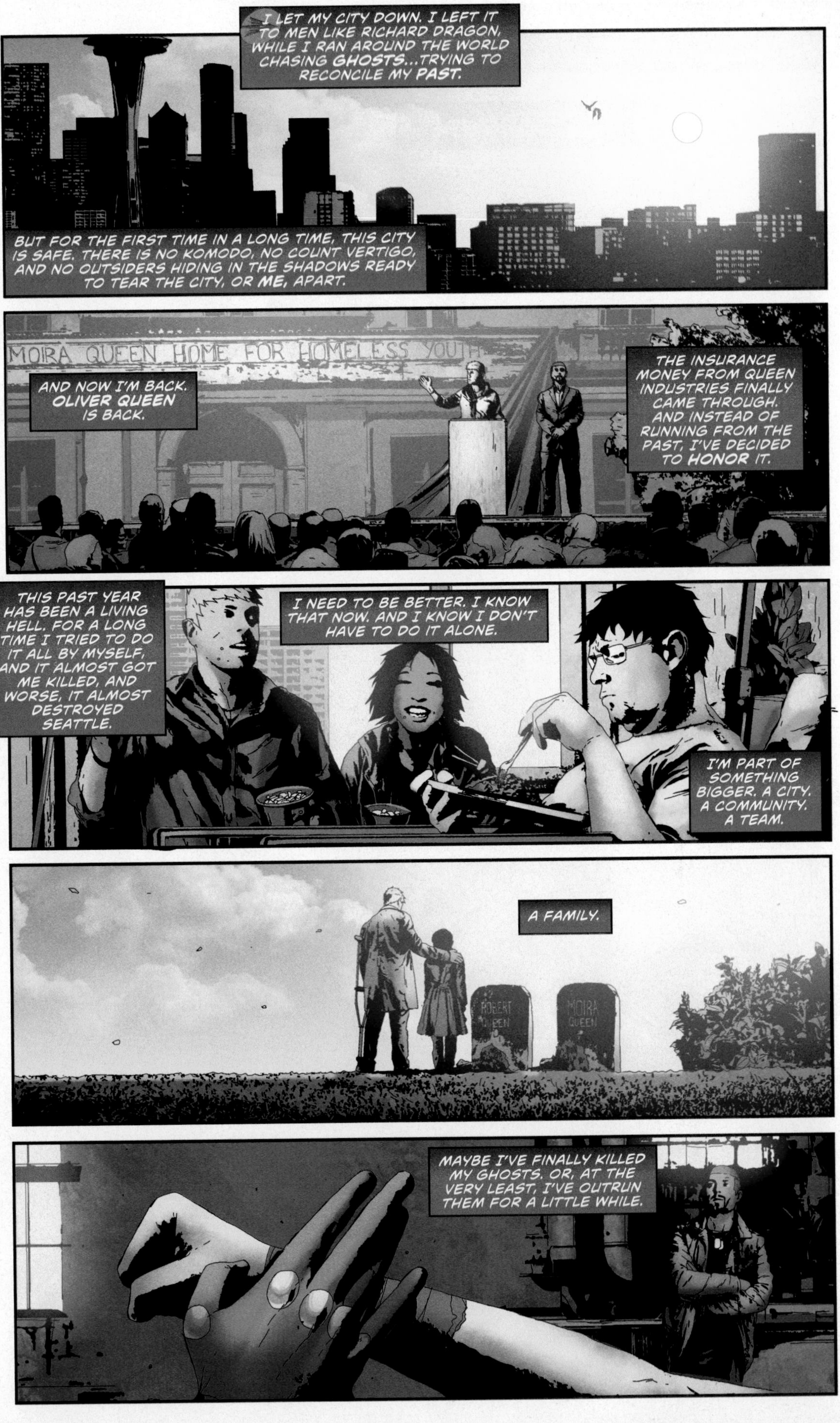
I LET MY CITY DOWN. I LEFT IT TO MEN LIKE RICHARD DRAGON, WHILE I RAN AROUND THE WORLD CHASING GHOSTS...TRYING TO RECONCILE MY PAST.
BUT FOR THE FIRST TIME IN A LONG TIME, THIS CITY IS SAFE. THERE IS NO KOMODO, NO COUNT VERTIGO, AND NO OUTSIDERS HIDING IN THE SHADOWS READY TO TEAR THE CITY, OR ME, APART.
MOIRA QUEEN HOME FOR HOMELESS YOUTH
AND NOW I'M BACK. OLIVER QUEEN IS BACK.
THE INSURANCE MONEY FROM QUEEN INDUSTRIES FINALLY CAME THROUGH. AND INSTEAD OF RUNNING FROM THE PAST, I'VE DECIDED TO HONOR IT.
THIS PAST YEAR HAS BEEN A LIVING HELL. FOR A LONG TIME I TRIED TO DO IT ALL BY MYSELF, AND IT ALMOST GOT ME KILLED, AND WORSE, IT ALMOST DESTROYED SEATTLE.
I NEED TO BE BETTER. I KNOW THAT NOW. AND I KNOW I DON'T HAVE TO DO IT ALONE.
I'M PART OF SOMETHING BIGGER. A CITY. A COMMUNITY. A TEAM.
A FAMILY.
ROBERT QUEEN
MOIRA QUEEN
MAYBE I'VE FINALLY KILLED MY GHOSTS. OR, AT THE VERY LEAST, I'VE OUTRUN THEM FOR A LITTLE WHILE.

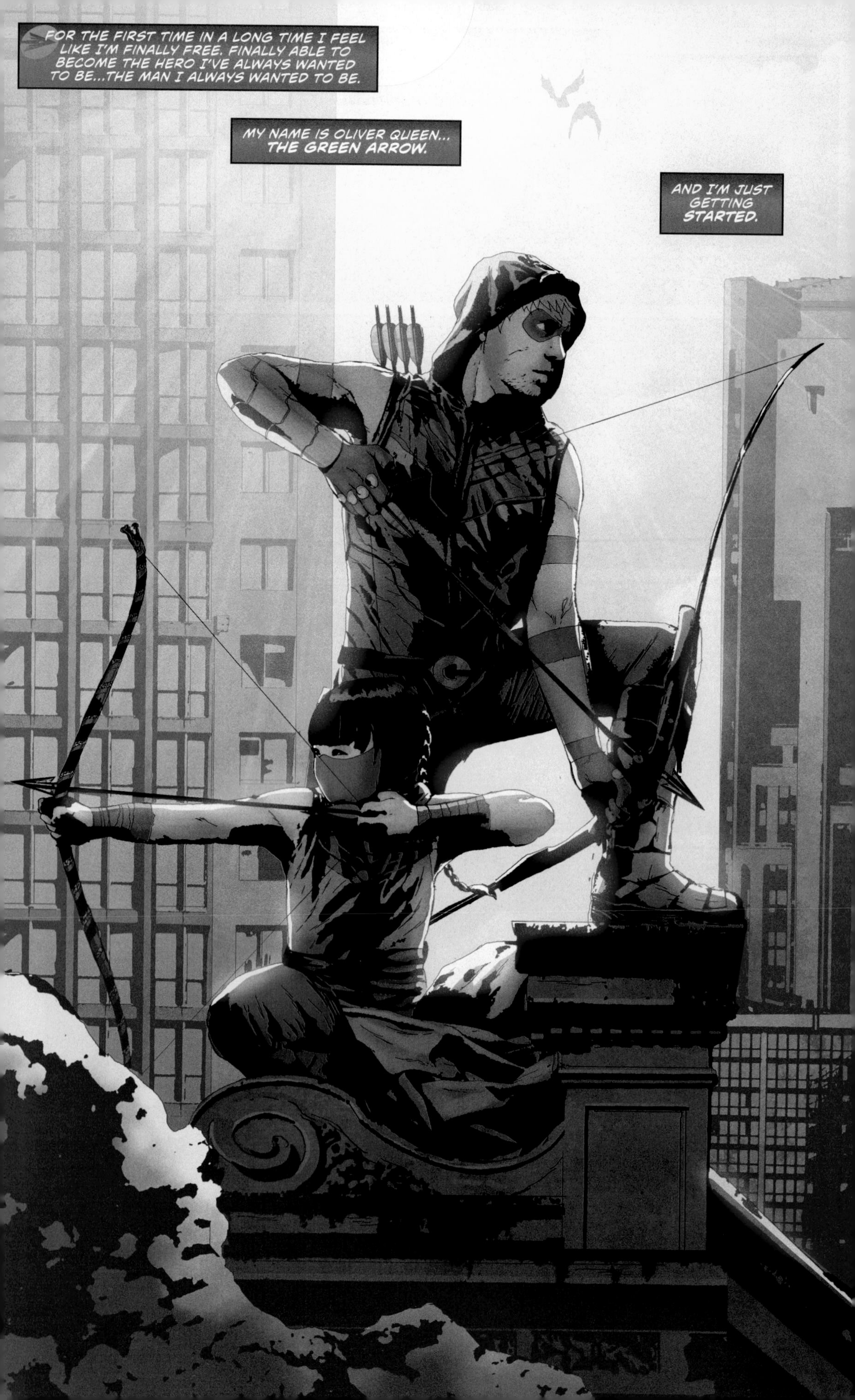
FOR THE FIRST TIME IN A LONG TIME I FEEL LIKE I'M FINALLY FREE. FINALLY ABLE TO BECOME THE HERO I'VE ALWAYS WANTED TO BE...THE MAN I ALWAYS WANTED TO BE.
MY NAME IS OLIVER QUEEN... THE GREEN ARROW.
AND I'M JUST GETTING STARTED.

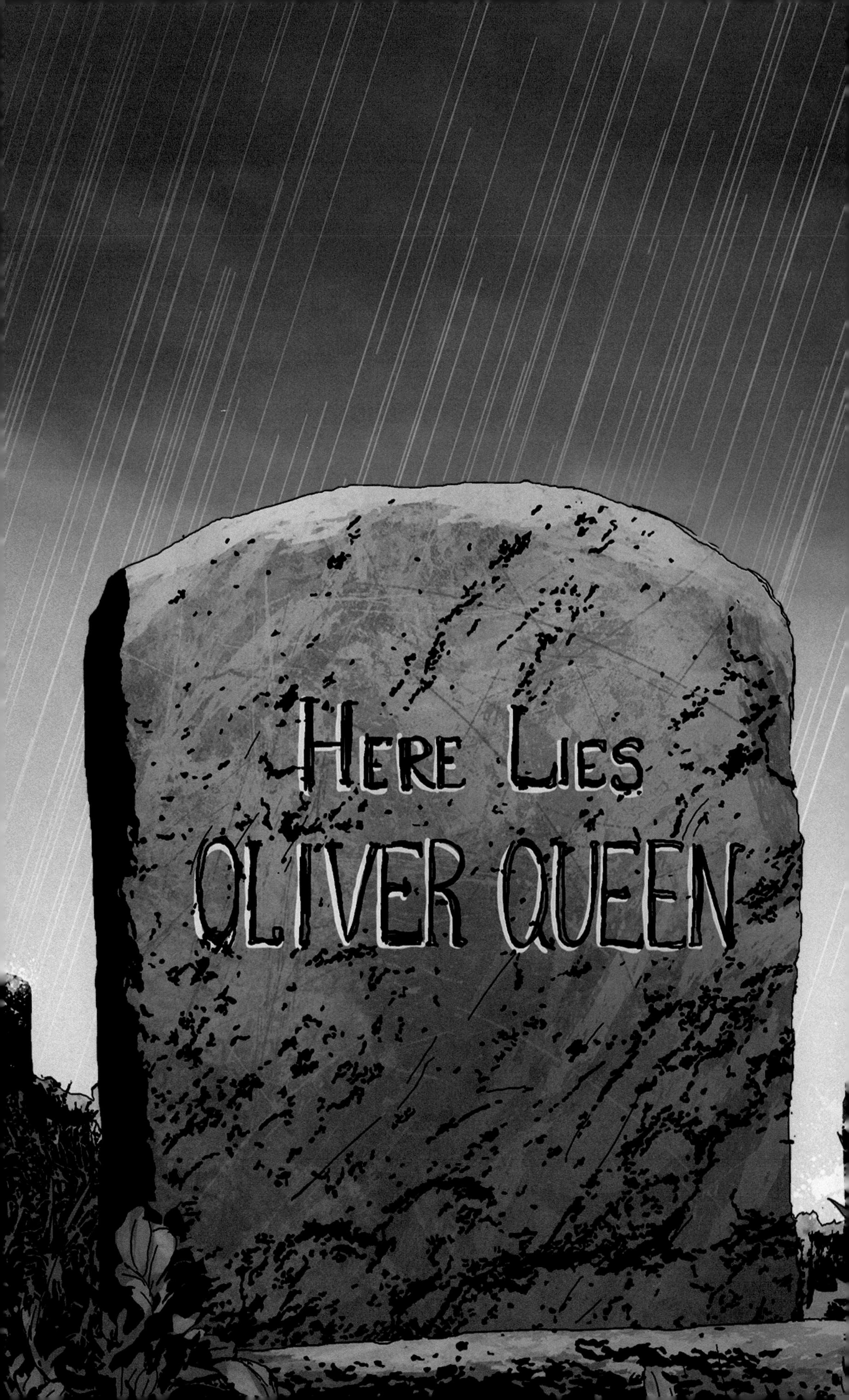
HERE LIES
OLIVER QUEEN

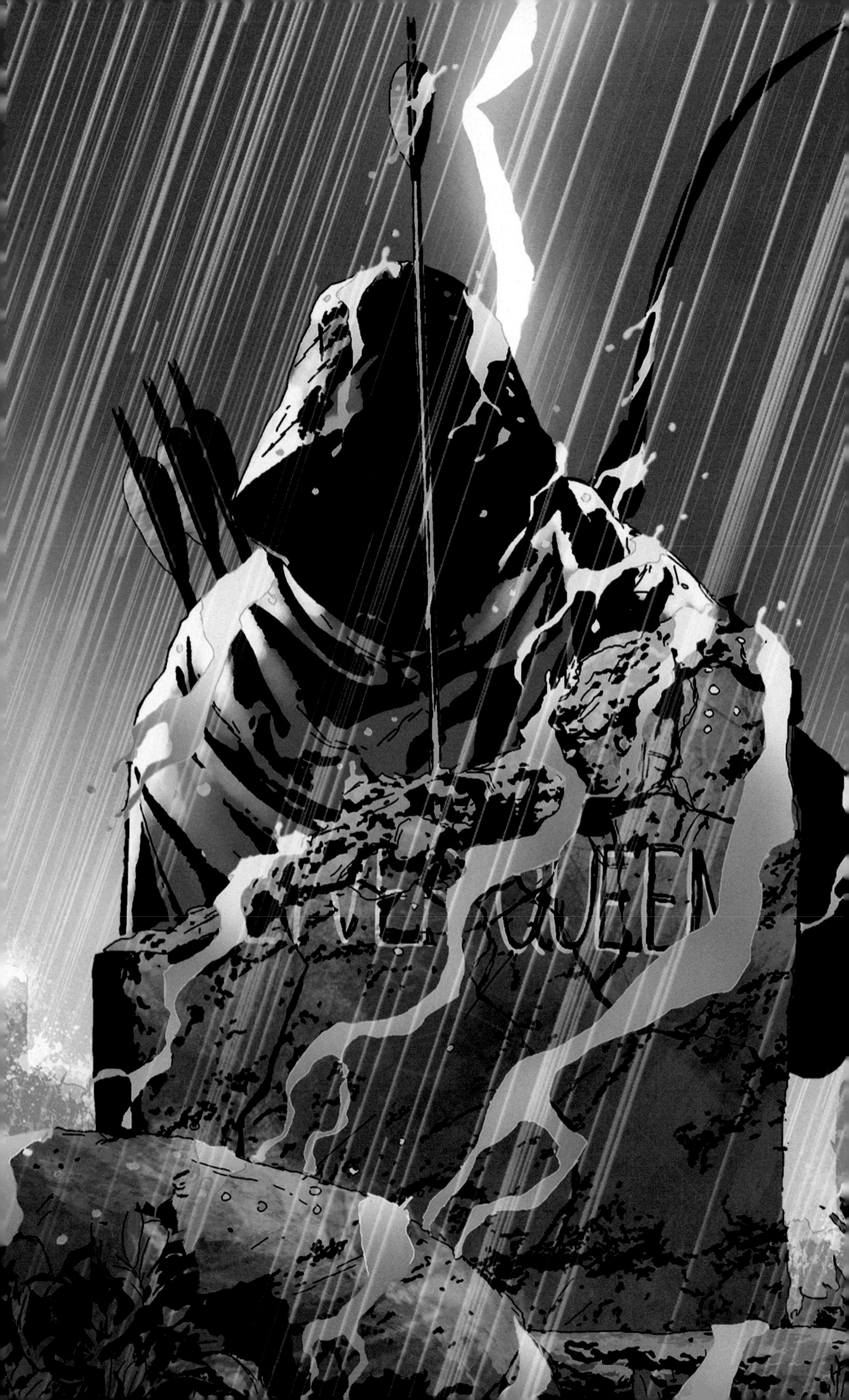
QUEEN

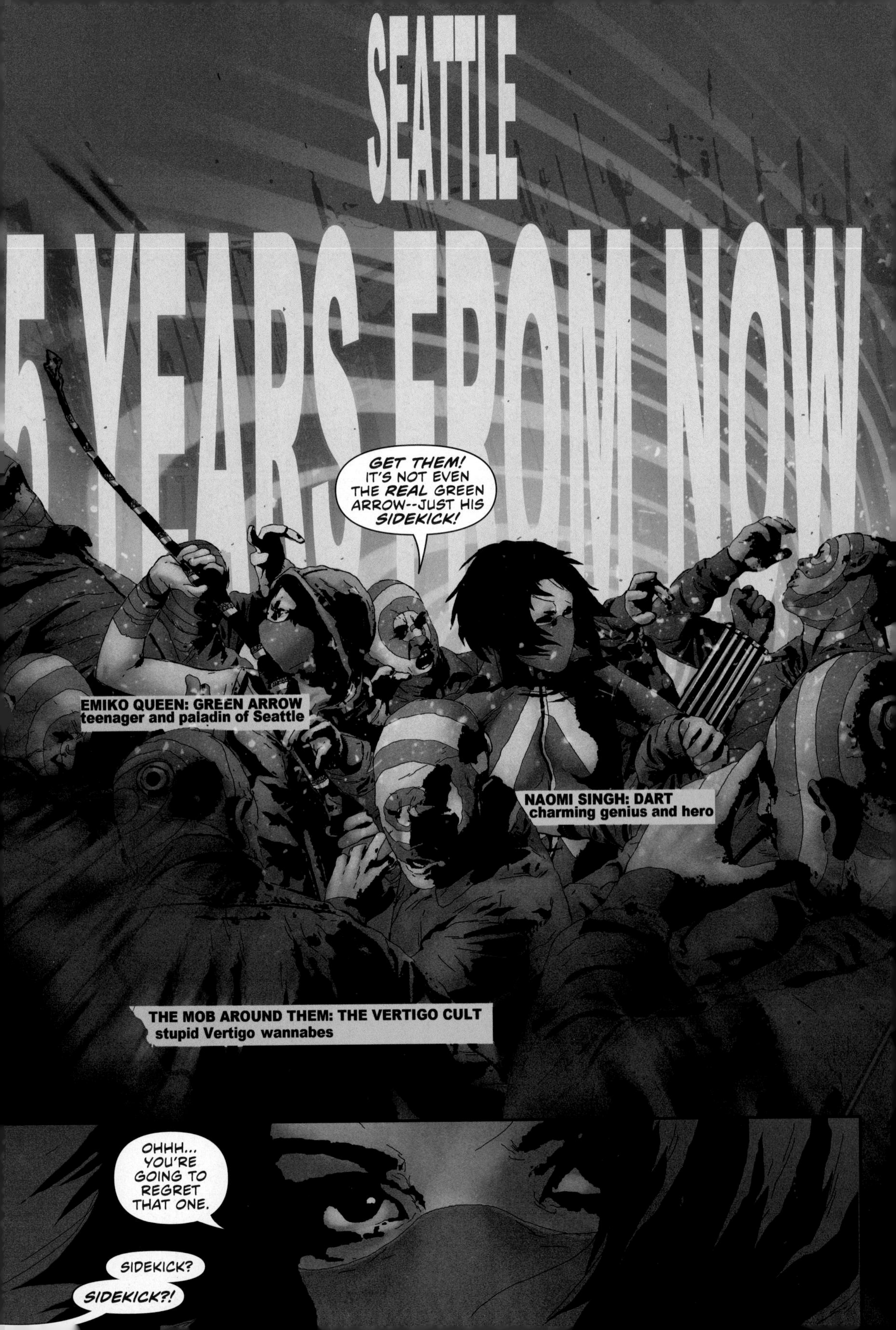

SEATTLE
5 YEARS FROM NOW
GET THEM! IT'S NOT EVEN THE REAL GREEN ARROW--JUST HIS SIDEKICK!
EMIKO QUEEN: GREEN ARROW teenager and paladin of Seattle
NAOMI SINGH: DART charming genius and hero
THE MOB AROUND THEM: THE VERTIGO CULT stupid Vertigo wannabes
OHHH... YOU'RE GOING TO REGRET THAT ONE.
SIDEKICK?
SIDEKICK?!

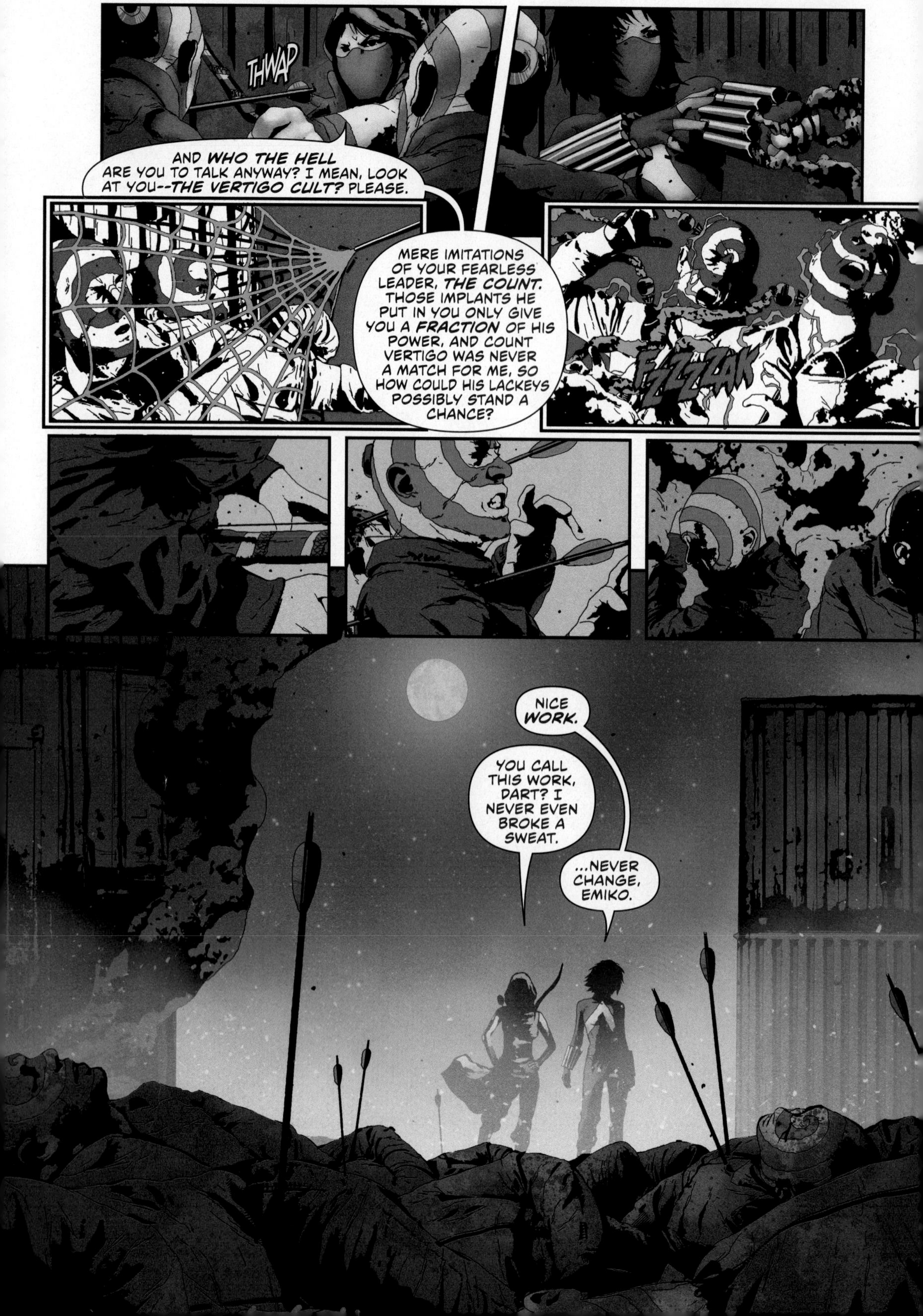
THWAP
AND WHO THE HELL ARE YOU TO TALK ANYWAY? I MEAN, LOOK AT YOU--THE VERTIGO CULT? PLEASE.
MERE IMITATIONS OF YOUR FEARLESS LEADER, THE COUNT. THOSE IMPLANTS HE PUT IN YOU ONLY GIVE YOU A FRACTION OF HIS POWER, AND COUNT VERTIGO WAS NEVER A MATCH FOR ME, SO HOW COULD HIS LACKEYS POSSIBLY STAND A CHANCE?
FZZZZAK
NICE WORK.
YOU CALL THIS WORK, DART? I NEVER EVEN BROKE A SWEAT.
...NEVER CHANGE, EMIKO.

I MUST SAY THOUGH, YOU'RE GETTING BETTER, NAOMI. WHEN YOU FIRST PROPOSED COMING INTO THE FIELD WITH ME AS DART, I WAS A BIT SKEPTICAL, BUT--

BEEP   BEEP

EMI--THE ARROW CAVE HAS BEEN BREACHED!

BLOOD?!

STAY HERE AND WATCH OUR BACKS...

BUT--

I SAID-- STAY HERE.

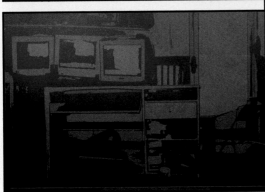

--GREEN ARROW.

SHOW YOURSELF!

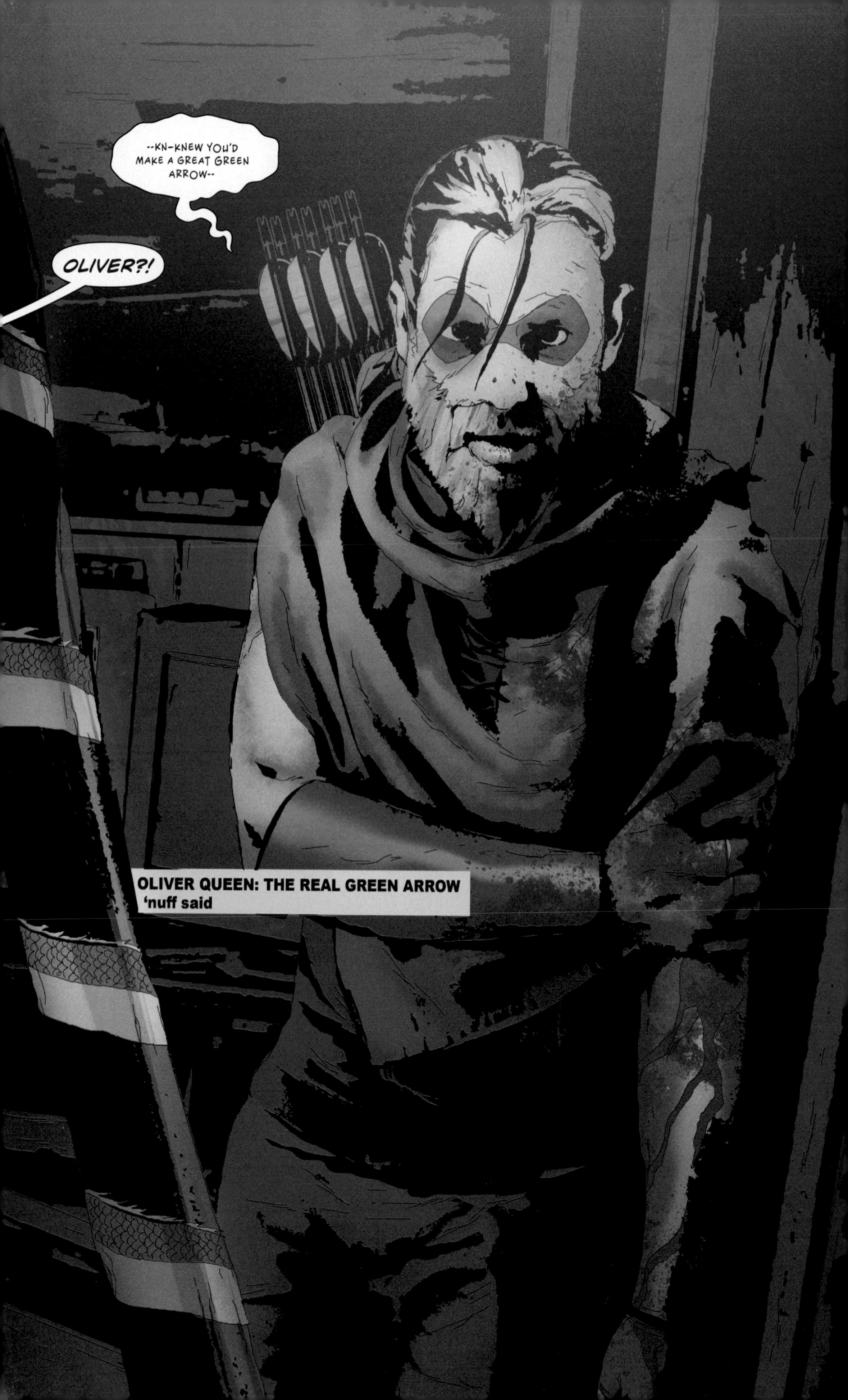

--KN-KNEW YOU'D MAKE A GREAT GREEN ARROW--
OLIVER?!
OLIVER QUEEN: THE REAL GREEN ARROW
'nuff said

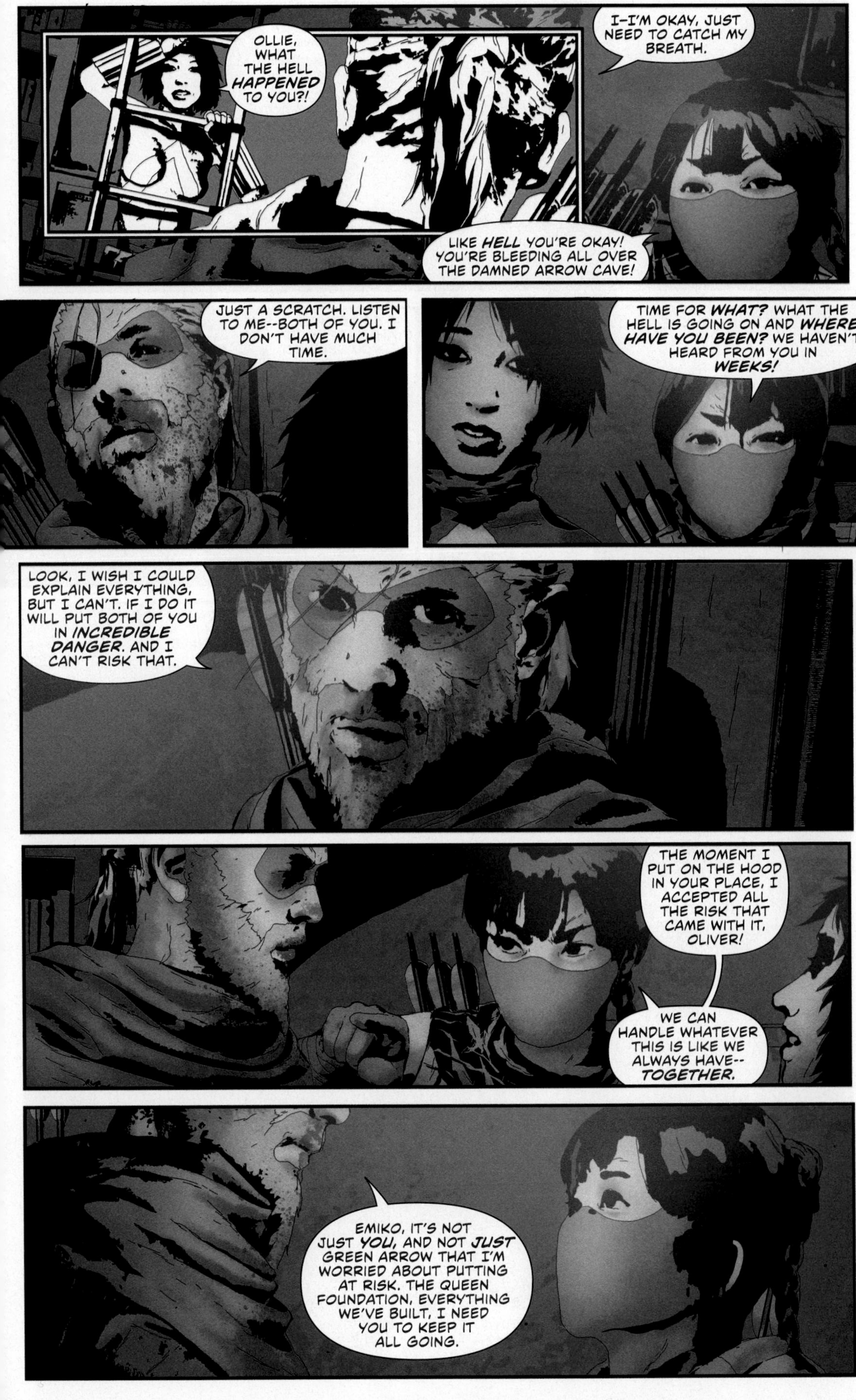
OLLIE, WHAT THE HELL HAPPENED TO YOU?!
I-I'M OKAY, JUST NEED TO CATCH MY BREATH.
LIKE HELL YOU'RE OKAY! YOU'RE BLEEDING ALL OVER THE DAMNED ARROW CAVE!
JUST A SCRATCH. LISTEN TO ME--BOTH OF YOU. I DON'T HAVE MUCH TIME.
TIME FOR WHAT? WHAT THE HELL IS GOING ON AND WHERE HAVE YOU BEEN? WE HAVEN'T HEARD FROM YOU IN WEEKS!
LOOK, I WISH I COULD EXPLAIN EVERYTHING, BUT I CAN'T. IF I DO IT WILL PUT BOTH OF YOU IN INCREDIBLE DANGER. AND I CAN'T RISK THAT.
THE MOMENT I PUT ON THE HOOD IN YOUR PLACE, I ACCEPTED ALL THE RISK THAT CAME WITH IT, OLIVER!
WE CAN HANDLE WHATEVER THIS IS LIKE WE ALWAYS HAVE-- TOGETHER.
EMIKO, IT'S NOT JUST YOU, AND NOT JUST GREEN ARROW THAT I'M WORRIED ABOUT PUTTING AT RISK. THE QUEEN FOUNDATION, EVERYTHING WE'VE BUILT, I NEED YOU TO KEEP IT ALL GOING.

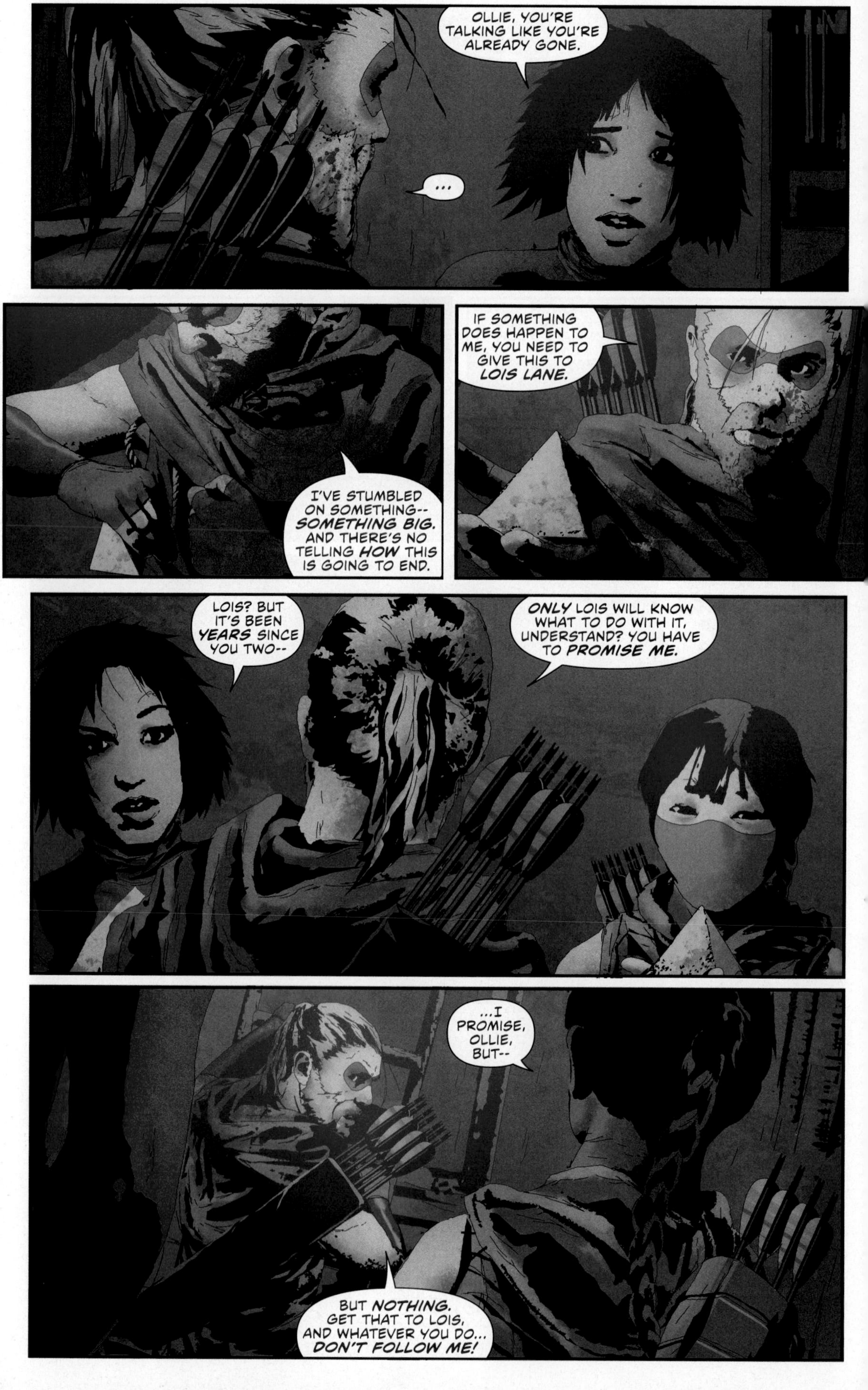
OLLIE, YOU'RE TALKING LIKE YOU'RE ALREADY GONE.
...
I'VE STUMBLED ON SOMETHING-- SOMETHING BIG. AND THERE'S NO TELLING HOW THIS IS GOING TO END.
IF SOMETHING DOES HAPPEN TO ME, YOU NEED TO GIVE THIS TO LOIS LANE.
LOIS? BUT IT'S BEEN YEARS SINCE YOU TWO--
ONLY LOIS WILL KNOW WHAT TO DO WITH IT, UNDERSTAND? YOU HAVE TO PROMISE ME.
...I PROMISE, OLLIE, BUT--
BUT NOTHING. GET THAT TO LOIS, AND WHATEVER YOU DO... DON'T FOLLOW ME!

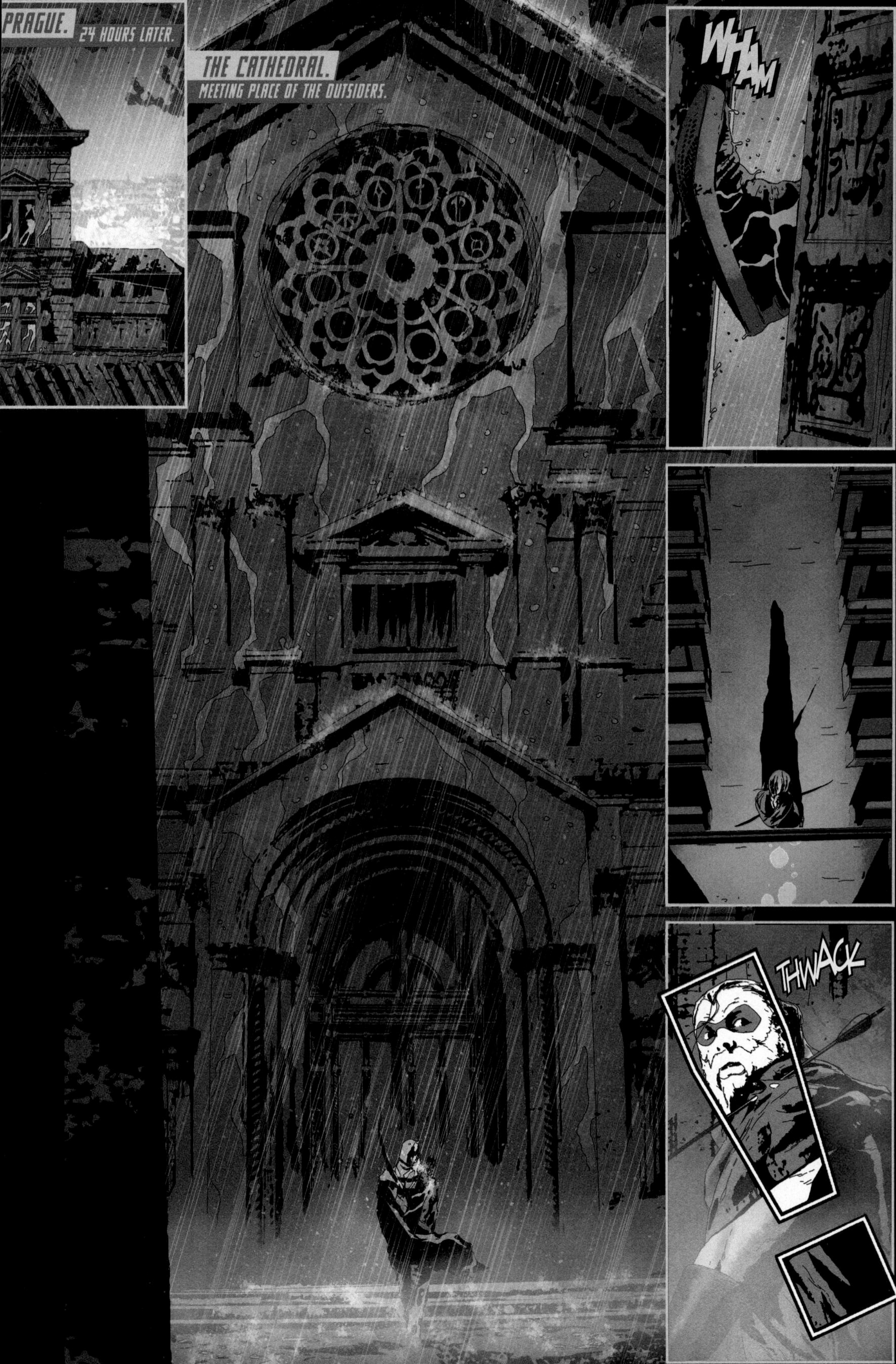
PRAGUE.
24 HOURS LATER.
THE CATHEDRAL.
MEETING PLACE OF THE OUTSIDERS.
WHAM
THWACK

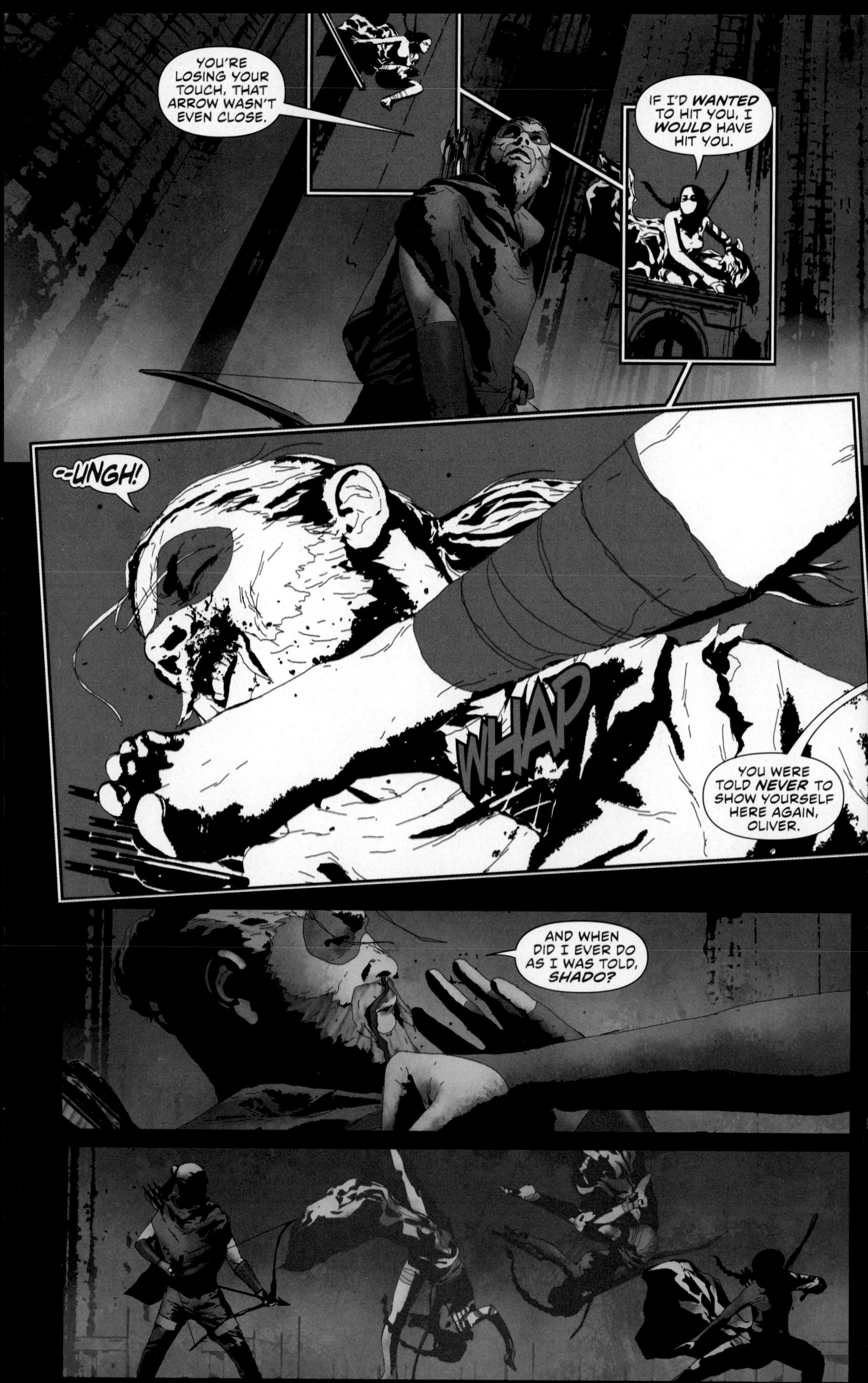
YOU'RE LOSING YOUR TOUCH, THAT ARROW WASN'T EVEN CLOSE.
IF I'D WANTED TO HIT YOU, I WOULD HAVE HIT YOU.
--UNGH!
WHAP
YOU WERE TOLD NEVER TO SHOW YOURSELF HERE AGAIN, OLIVER.
AND WHEN DID I EVER DO AS I WAS TOLD, SHADO?

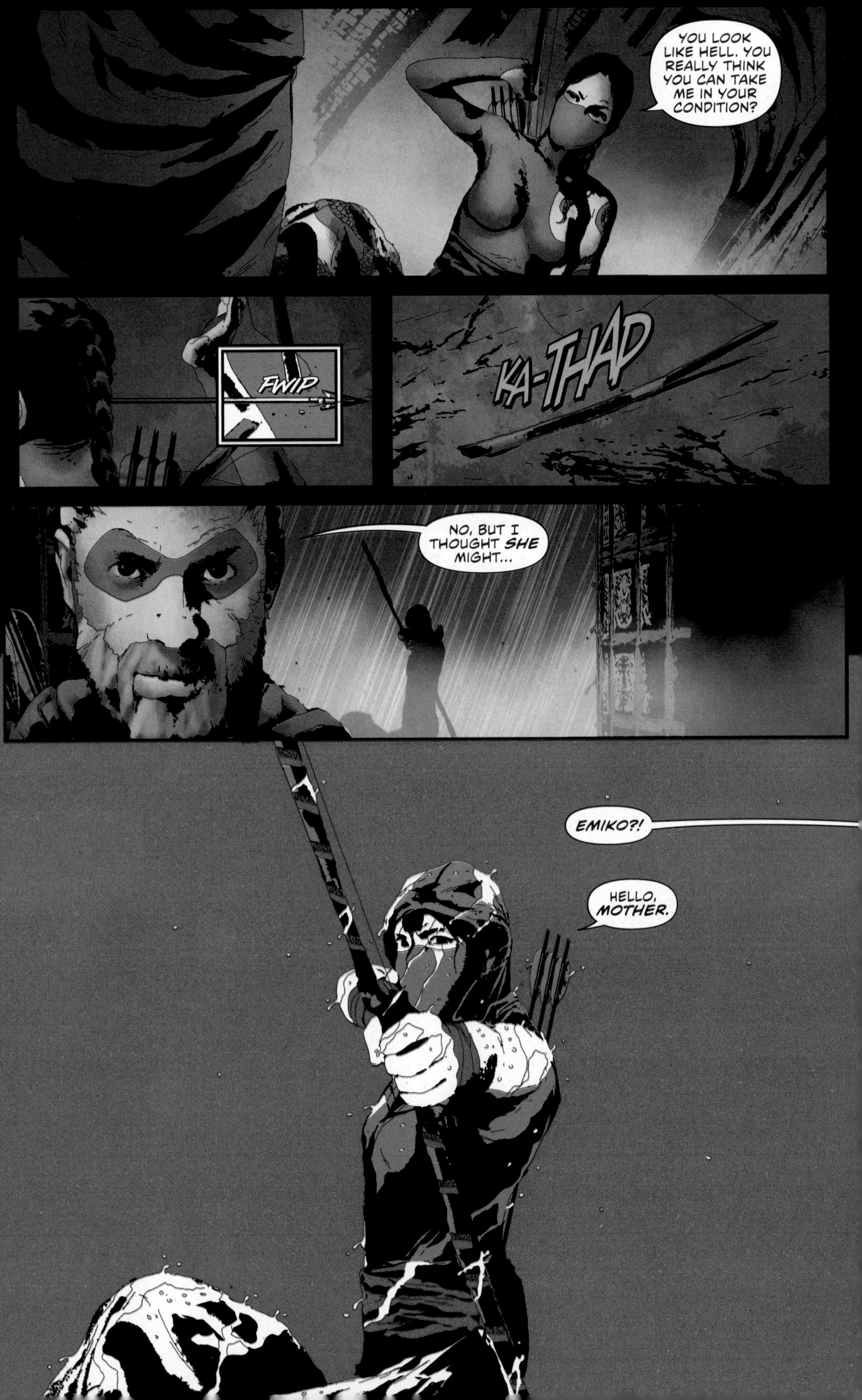
YOU LOOK LIKE HELL. YOU REALLY THINK YOU CAN TAKE ME IN YOUR CONDITION?
FWIP
KA-THAD
NO, BUT I THOUGHT SHE MIGHT...
EMIKO?!
HELLO, MOTHER.

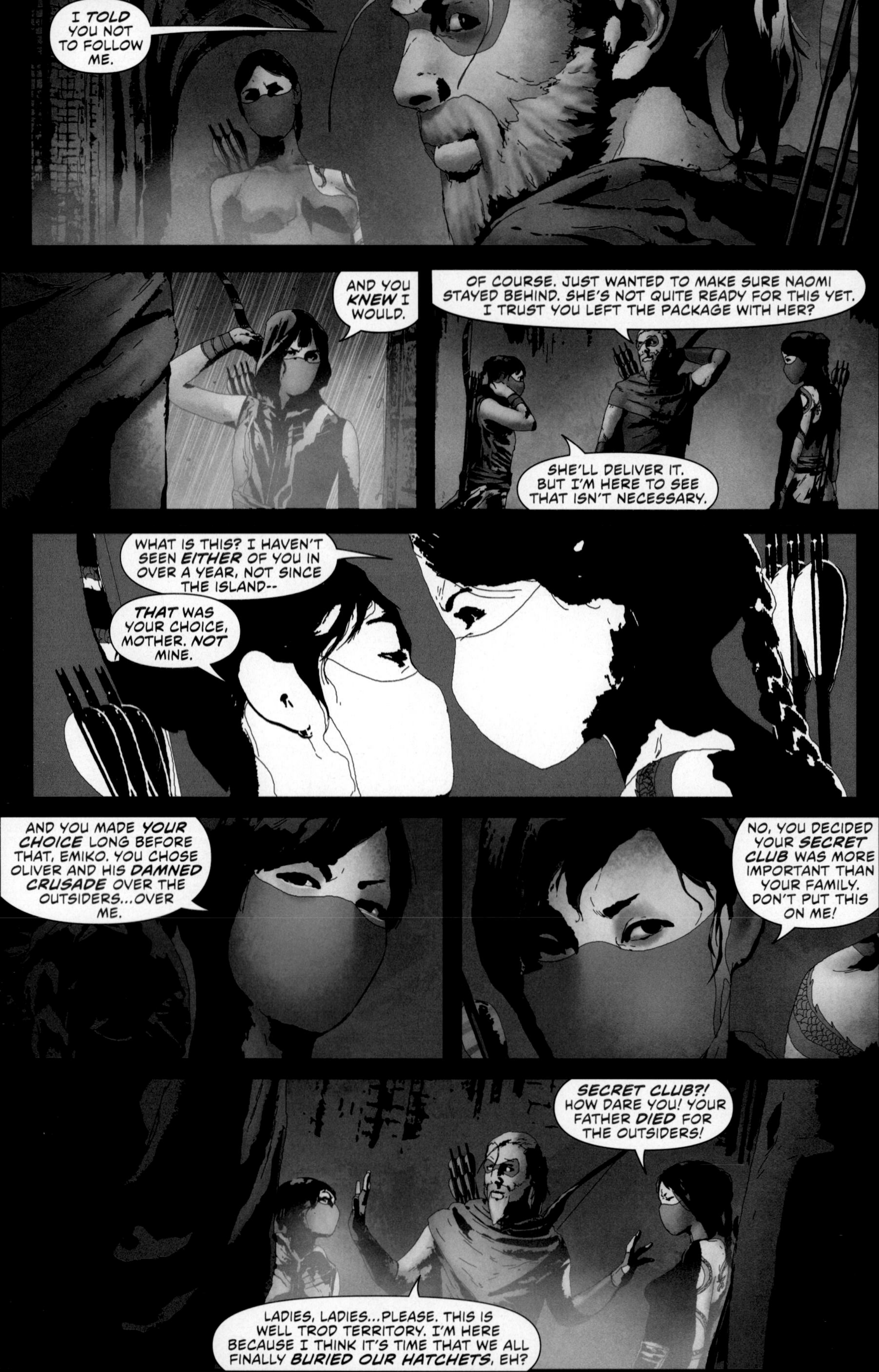
I TOLD YOU NOT TO FOLLOW ME.
AND YOU KNEW I WOULD.
OF COURSE. JUST WANTED TO MAKE SURE NAOMI STAYED BEHIND. SHE'S NOT QUITE READY FOR THIS YET. I TRUST YOU LEFT THE PACKAGE WITH HER?
SHE'LL DELIVER IT. BUT I'M HERE TO SEE THAT ISN'T NECESSARY.
WHAT IS THIS? I HAVEN'T SEEN EITHER OF YOU IN OVER A YEAR, NOT SINCE THE ISLAND--
THAT WAS YOUR CHOICE, MOTHER. NOT MINE.
AND YOU MADE YOUR CHOICE LONG BEFORE THAT, EMIKO. YOU CHOSE OLIVER AND HIS DAMNED CRUSADE OVER THE OUTSIDERS...OVER ME.
NO, YOU DECIDED YOUR SECRET CLUB WAS MORE IMPORTANT THAN YOUR FAMILY. DON'T PUT THIS ON ME!
SECRET CLUB?! HOW DARE YOU! YOUR FATHER DIED FOR THE OUTSIDERS!
LADIES, LADIES...PLEASE. THIS IS WELL TROD TERRITORY. I'M HERE BECAUSE I THINK IT'S TIME THAT WE ALL FINALLY BURIED OUR HATCHETS, EH?

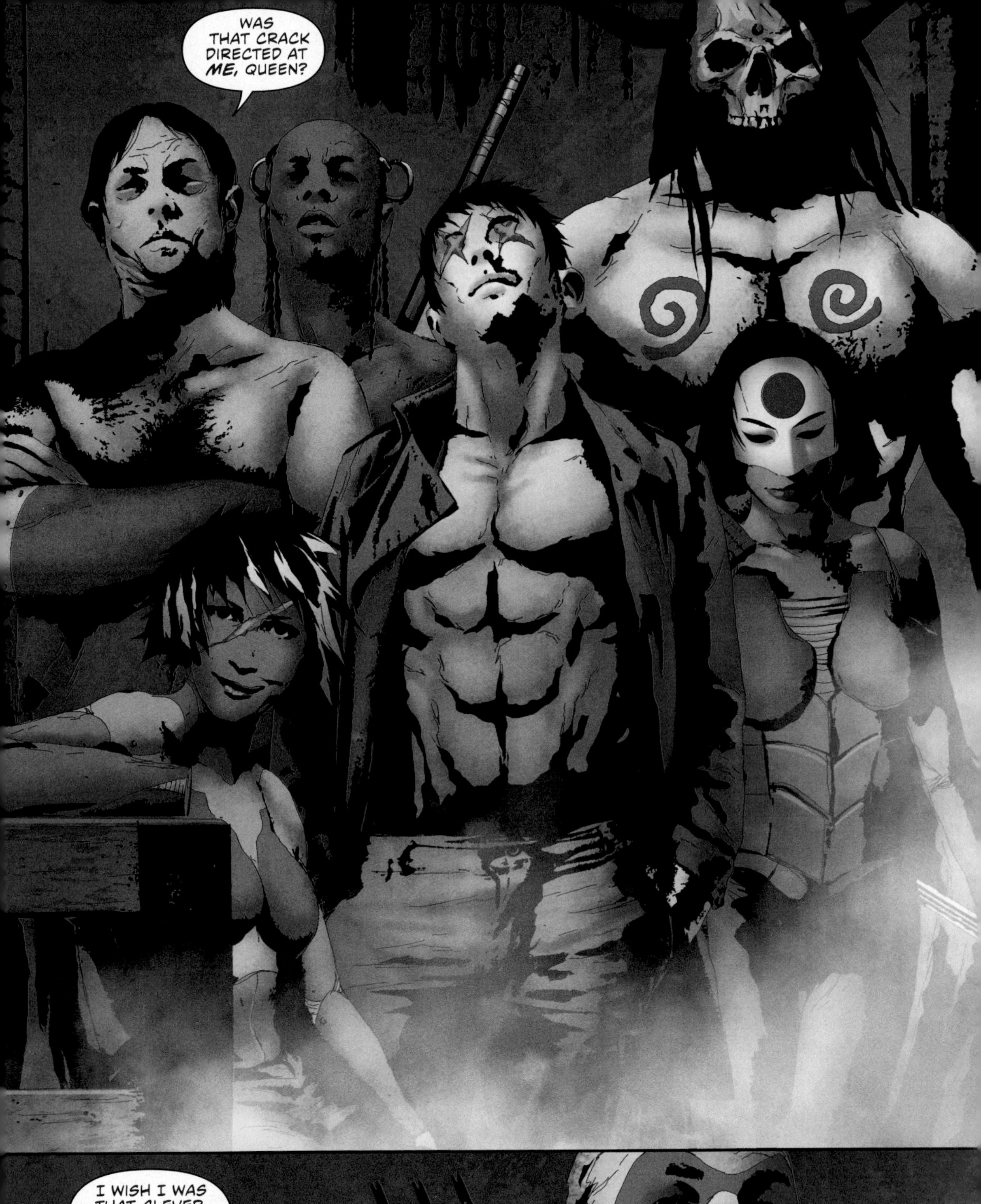
WAS THAT CRACK DIRECTED AT ME, QUEEN?

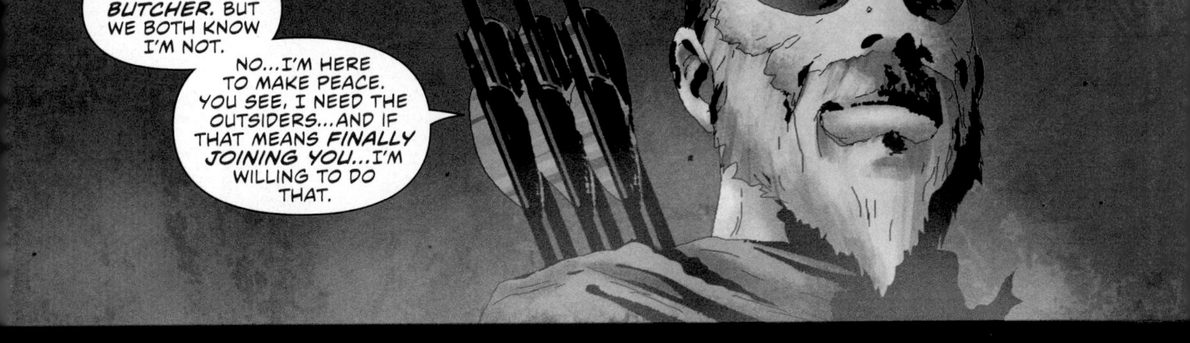
I WISH I WAS THAT CLEVER, BUTCHER. BUT WE BOTH KNOW I'M NOT.
NO...I'M HERE TO MAKE PEACE. YOU SEE, I NEED THE OUTSIDERS...AND IF THAT MEANS FINALLY JOINING YOU...I'M WILLING TO DO THAT.

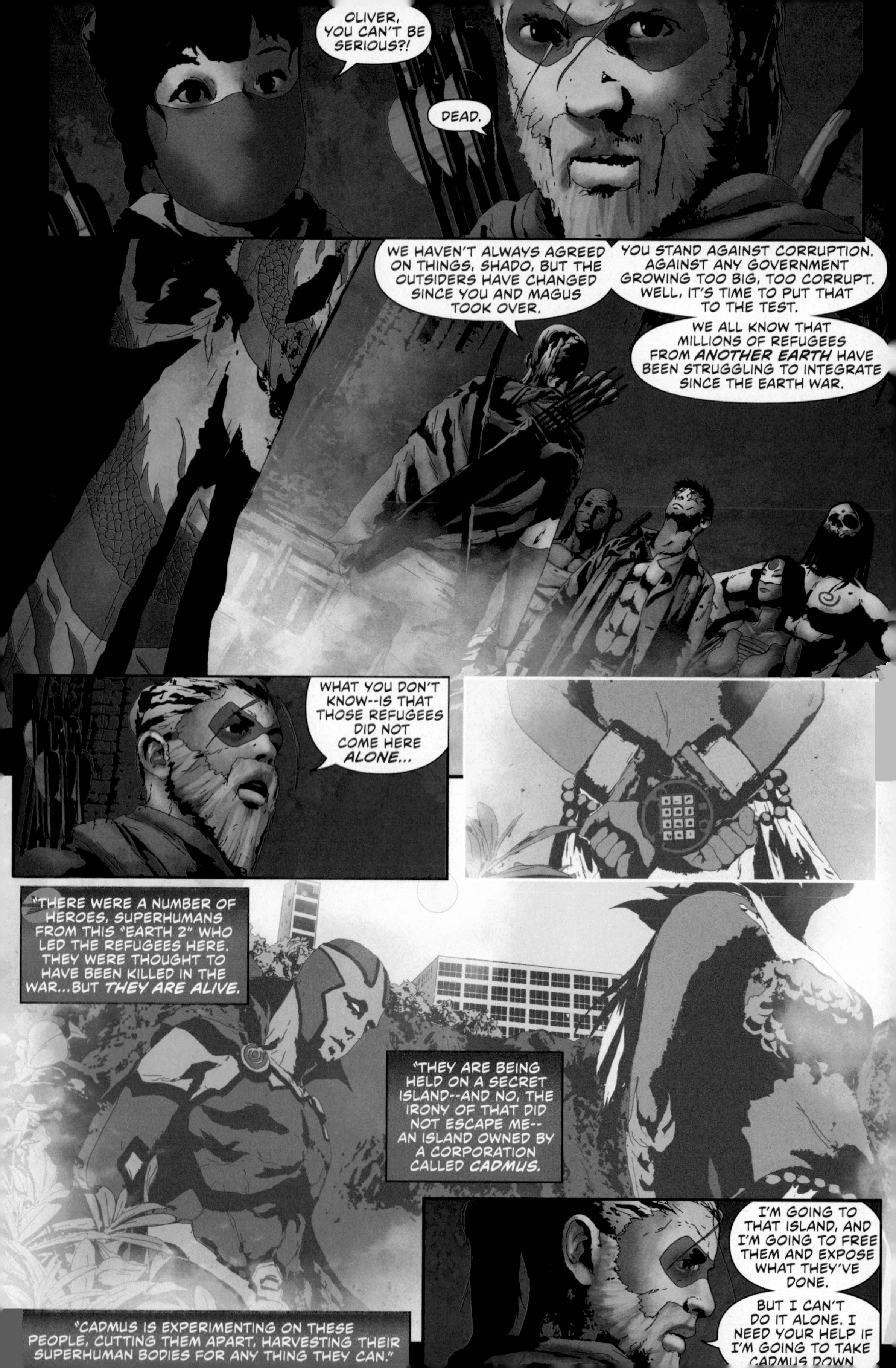
OLIVER, YOU CAN'T BE SERIOUS?!
DEAD.
WE HAVEN'T ALWAYS AGREED ON THINGS, SHADO, BUT THE OUTSIDERS HAVE CHANGED SINCE YOU AND MAGUS TOOK OVER.
YOU STAND AGAINST CORRUPTION. AGAINST ANY GOVERNMENT GROWING TOO BIG, TOO CORRUPT. WELL, IT'S TIME TO PUT THAT TO THE TEST.
WE ALL KNOW THAT MILLIONS OF REFUGEES FROM ANOTHER EARTH HAVE BEEN STRUGGLING TO INTEGRATE SINCE THE EARTH WAR.
WHAT YOU DON'T KNOW--IS THAT THOSE REFUGEES DID NOT COME HERE ALONE...
"THERE WERE A NUMBER OF HEROES, SUPERHUMANS FROM THIS "EARTH 2" WHO LED THE REFUGEES HERE. THEY WERE THOUGHT TO HAVE BEEN KILLED IN THE WAR...BUT THEY ARE ALIVE.
"THEY ARE BEING HELD ON A SECRET ISLAND--AND NO, THE IRONY OF THAT DID NOT ESCAPE ME--AN ISLAND OWNED BY A CORPORATION CALLED CADMUS.
"CADMUS IS EXPERIMENTING ON THESE PEOPLE, CUTTING THEM APART, HARVESTING THEIR SUPERHUMAN BODIES FOR ANY THING THEY CAN."
I'M GOING TO THAT ISLAND, AND I'M GOING TO FREE THEM AND EXPOSE WHAT THEY'VE DONE.
BUT I CAN'T DO IT ALONE. I NEED YOUR HELP IF I'M GOING TO TAKE CADMUS DOWN

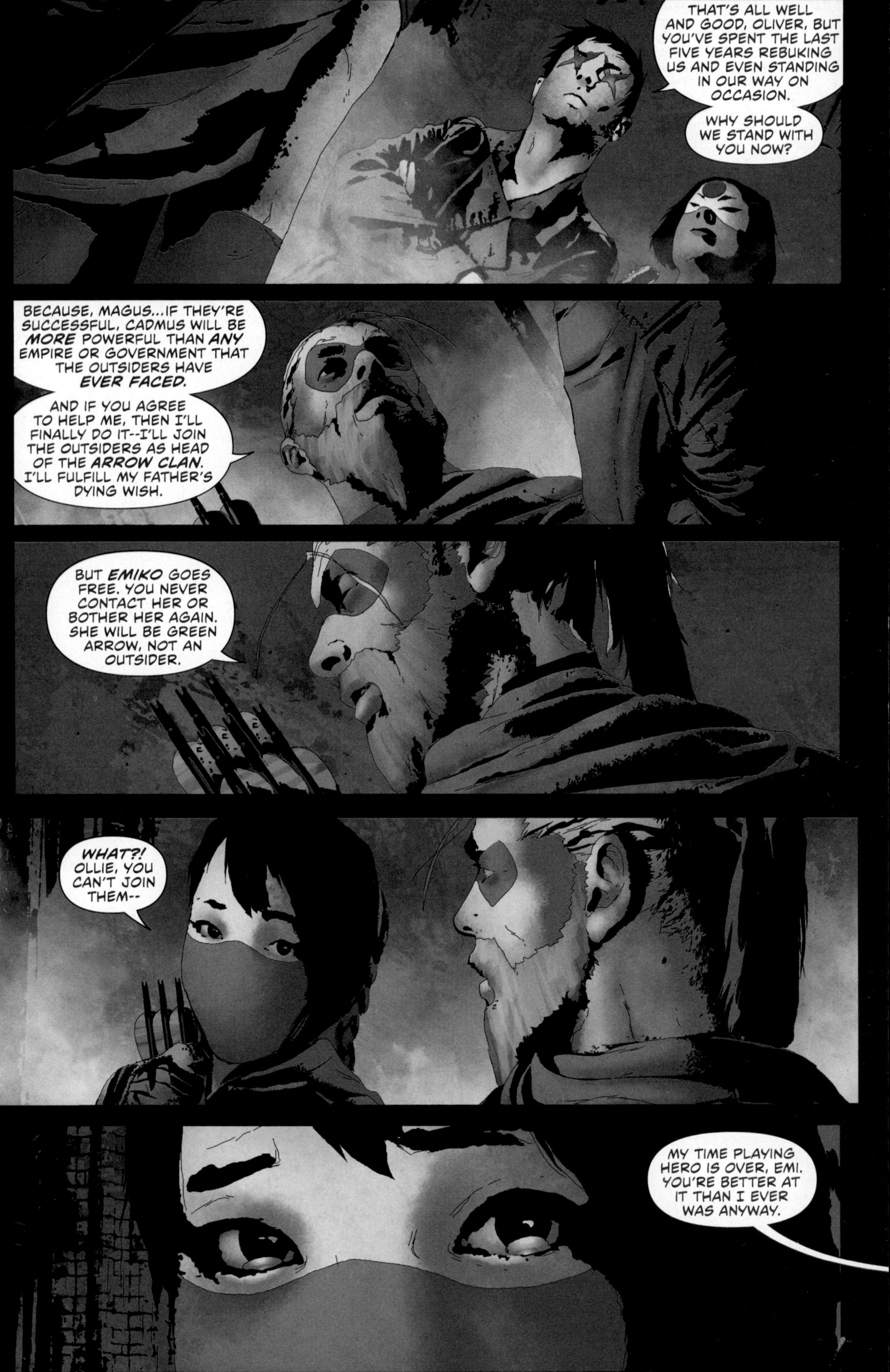
THAT'S ALL WELL AND GOOD, OLIVER, BUT YOU'VE SPENT THE LAST FIVE YEARS REBUKING US AND EVEN STANDING IN OUR WAY ON OCCASION.
WHY SHOULD WE STAND WITH YOU NOW?
BECAUSE, MAGUS...IF THEY'RE SUCCESSFUL, CADMUS WILL BE **MORE** POWERFUL THAN **ANY** EMPIRE OR GOVERNMENT THAT THE OUTSIDERS HAVE **EVER FACED**.
AND IF YOU AGREE TO HELP ME, THEN I'LL FINALLY DO IT--I'LL JOIN THE OUTSIDERS AS HEAD OF THE **ARROW CLAN**. I'LL FULFILL MY FATHER'S DYING WISH.
BUT **EMIKO** GOES FREE. YOU NEVER CONTACT HER OR BOTHER HER AGAIN. SHE WILL BE GREEN ARROW, NOT AN OUTSIDER.
WHAT?! OLLIE, YOU CAN'T JOIN THEM--
MY TIME PLAYING HERO IS OVER, EMI. YOU'RE BETTER AT IT THAN I EVER WAS ANYWAY.

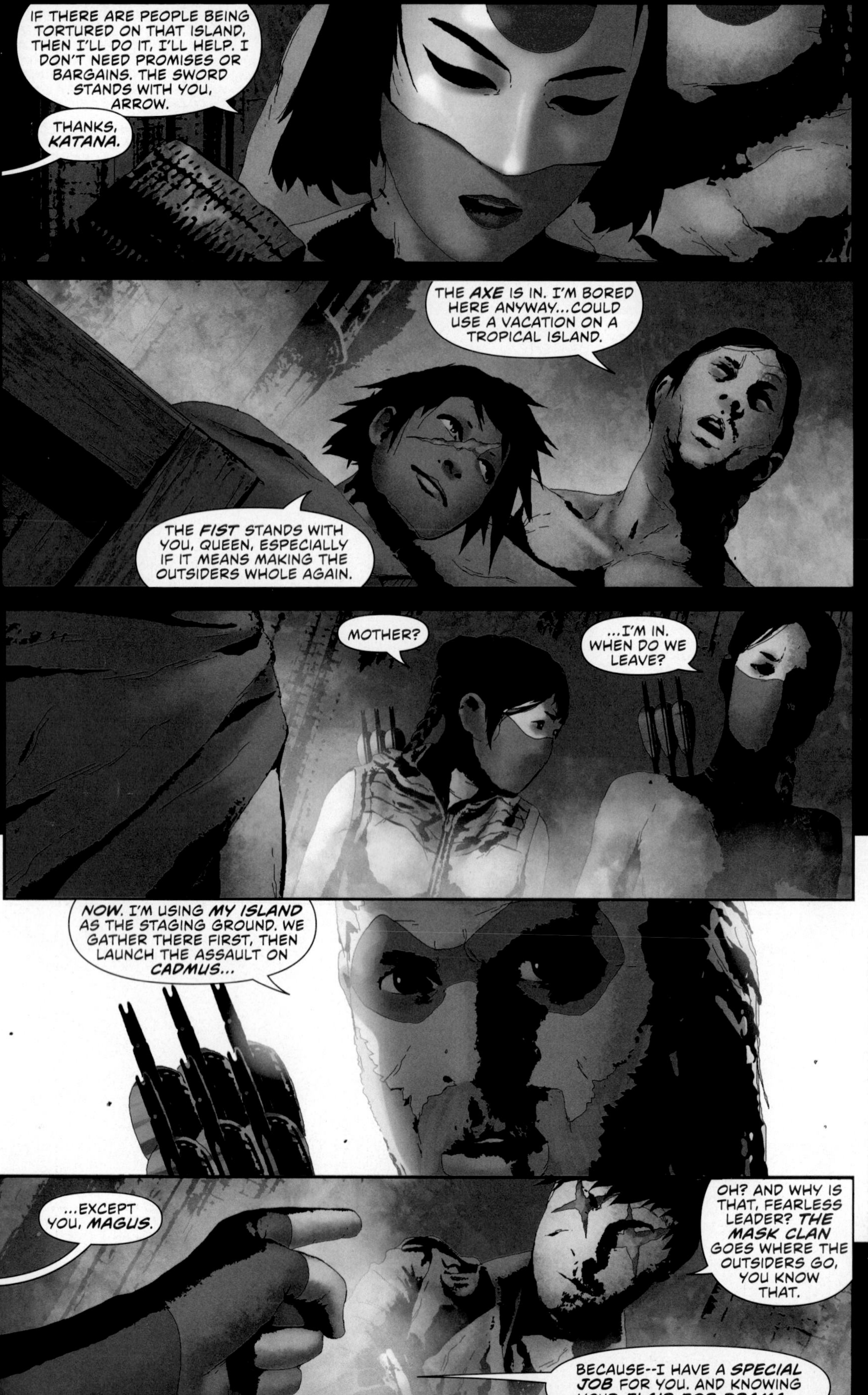
IF THERE ARE PEOPLE BEING TORTURED ON THAT ISLAND, THEN I'LL DO IT, I'LL HELP. I DON'T NEED PROMISES OR BARGAINS. THE SWORD STANDS WITH YOU, ARROW.
THANKS, KATANA.
THE AXE IS IN. I'M BORED HERE ANYWAY...COULD USE A VACATION ON A TROPICAL ISLAND.
THE FIST STANDS WITH YOU, QUEEN, ESPECIALLY IF IT MEANS MAKING THE OUTSIDERS WHOLE AGAIN.
MOTHER?
...I'M IN. WHEN DO WE LEAVE?
NOW. I'M USING MY ISLAND AS THE STAGING GROUND. WE GATHER THERE FIRST, THEN LAUNCH THE ASSAULT ON CADMUS...
...EXCEPT YOU, MAGUS.
OH? AND WHY IS THAT, FEARLESS LEADER? THE MASK CLAN GOES WHERE THE OUTSIDERS GO, YOU KNOW THAT.
BECAUSE--I HAVE A SPECIAL JOB FOR YOU. AND KNOWING YOUR FLAIR FOR DRAMA...

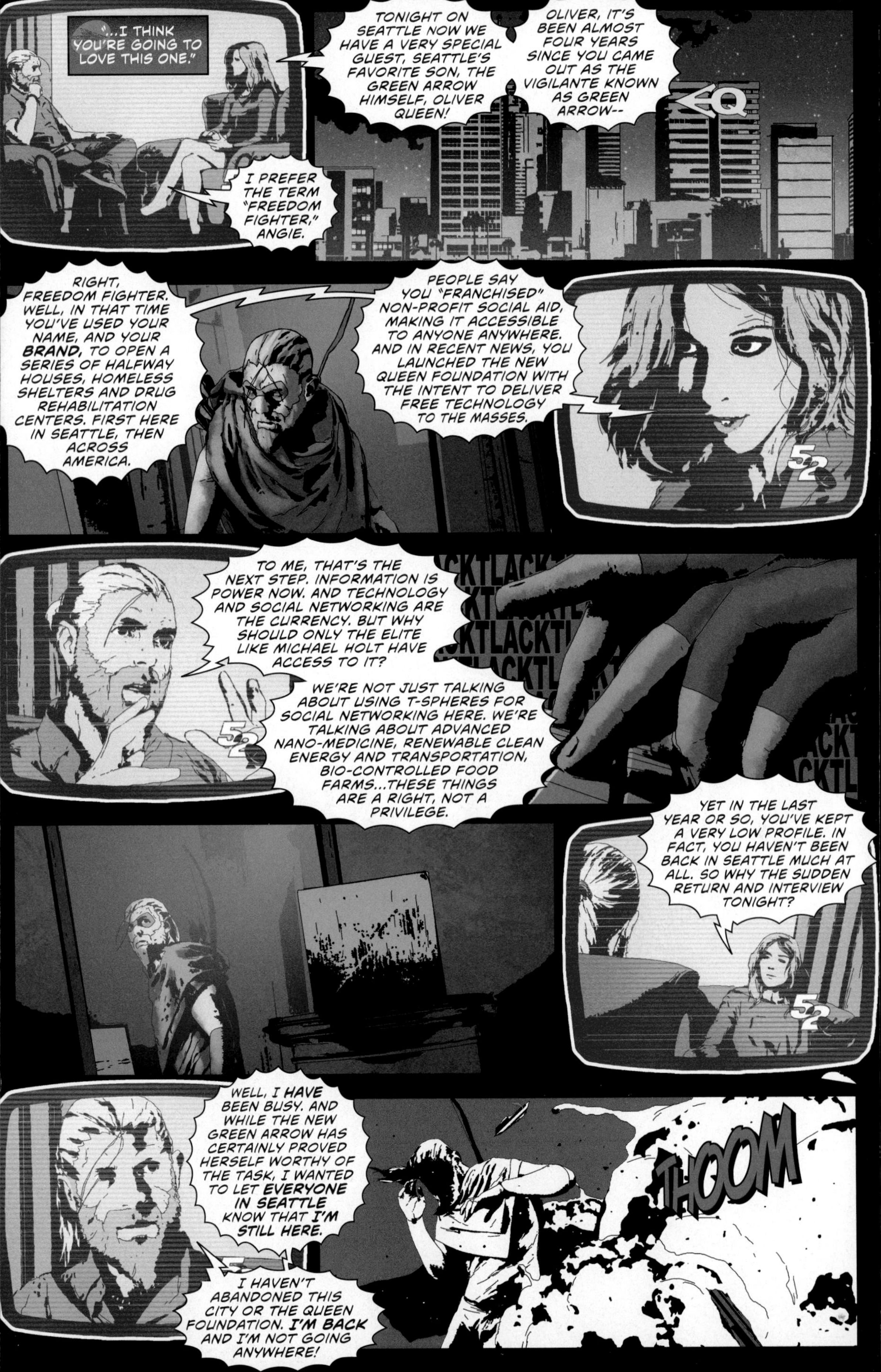
"...I THINK YOU'RE GOING TO LOVE THIS ONE."
TONIGHT ON SEATTLE NOW WE HAVE A VERY SPECIAL GUEST, SEATTLE'S FAVORITE SON, THE GREEN ARROW HIMSELF, OLIVER QUEEN!
OLIVER, IT'S BEEN ALMOST FOUR YEARS SINCE YOU CAME OUT AS THE VIGILANTE KNOWN AS GREEN ARROW--
I PREFER THE TERM "FREEDOM FIGHTER," ANGIE.
RIGHT, FREEDOM FIGHTER. WELL, IN THAT TIME YOU'VE USED YOUR NAME, AND YOUR BRAND, TO OPEN A SERIES OF HALFWAY HOUSES, HOMELESS SHELTERS AND DRUG REHABILITATION CENTERS. FIRST HERE IN SEATTLE, THEN ACROSS AMERICA.
PEOPLE SAY YOU "FRANCHISED" NON-PROFIT SOCIAL AID, MAKING IT ACCESSIBLE TO ANYONE ANYWHERE. AND IN RECENT NEWS, YOU LAUNCHED THE NEW QUEEN FOUNDATION WITH THE INTENT TO DELIVER FREE TECHNOLOGY TO THE MASSES.
TO ME, THAT'S THE NEXT STEP. INFORMATION IS POWER NOW. AND TECHNOLOGY AND SOCIAL NETWORKING ARE THE CURRENCY. BUT WHY SHOULD ONLY THE ELITE LIKE MICHAEL HOLT HAVE ACCESS TO IT?
WE'RE NOT JUST TALKING ABOUT USING T-SPHERES FOR SOCIAL NETWORKING HERE. WE'RE TALKING ABOUT ADVANCED NANO-MEDICINE, RENEWABLE CLEAN ENERGY AND TRANSPORTATION, BIO-CONTROLLED FOOD FARMS...THESE THINGS ARE A RIGHT, NOT A PRIVILEGE.
KTLACKTLACKTL
YET IN THE LAST YEAR OR SO, YOU'VE KEPT A VERY LOW PROFILE. IN FACT, YOU HAVEN'T BEEN BACK IN SEATTLE MUCH AT ALL. SO WHY THE SUDDEN RETURN AND INTERVIEW TONIGHT?
WELL, I HAVE BEEN BUSY. AND WHILE THE NEW GREEN ARROW HAS CERTAINLY PROVED HERSELF WORTHY OF THE TASK, I WANTED TO LET EVERYONE IN SEATTLE KNOW THAT I'M STILL HERE.
I HAVEN'T ABANDONED THIS CITY OR THE QUEEN FOUNDATION. I'M BACK AND I'M NOT GOING ANYWHERE!
THOOM

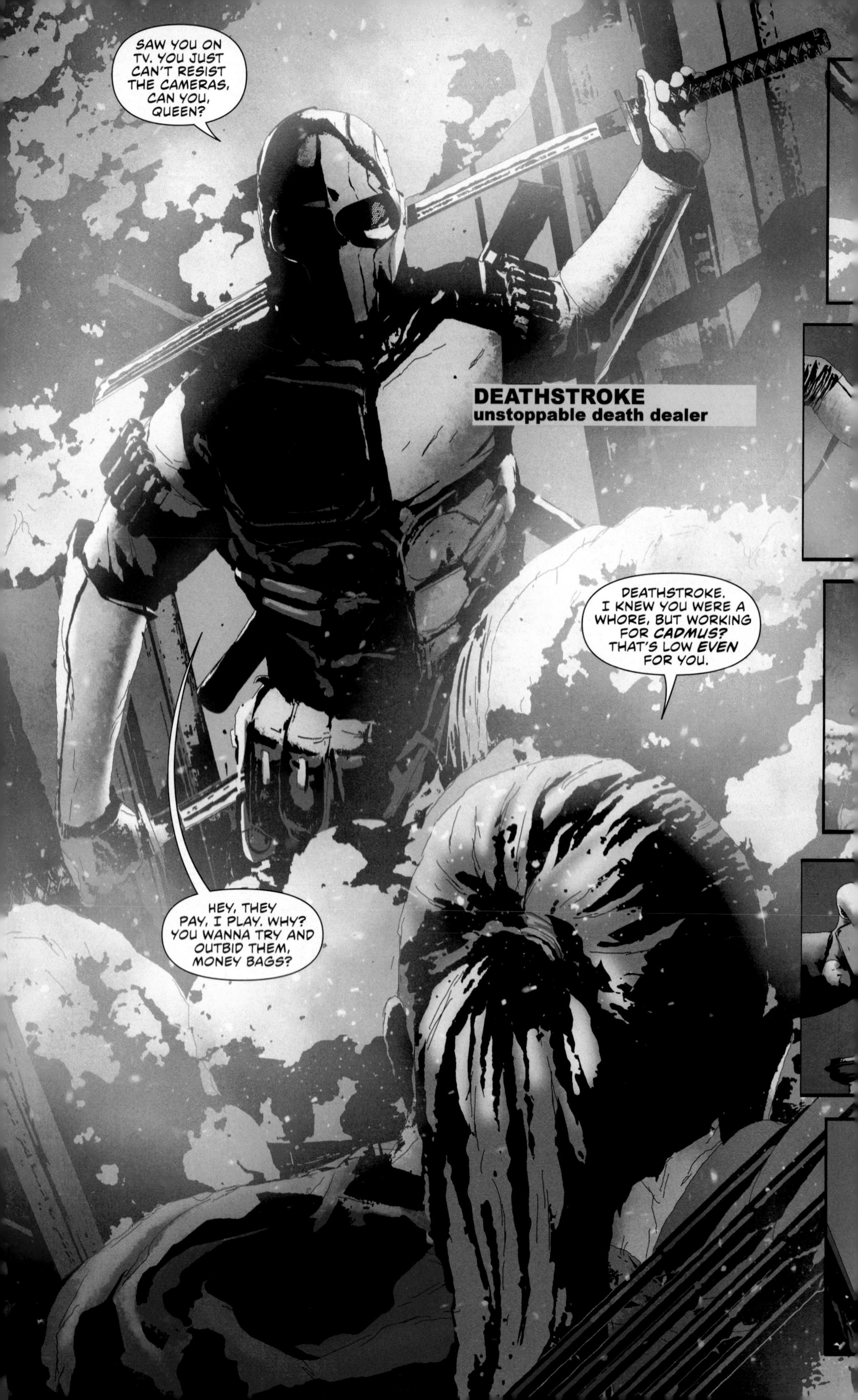
SAW YOU ON TV. YOU JUST CAN'T RESIST THE CAMERAS, CAN YOU, QUEEN?
DEATHSTROKE
unstoppable death dealer
DEATHSTROKE. I KNEW YOU WERE A WHORE, BUT WORKING FOR CADMUS? THAT'S LOW EVEN FOR YOU.
HEY, THEY PAY, I PLAY. WHY? YOU WANNA TRY AND OUTBID THEM, MONEY BAGS?

NO THANKS. I DON'T HIRE KILLERS.

--UNGH!

UNGH!

NICE TRICK.

AGH!

BUT I'M NOT SCARED OF YOU OR ANYTHING *CADMUS* CAN THROW AT ME, SLADE. I'M GOING TO EXPOSE IT ALL. I'M GOING TO BRING *CADMUS* DOWN!

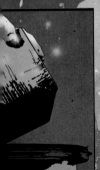

YEAH, YEAH. BUT SERIOUSLY, YOU SHOULD NEVER HAVE GONE ON TELEVISION.

WE'VE BEEN LOOKING FOR YOU FOR A WHILE NOW. NEVER WOULD'VE KNOWN YOU WERE BACK IN TOWN.

IT'S ALMOST LIKE YOU *WANT* TO DIE.

FWP

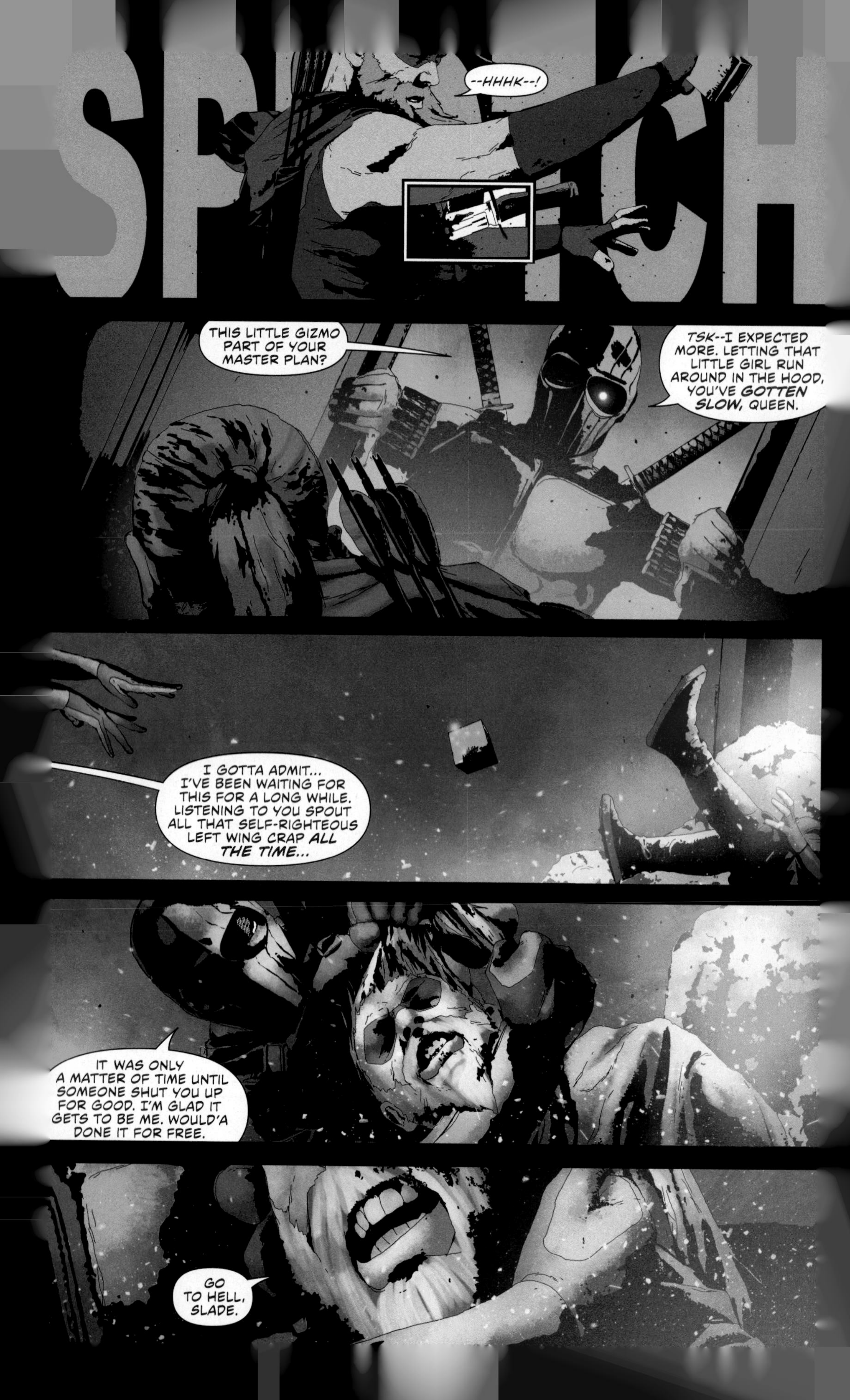
SPLTCH
--HHHK--!
THIS LITTLE GIZMO PART OF YOUR MASTER PLAN?
TSK--I EXPECTED MORE. LETTING THAT LITTLE GIRL RUN AROUND IN THE HOOD, YOU'VE GOTTEN SLOW, QUEEN.
I GOTTA ADMIT... I'VE BEEN WAITING FOR THIS FOR A LONG WHILE. LISTENING TO YOU SPOUT ALL THAT SELF-RIGHTEOUS LEFT WING CRAP ALL THE TIME...
IT WAS ONLY A MATTER OF TIME UNTIL SOMEONE SHUT YOU UP FOR GOOD. I'M GLAD IT GETS TO BE ME. WOULD'A DONE IT FOR FREE.
GO TO HELL, SLADE.

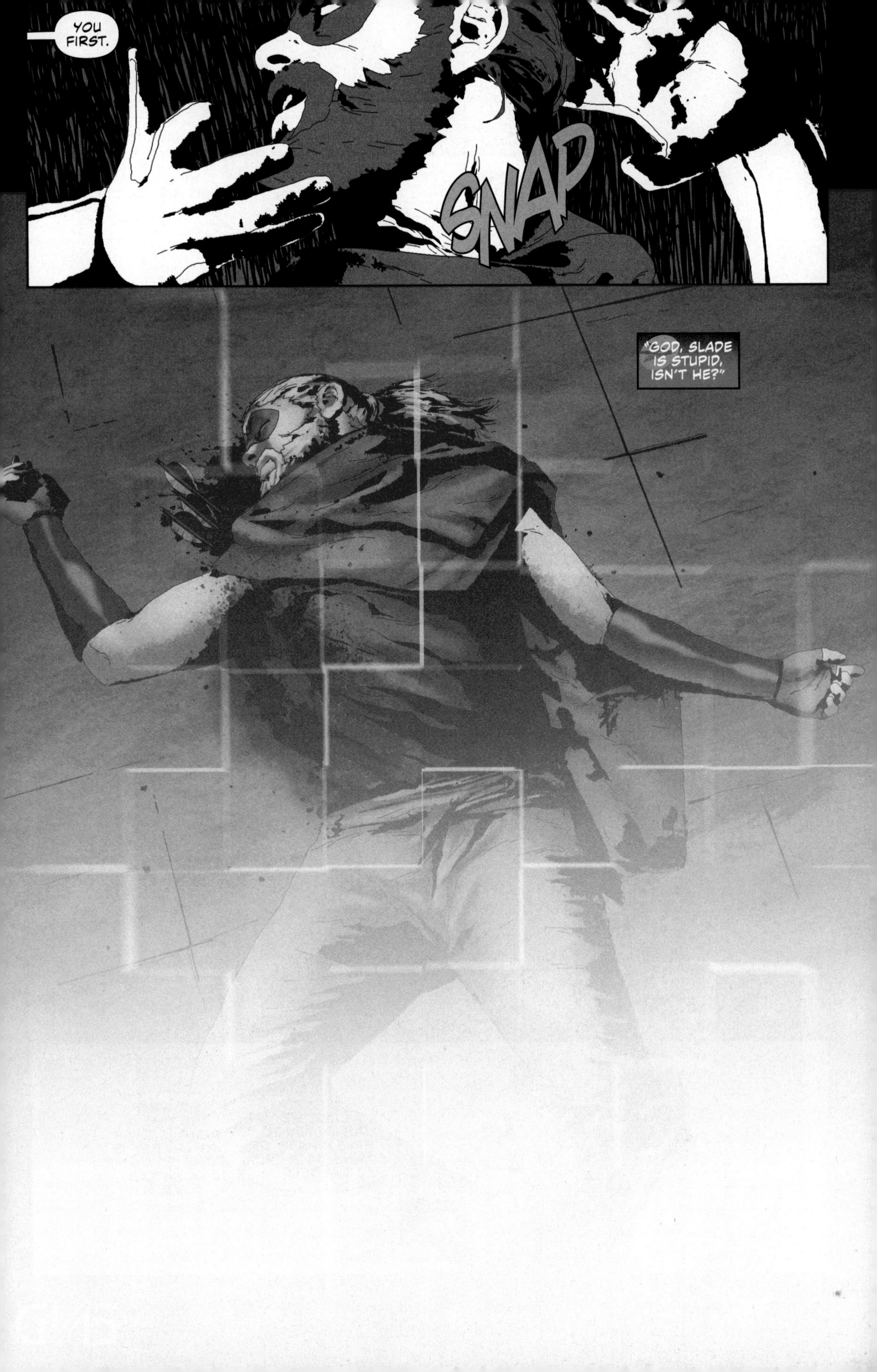
YOU FIRST.
SNAP
"GOD, SLADE IS STUPID, ISN'T HE?"

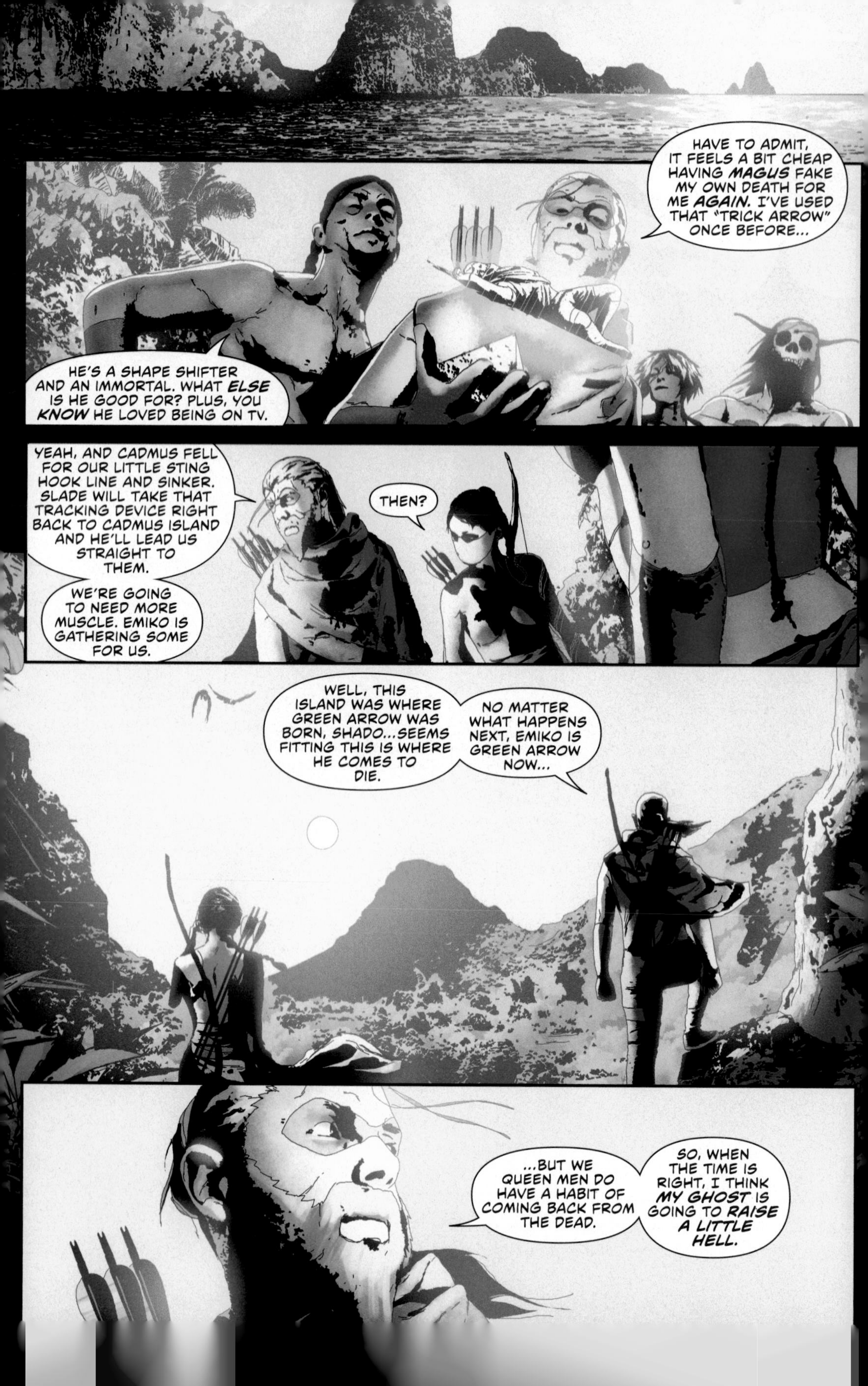
HAVE TO ADMIT, IT FEELS A BIT CHEAP HAVING MAGUS FAKE MY OWN DEATH FOR ME AGAIN. I'VE USED THAT "TRICK ARROW" ONCE BEFORE...
HE'S A SHAPE SHIFTER AND AN IMMORTAL. WHAT ELSE IS HE GOOD FOR? PLUS, YOU KNOW HE LOVED BEING ON TV.
YEAH, AND CADMUS FELL FOR OUR LITTLE STING HOOK LINE AND SINKER. SLADE WILL TAKE THAT TRACKING DEVICE RIGHT BACK TO CADMUS ISLAND AND HE'LL LEAD US STRAIGHT TO THEM.
THEN?
WE'RE GOING TO NEED MORE MUSCLE. EMIKO IS GATHERING SOME FOR US.
WELL, THIS ISLAND WAS WHERE GREEN ARROW WAS BORN, SHADO...SEEMS FITTING THIS IS WHERE HE COMES TO DIE.
NO MATTER WHAT HAPPENS NEXT, EMIKO IS GREEN ARROW NOW...
...BUT WE QUEEN MEN DO HAVE A HABIT OF COMING BACK FROM THE DEAD.
SO, WHEN THE TIME IS RIGHT, I THINK MY GHOST IS GOING TO RAISE A LITTLE HELL.

GREEN ARROW #32
BROKEN: PART 1

NOTE: THIS ENTIRE 3-ISSUE ARC HAPPENS OVER THE COURSE OF ONE NIGHT IN SEATTLE.

PAGE 1.

We open on a series of widescreen panels... vignettes of SEATTLE under siege by crime. Green Arrow has been away, dealing with The Outsiders, and in his absence the city is on the verge of collapse. Richard Dragon has seized the underworld and the police are on the brink of losing control...

1. In the foreground we see a POLICE DO NOT CROSS TAPE LINE draped across a downtown street <u>at night</u>. POLICE CARS surround a crime scene. TWO BODIES lay in the streets, both victims of gunshots. Uniformed Police Officers try to keep a crowd back, while detectives investigate.

NEWS CAPTION: --SEATTLE UNDER SIEGE! As the crime wave that has gripped Seattle enters its second week, Police urged citizens in the city's downtown core to adhere to the new curfews, and avoid going out after dark.

2. We cut to a rough-looking downtown street corner. A THUG IN A HOODIE sells drugs to someone in a car that has pulled up. Behind them 2 MORE THUGS stand with assault rifles blatantly out in the open.

NEWS CAPTION: The mayor continued to urge calm, but with armed criminals blatantly controlling major areas of the city with assault rifles and widespread looting being reported, it's clear that Police have lost control.

3. We cut above the city. A wide aerial shot as a POLICE HELICOPTER hovers overhead, shining its spotlight down. We see smoke rising from downtown in multiple areas, as if a number of fires are burning.

NEWS CAPTION: The White House suggested that the National Guard might be mobilized within days if the situation isn't resolved...

4. We cut to the WATERFRONT area. We are up on a warehouse rooftop with GREEN ARROW. He crouches in the foreground, cast in shadow, his hood is up. He is looking down at the HARBOUR where ARMED CRIMINALS guard others who unload a ship. Arrow has one hand to his ear, listening to the news report on his earpiece.

NEWS (from radio earpiece): ...And the biggest mystery of all, where is Seattle's guardian angel in all this chaos? Has the hooded vigilante known as *The Green Arrow* abandoned us?

PAGE 2.

1. We cut to the GREEN ARROW WAREHOUSE HEADQUARTERS. It's dark, seemingly empty. We are looking at the main training area, with targets on one wall, and GREEN ARROW's SPARE COSTUMES and BOWS/ARROWS/QUIVERS hanging on another. There is a small hatch above this training area that now opens, moonlight pouring in from above. A ladder leads up to the hatch.

2. GREEN ARROW jumps down into the bunker from above.

SFX: THUMP!

3. Suddenly an ARROW zips by Ollie, just missing his head and slamming into a target on the wall behind him. Ollie looks wide-eyed and surprised!

SFX: FWIP!

4. Reverse. Over Ollie's shoulder, looking into the other half of the warehouse. NAOMI stands there with one of Ollie's spare bows, having just fired at him. She looks panicked and scared. FYFF cowers behind the computer terminal, peeking out at Ollie.

OLLIE: Naomi?! What the hell are you--?!

NAOMI: Ollie?!

FYFF: Dude--you almost killed him!

5. Naomi runs and hugs Ollie tightly, relieved. Ollie is confused. Fyff stands behind them, looking uncomfortable at Naomi's clear affection for Ollie.

NAOMI: Oh, thank God you're back!

OLLIE: I--I was headed back from Prague when the *villain uprising* hit.

OLLIE: My God, Naomi, *what the hell happened here?!*

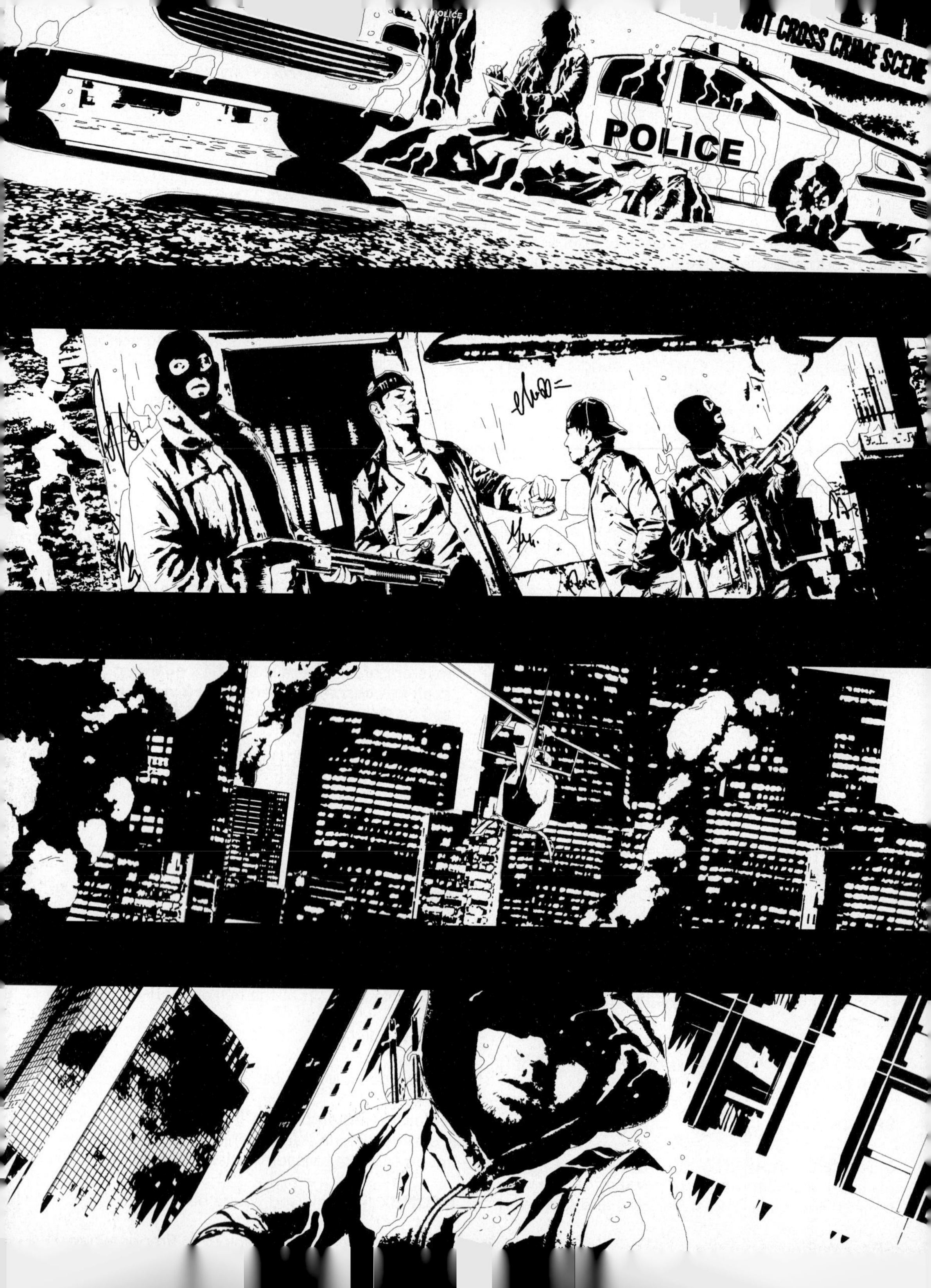
POLICE
CROSS CRIME SCENE
POLICE

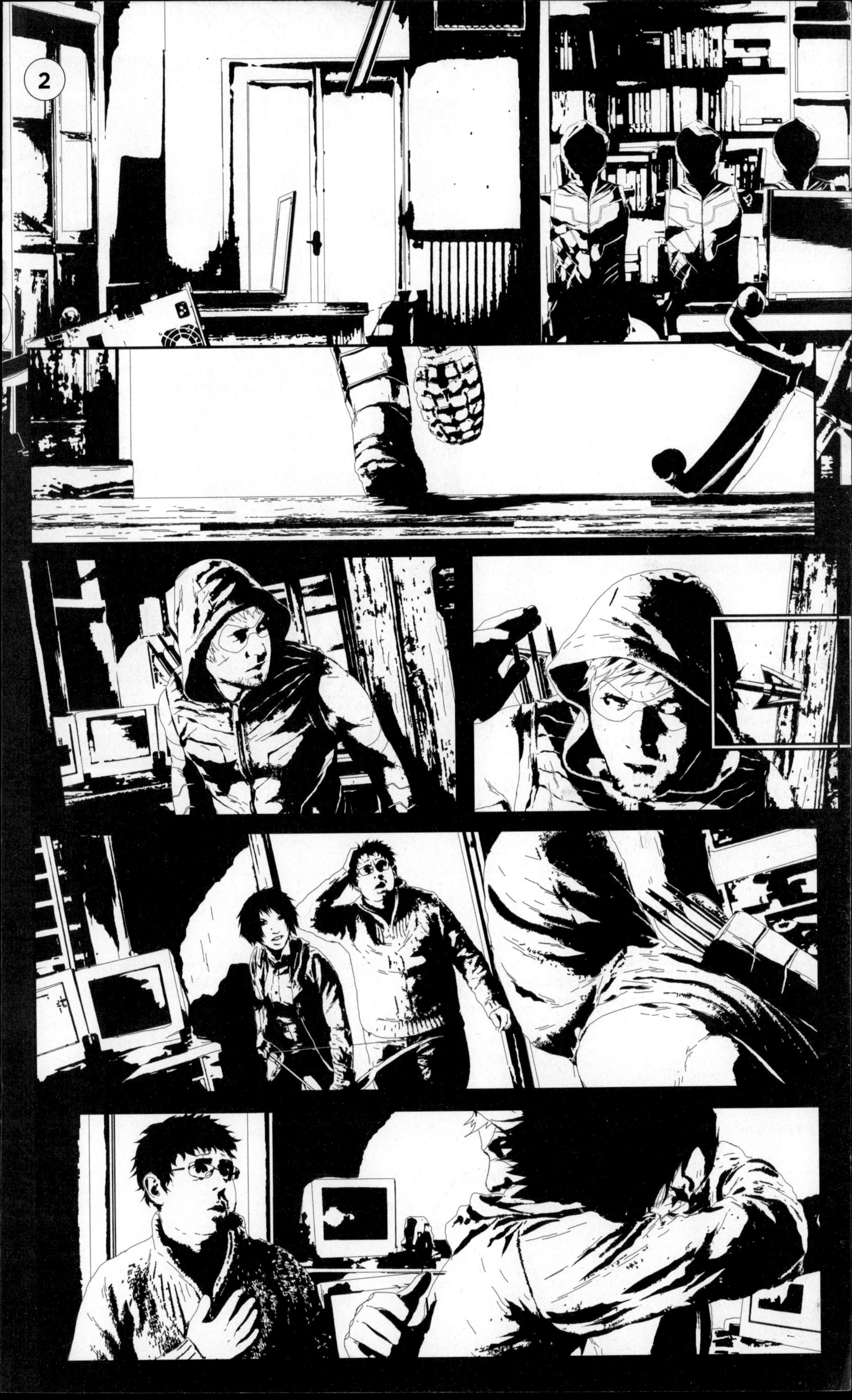
2

PAGE 3.

1. Close on Fyff. He looks at them with unease.

FYFF: It's Dragon, Ollie...*Richard Dragon* has taken the city. And he has Diggle too.

2. Ollie looks at Fyff, stunned.

OLLIE: Diggle?! Diggle is back?!

NAOMI: He was. He--he tried to stop Dragon. Diggle formed an alliance with Billy Tockman, we were going to hit Dragon.

3. Close on Naomi, she looks up, sad and freaked out.

NAOMI: But Tockman sold us out. Th--they took, Diggle. Fyff and I barely got away.

4. Ollie is mad, he snaps at them accusingly.

ARROW: Tockman?! What the hell were you two thinking?!

ARROW: You had no business trying to go after Dragon without me!

5. Naomi gets mad now, pointing at Ollie. Fyff stands behind her.

NAOMI: Are you--Are you *serious?!* Have you seen what happened to Seattle while you were off chasing Shado and Komodo on some damned personal crusade?!

NAOMI: You abandoned the city, Ollie-- you abandoned us! Someone had to do something!

PAGE 4.

1. Ollie starts to answer, but a noise from above interrupts. The lights in the warehouse suddenly turn EMERGENCY YELLOW.

OLLIE: Naomi, that's not fair! The Outsiders were—

SFX: THUNK!!

FYFF: What the hell?!

2. Ollie runs to the hatch/ladder.

OLLIE: The proximity alert! Someone's on the roof!

OLLIE: You two didn't escape, Dragon's men, they *let you go*...they *followed* you here!

3. Suddenly an explosion blasts through the roof near the ladder/hatch! Concrete and rubble rain down, Ollie is blown back.

SFX: KA-THOOM!!

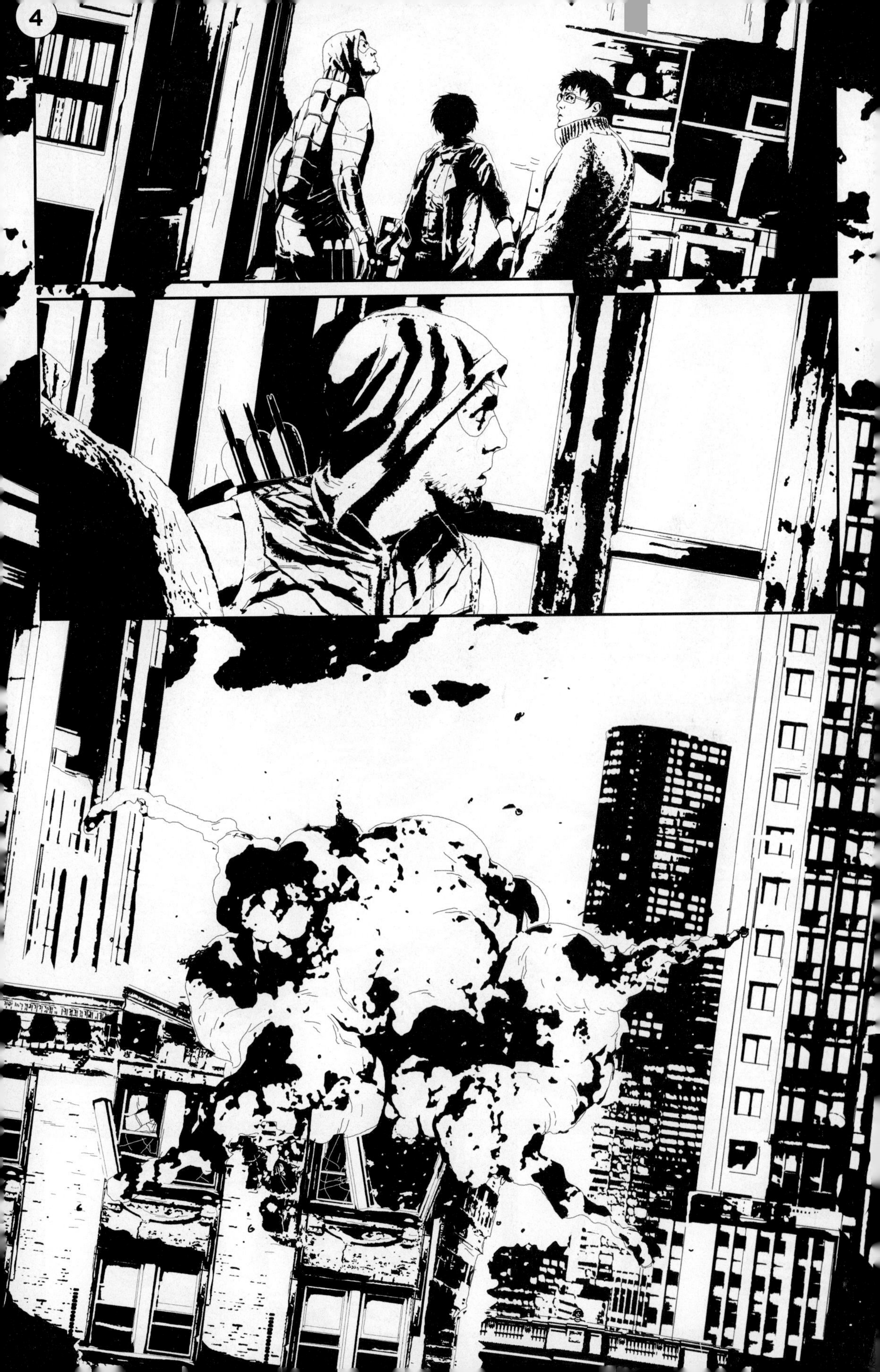

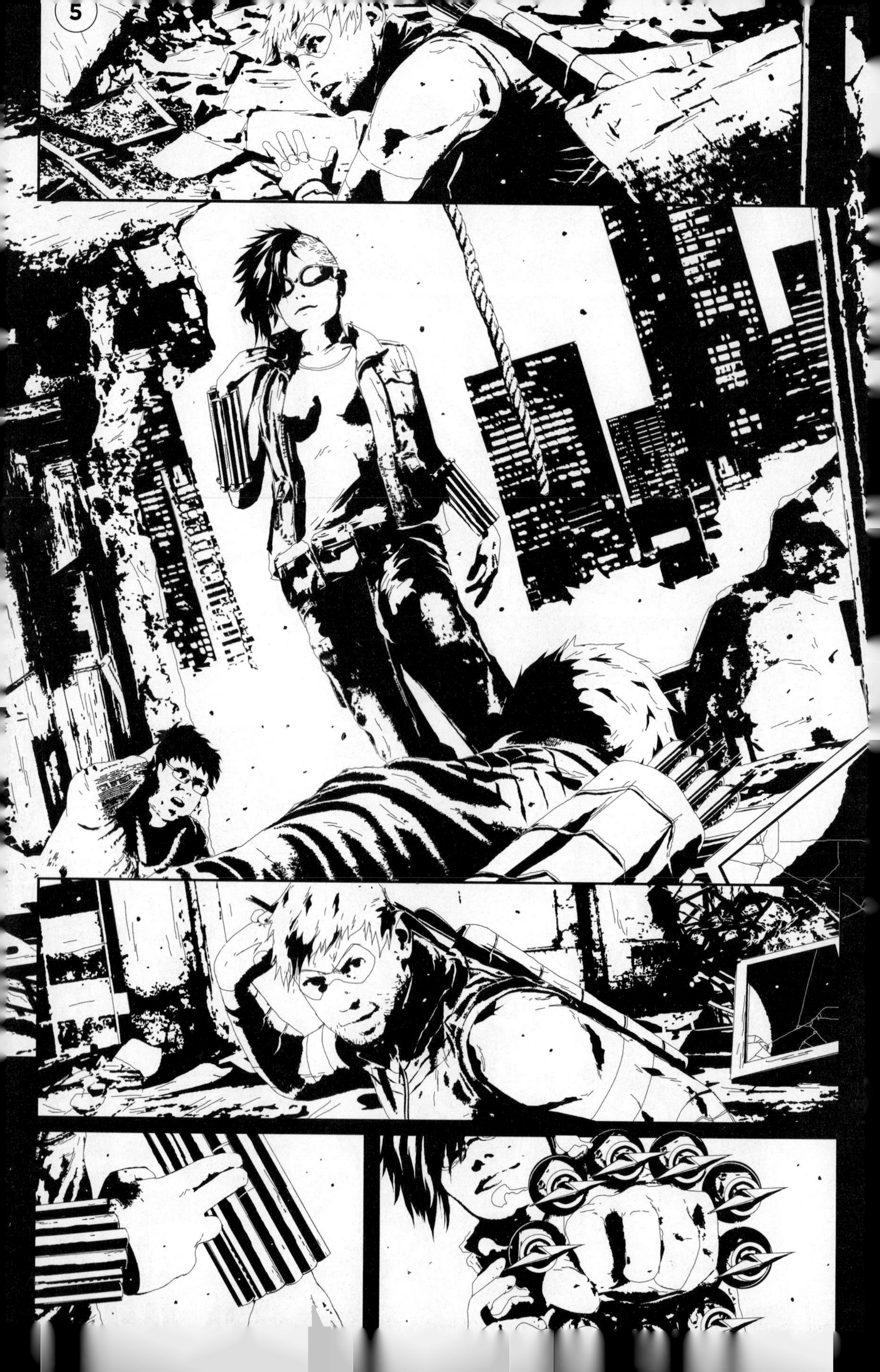

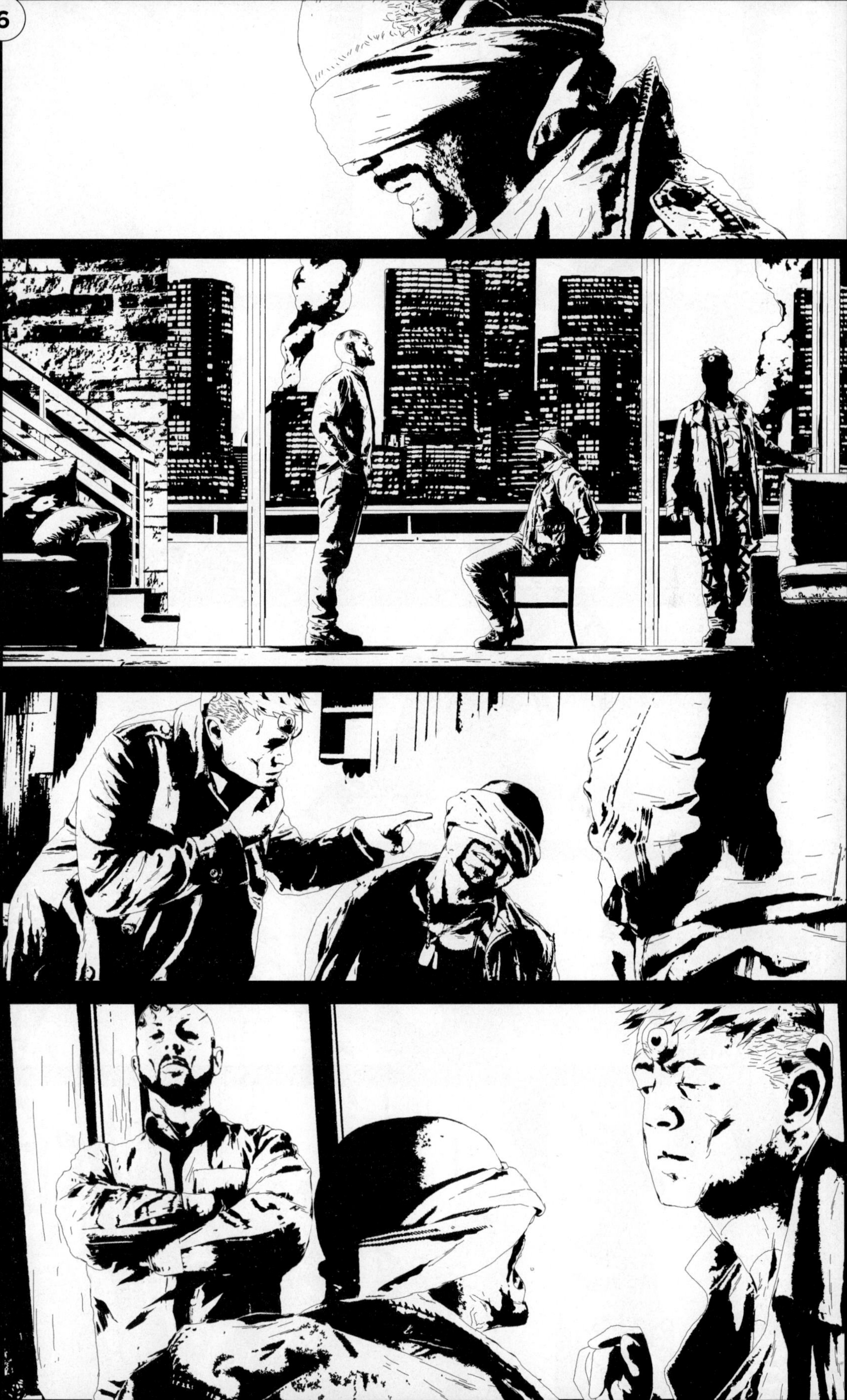

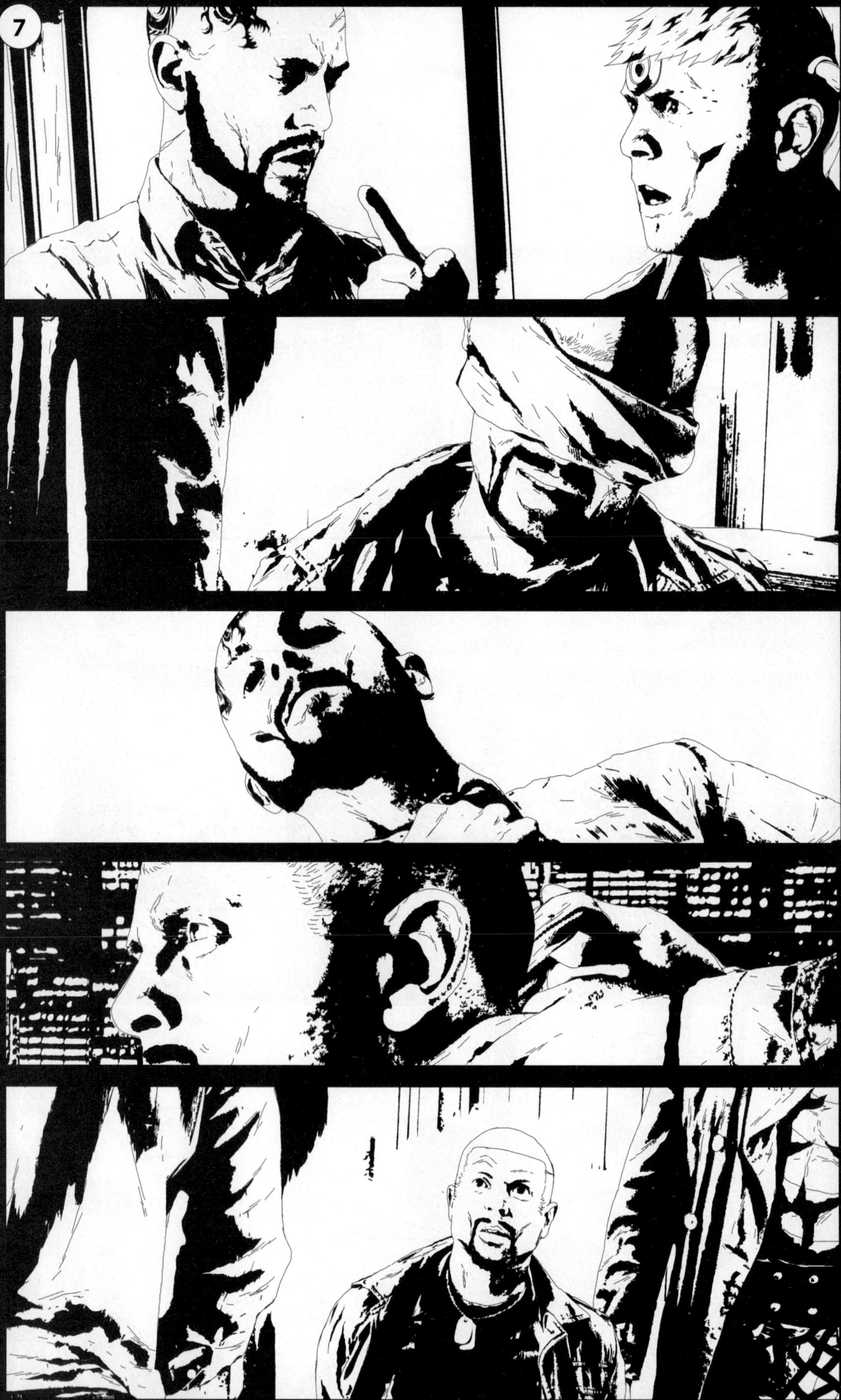

7

PAGE 5.

1. BIG PANEL: Ollie is on the ground amidst the rubble. Smoke and debris cloud the air as THE RED DART leaps down from above into the warehouse. A dynamic full-body shot of the New 52 version of RED DART, revealing her for the first time. She wears a tight red bodysuit with a sleek helmet and goggles. She has a metallic, rectangular pack strapped to her back with metallic cables leading from it, down her arms to TWO WRIST GAUNTLETS on each arm, which fire her darts. This new costume is sexy and very utilitarian.

ARROW: Who—who the hell—?!

DART: Oh, I'm hurt that you haven't heard of me, Arrow. But I guess you at least deserve to know the name of the woman who is going to *kill you*...they call me The Dart. THE RED DART.

DART: ...Richard Dragon sends his love. See, he just put a thirty-million-dollar bounty on your head, and I aim to collect.

2. Close on Ollie, who draws an arrow from his quiver. Naomi and Fyff scramble for cover behind him.

OLLIE: *Red Dart?* Are you serious?

3. Close on Dart, she aims one of her gauntlets right at us and fires. A silver dart flies right at us.

DART: Very.

DART: Trick Darts versus Trick Arrow. *Let's do this...*

SFX: THWIP!

PAGE 6.

1. We cut to DIGGLE. Close on his face, he has a blindfold on. His lip is bruised and bloody.

DRAGON (OP): Well, Mr. Diggle, it would seem your friend in the hood has finally returned home to join our little party...

2. We pull out and see that Diggle is in a posh PENTHOUSE apartment in the downtown area. DIGGLE is tied to a chair, with a blindfold on, in front of glass doors that lead to a balcony overlooking Seattle. RICHARD DRAGON stands there, hands behind his back, looking at Diggle. Dragon wears a white button-up shirt with a tie. COUNT VERTIGO is coming inside the penthouse from the balcony, behind Dig.

VERTIGO: Then, let's get on with this, already, Dragon. I'm tired of waiting up here. I want Green Arrow's head.

DRAGON: Patience, Vertigo, patience. You need to learn to savor victory.

DIGGLE: You two clowns haven't won anything yet. If Arrow is back, it's only a matter of time until he comes for you.

3. Vertigo slaps Diggle on the back of the head.

VERTIGO: Can't I just kill this one, already? Never shuts his big mouth.

SFX: WHAP!

4. Diggle sneers up at him from behind the blindfold.

DIGGLE: Why don't you undo these ropes and give it a shot, Count Chochula?

DRAGON: Gentlemen, gentlemen...please. Can't we keep this civilized? There will be plenty of time for violence soon.

PAGE 7.

1. Vertigo points at Dragon, angry. Dragon calmly looks at him.

VERTIGO: You promised me a shot at Green Arrow!

DRAGON: I promised you a lot more than that, Vertigo. When we're done here with Green Arrow, I plan on expanding. And I'll need your power to do it.

DRAGON: You want back to Vlatavia, you help me. That's the deal. Green Arrow is secondary to the *larger cause.*

2. Diggle smiles up at them.

DIGGLE: Larger cause? Please. You can spout all the rhetoric you want. This is about one thing, and that's power. It's about Money.

3. Dragon looks down at him, smirking.

DRAGON: Of course it's about money. This is America.

DRAGON: That's one of the first lessons *my Father* taught me. But before money comes honor. And to honor him, I need to make you and Green Arrow suffer.

4. Vertigo watches as Dragon starts to remove Diggle's blindfold.

DIGGLE: Who the hell are you, Dragon?

DRAGON: I'm not surprised you don't remember me. I was very young the last time we met...

5. Close on Diggle's surprised face, looking up at him.

DRAGON: Let me help...surely you remember my Father? *You killed him,* after all. His name was Ricardo Diaz.

DIGGLE: --Diaz?!

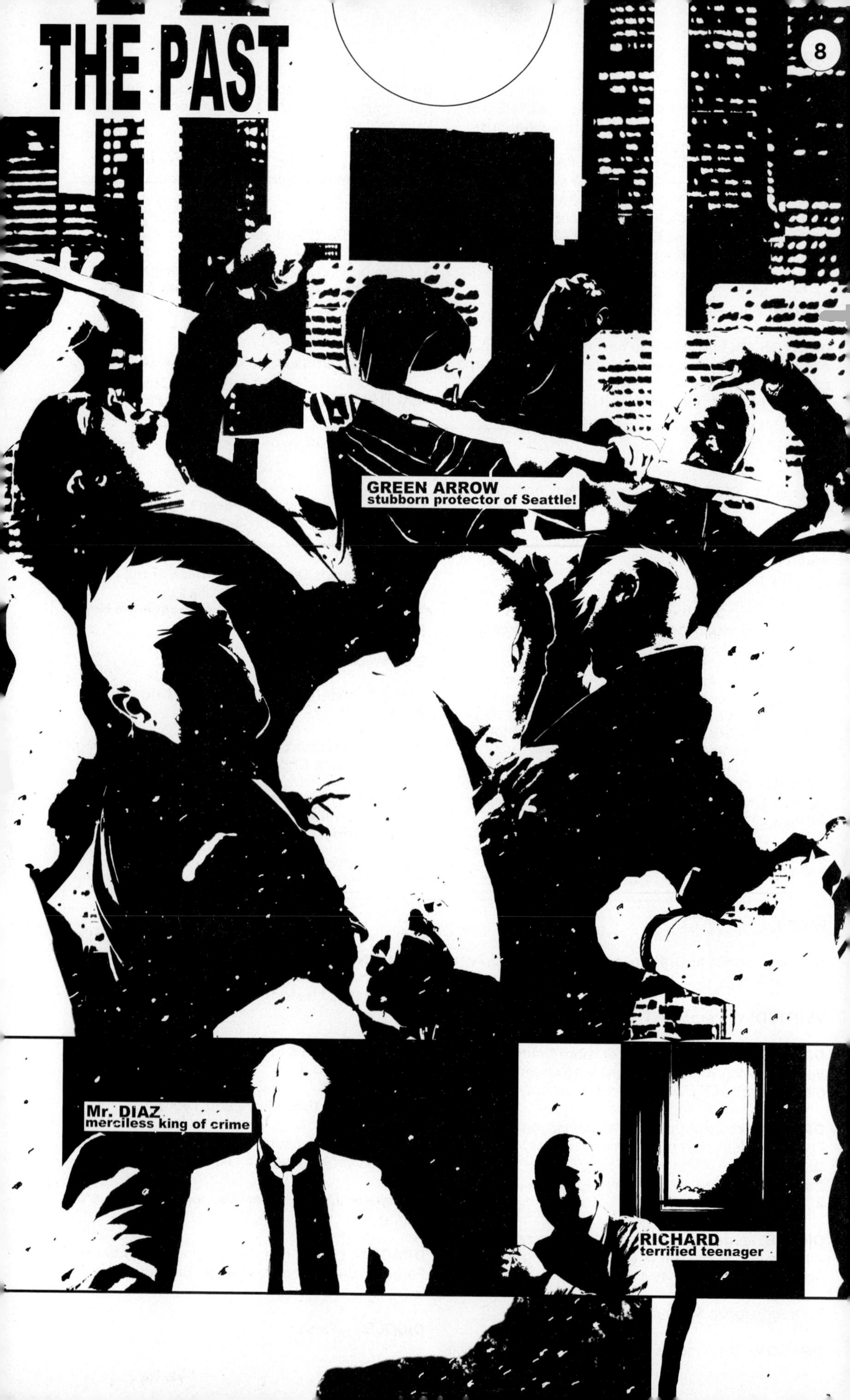
THE PAST
8
GREEN ARROW
stubborn protector of Seattle!
Mr. DIAZ
merciless king of crime
RICHARD
terrified teenager

PAGE 8.

SPLASH.

We cut to a flashback. We are in this very penthouse, years earlier. GREEN ARROW is fighting half a dozen THUGS in suits. A middle-aged man, who looks a lot like DRAGON except older and not nearly as fit, watches. RICHARD DRAGON is there too, but he is only a teenager, skinny and terrified, cowering behind his father.

GREEN ARROW'S HOOD IS UP. This is important, because next issue we will reveal that for a short time, Ollie was out of commission and DIGGLE wore the Green Arrow costume. So the hood should help hide the fact that this isn't Ollie, but Diggle. And also, Green Arrow wears a FULL MASK here, one that covers all of his face, kind of like a green version of GRIFTER'S mask.

An action-packed panel. Diggle/Green Arrow takes out all of Diaz' bodyguards as Diaz and Ricardo Diaz Jr. (DRAGON) watch. Diggle/Arrow uses his bow as a weapon, swinging it up and taking out another guard.

DRAGON CAPTION: --That's right. My Father was the king of this city. He ruled it firmly and fairly... like a business.

DRAGON CAPTION: But then the Green Arrow had to show up and ruin everything with his self-righteous "war on crime."

DRAGON CAPTION: You see, my Father was civilized, honorable. Then Arrow showed up and everything changed. And you were his right hand man weren't you, Diggle? See, I did some digging of my own. I know you worked with him back then.

PAGE 9.

1. Cut back to the present. Close on Diggle's surprised face.

DIGGLE: You!—You were there—his kid!

2. Closer on young Dragon/Diaz Jr. watching in horror as Green Arrow grabs Diaz Sr. by the collar and punches him in the face.

DRAGON CAPTION: Oh, yes...I was there. Right here, in this apartment the night you and Green Arrow stormed in and brought all your *violence and fear* with you.

DRAGON CAPTION: Before that night, I thought my father was *invincible.*

3. Arrow punches Diaz Sr. again and again, the man's face is a bloody pulp. Diaz Jr. watches in horror.

DRAGON CAPTION: --But you showed me how soft he really was. You exposed him...*humiliated* him.

4. We cut back to the present. Dragon starts to unbutton his shirt, Diggle watches.

DIGGLE: Your Father was a murderer, a pimp, a drug dealer and a thug. There was nothing honorable about him.

DRAGON: This country was built on the backs of men like my Father, Diggle.

5. Dragon removes his shirt, revealing his tattoos and turns back to Diggle, cracking his knuckles.

DRAGON: And now I'm going to take back what was his. I'm going to take Seattle.

DRAGON: But first I'm going to do to you and Arrow what you did to him... going to *humiliate you.* I'm going to show you *how soft* you really are.

PAGE 10.

1. We cut back to the battle between Green Arrow and Red Dart at the warehouse. A close-up on a number of DARTS flying through the air.

DART (OP): --Let's see how fast you are, Arrow.

2. Pull out to an establishing shot of the battle. Dart stands firing multiple arts from both wrists.

Green Arrow dives and rolls, the darts hitting the floor all around him and exploding into small fireballs. Naomi and Fyff hide behind the computer terminal.

DART: Not bad, but you can't dodge them all.

SFX: FOOM! FOOM! FOOM!

3. Arrow loads his bow, but a dart hits him in the shoulder. And ELECTROCUTES HIM! He writhes in pain, electricity surging through his body.

ARROW: ARRRGH!!!

4. Dart smiles and presses a button on her gauntlet as Arrow stumbles to his feet, smoke rising off of him.

DART: Electro-Dart. Love that one. Not enough to kill, just enough to stun.

ARROW: --Th—that--

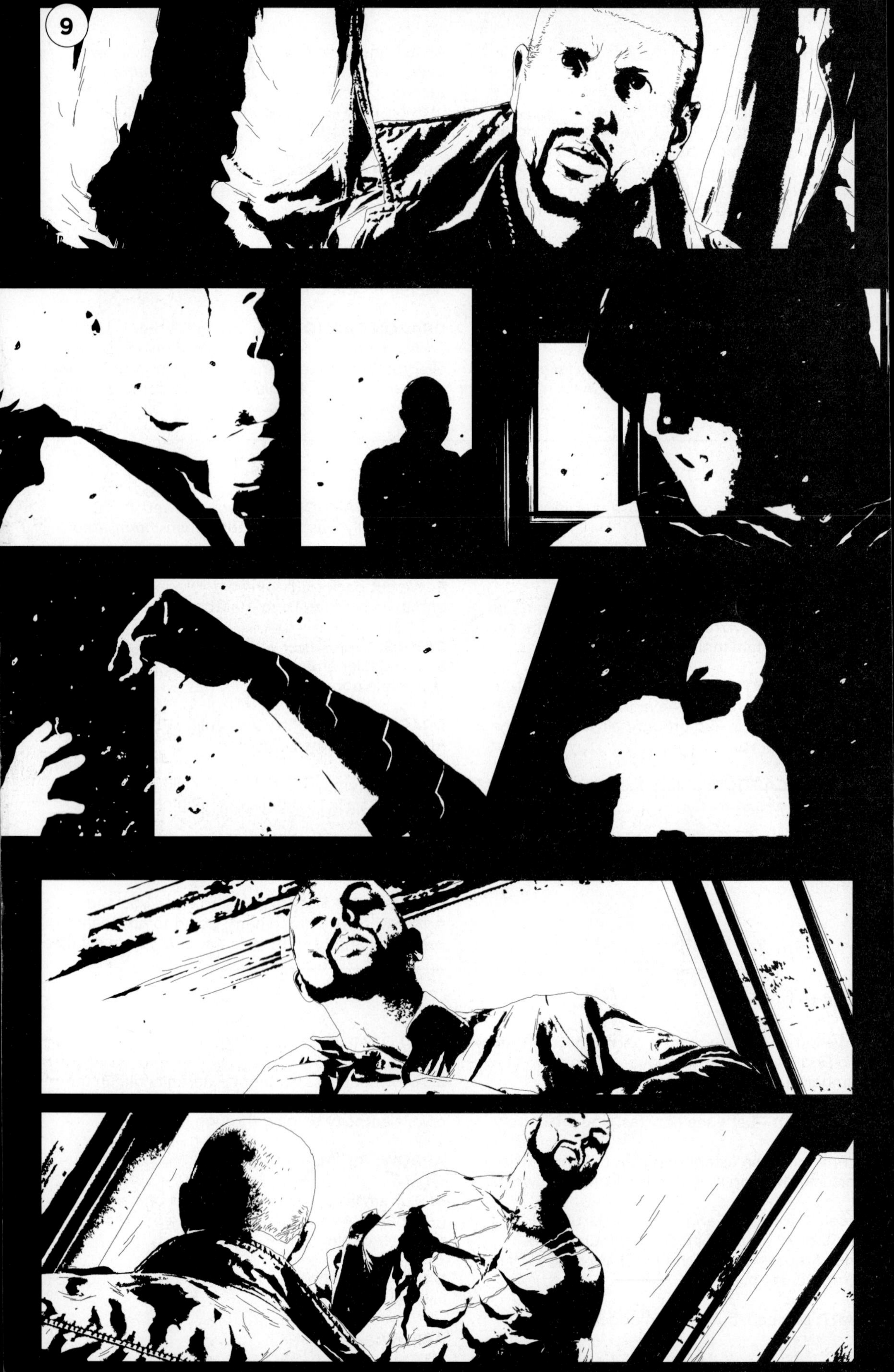
9

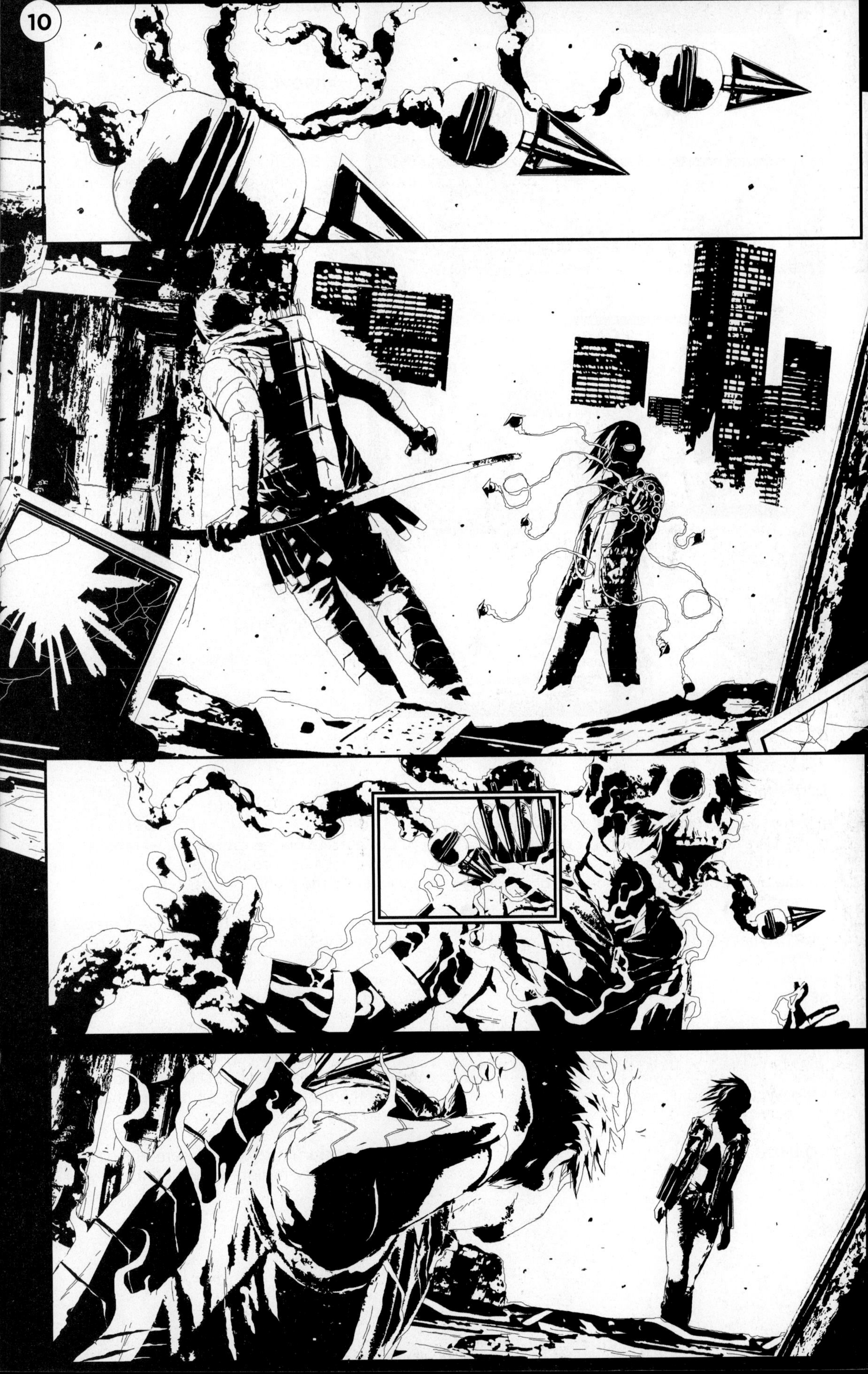
10

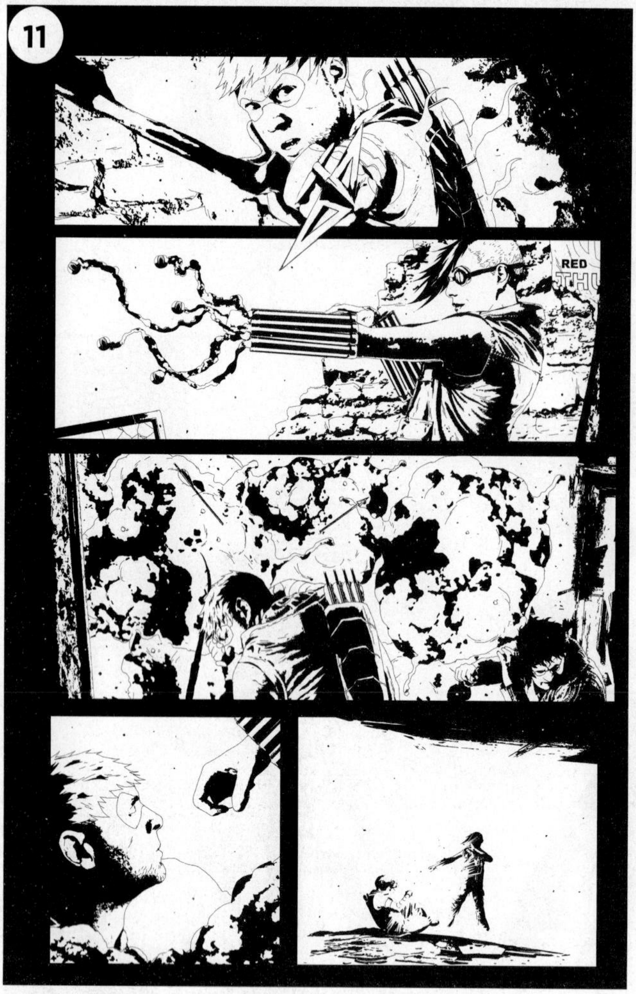
11
RED

PAGE 11.

1. Ollie fires an arrow at her.

ARROW: --Hurt!

SFX: FWIP!

2. She smiles, both wrist gauntlets raised, firing a cluster of darts back at him.

DART: Uh, oh--Cluster fire!

SFX: THWIP! THWIP! THWIP!

3. The cluster of darts explodes mid-air, blowing his arrow apart.

SFX: CHOOM! CHOOM! CHOOM!

4. She fires again.

DART: Let's try this one—Flash-Dart!

5. The dart explodes right in front of Ollie's face into a blast of blinding light! Ollie staggers back, covering his eyes. Naomi and Fyff are blinded too.

OLLIE: Arrgh!

SFX: FWOOSH!

PAGE 12.

1. Arrow tries to fire at her, but he is disoriented, his aim is all off. The arrowhead explodes into a NET, which misses her as she acrobatically jumps up and out of the hole in the ceiling blown in by the explosion.

DART: What's the matter, hot shot? Aim a little off?

SFX: FWIP!

2. A bit disoriented, Ollie turns back to Fyff and Naomi. They both rub their eyes.

ARROW: Fyff, Naomi, no matter what happens, stay down here!

NOAMI: But, Ollie—

ARROW: No buts! Stay put!

3. Cut outside on the roof of the warehouse. Arrow climbs up through the jagged hole in the ceiling into the night.

4. An arrow loaded into his bow, GA stumbles a bit, scanning the rooftop.

5. Someone yells to him from behind, he swings around.

DART: Over here, handsome.

6. He turns and aims at RED DART who stands across the rooftop, hands on her hips, head cocked playfully.

DART: So...I forgot to tell you something. You know that thirty-million-dollar bounty on your head?

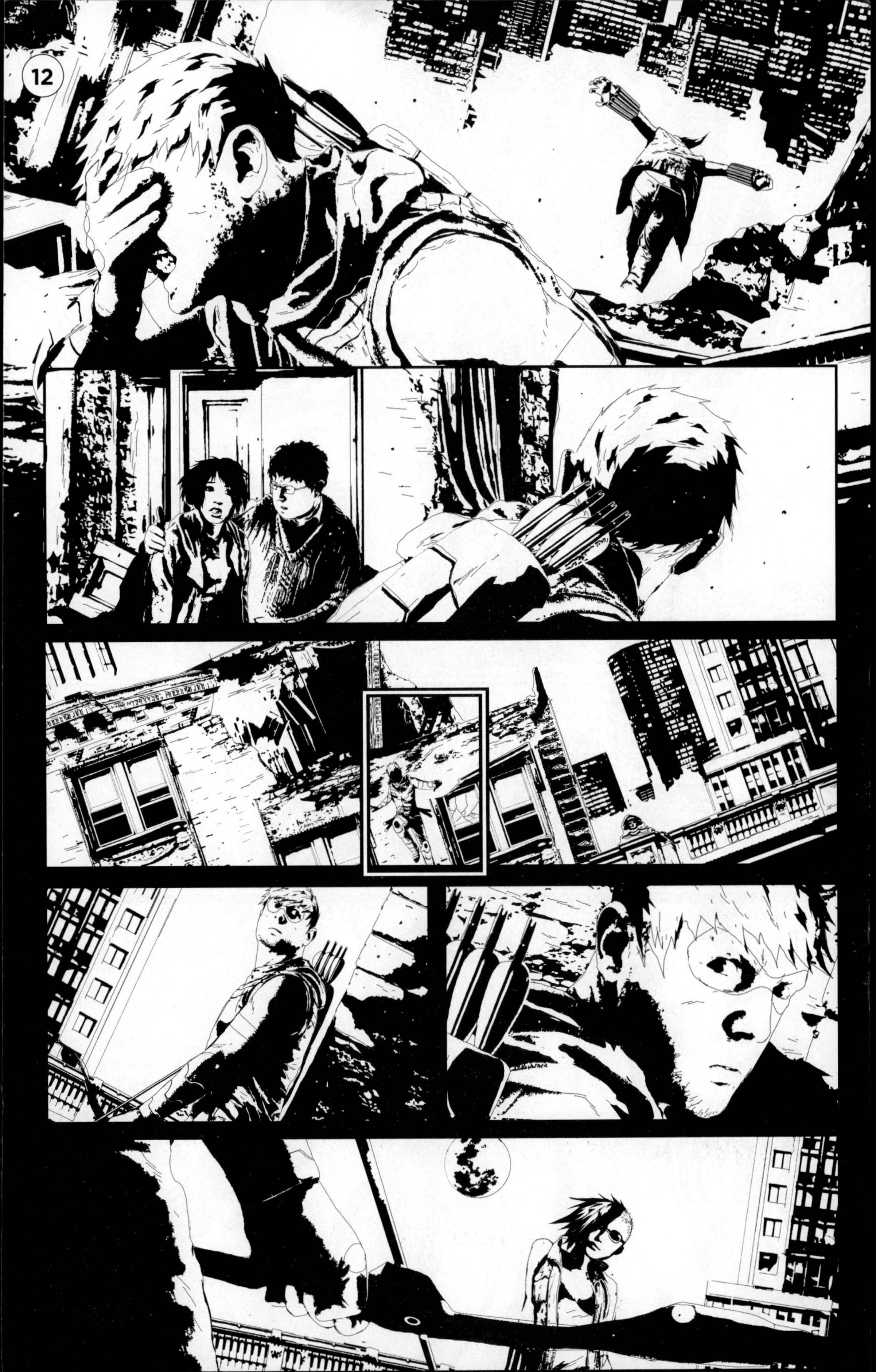

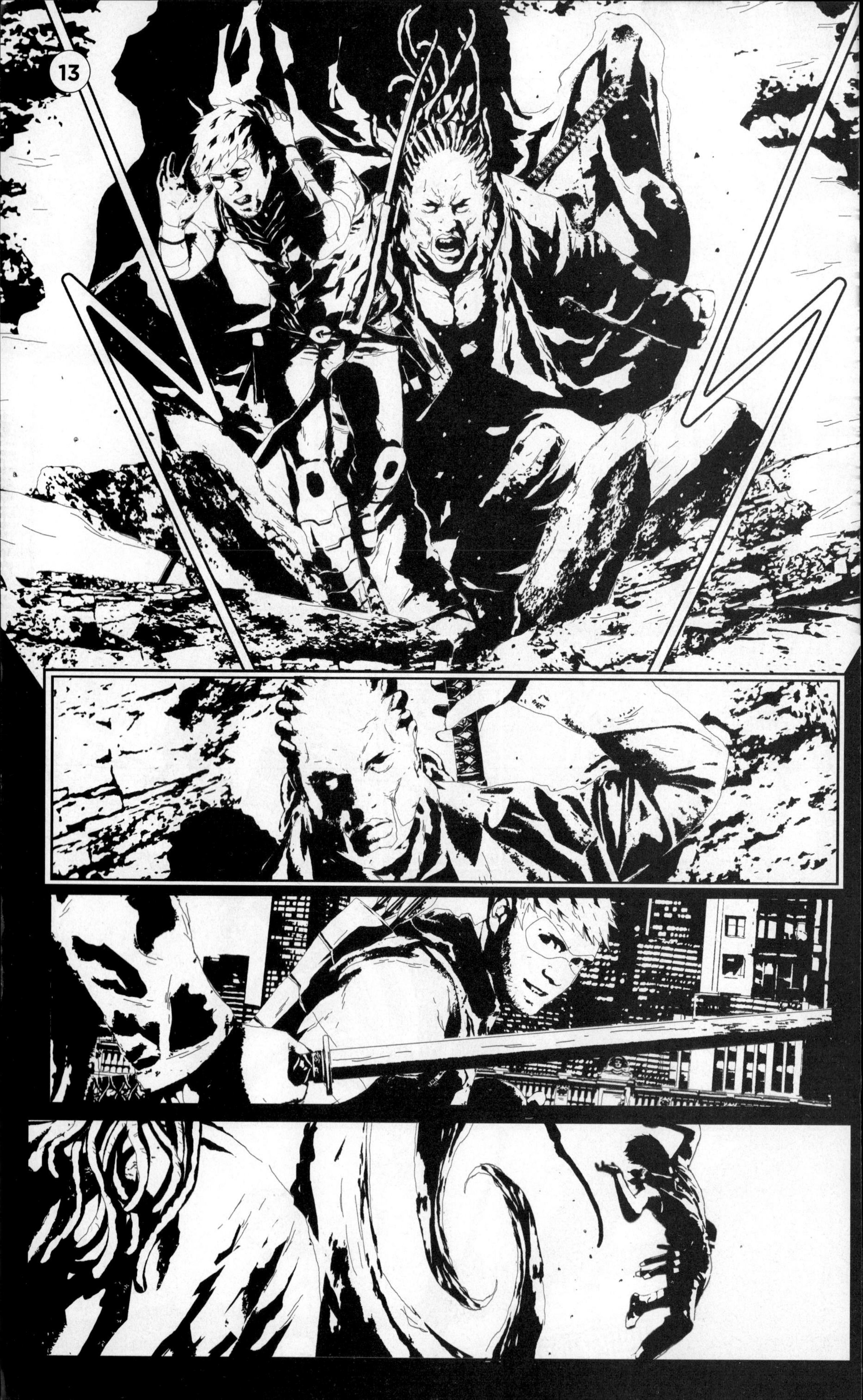
13

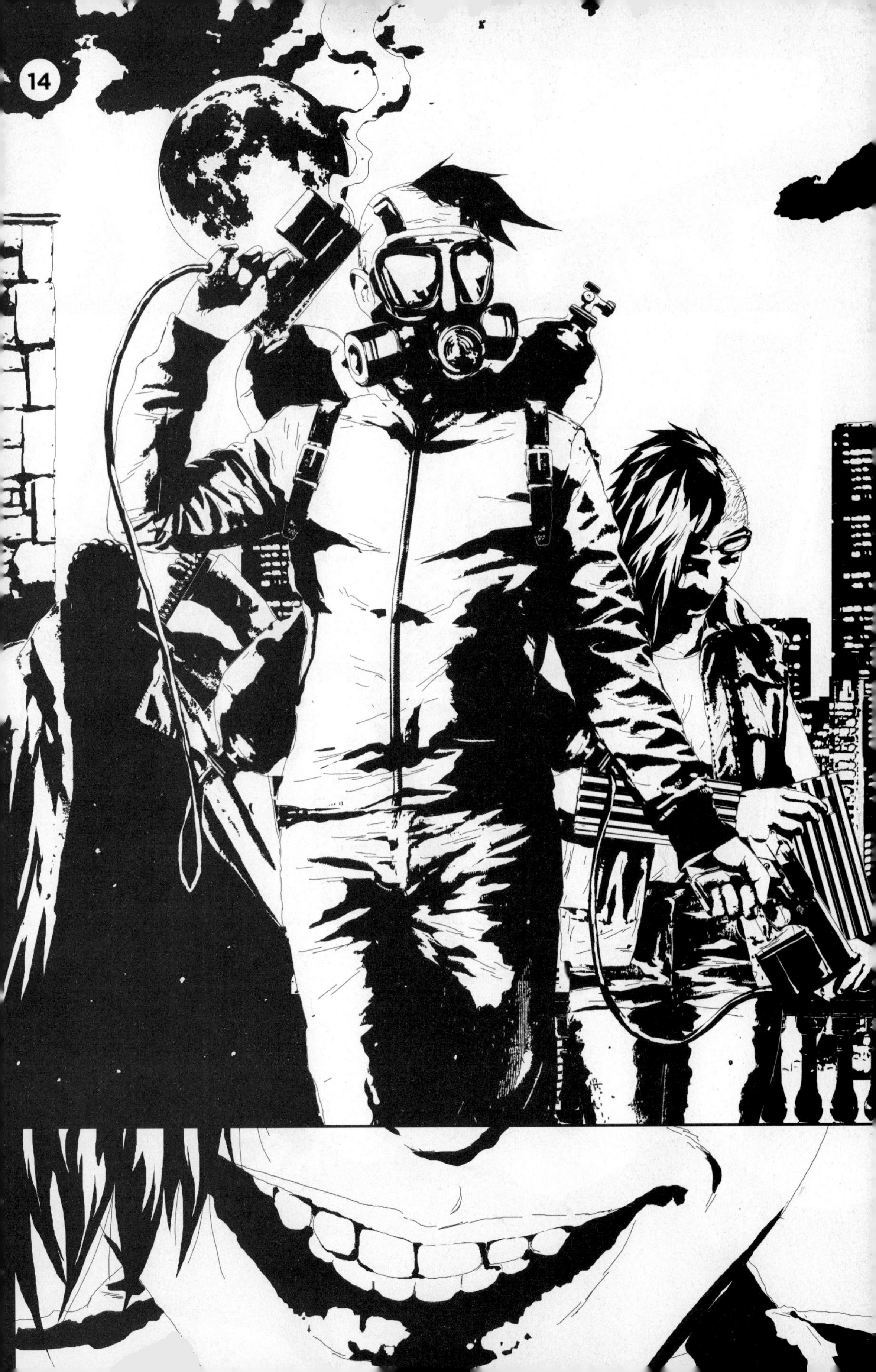
14

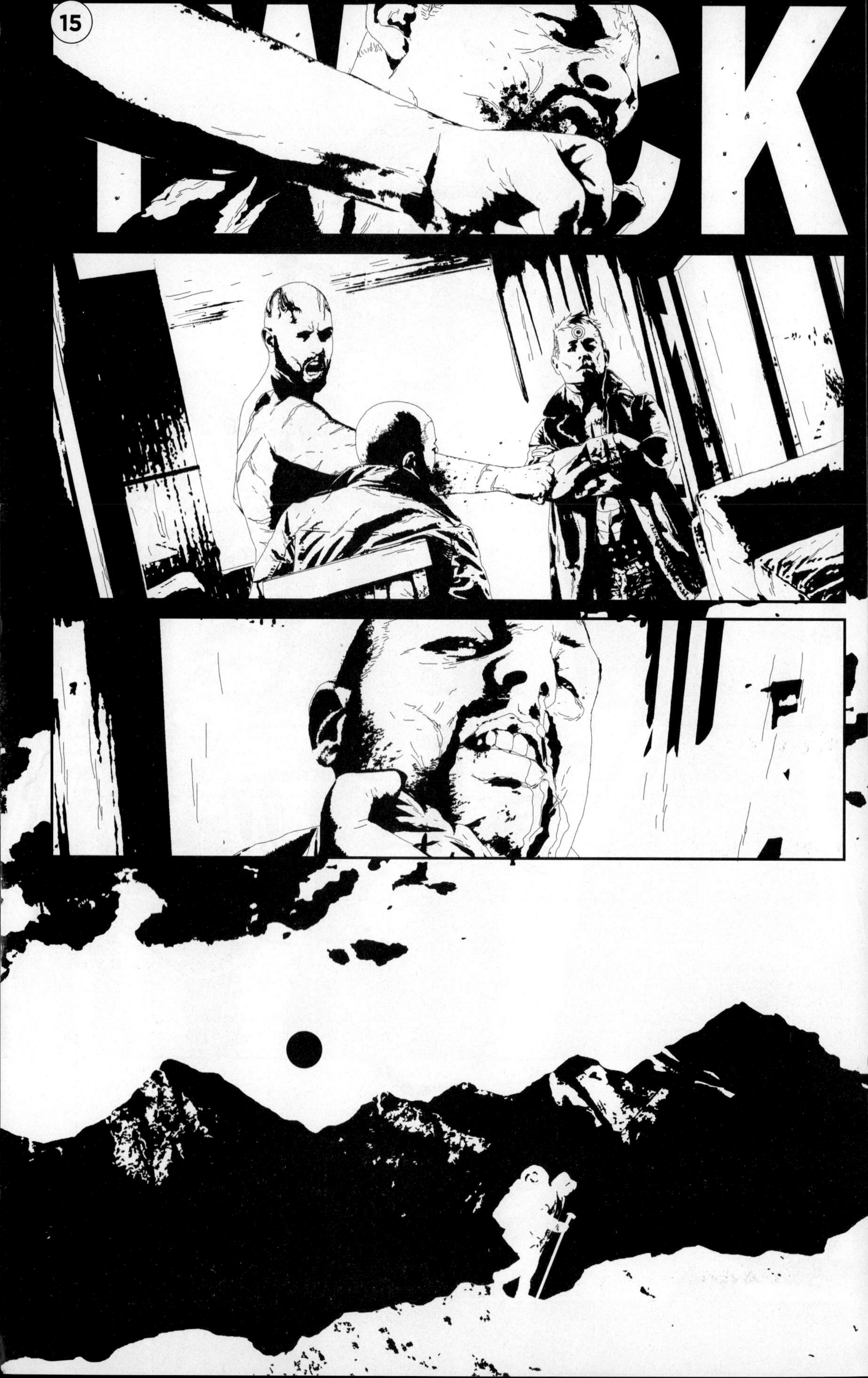

PAGE 13.

1. Suddenly BRICK, a massive villain, jumps down onto the roof from above, the impact throws Ollie flying back.

DART: We decided to split it three ways.

SFX: THOOM!!

2. Ollie groggily gets to his knees trying to load another arrow at Brick, who lumbers towards him growling.

BRICK: Gonna snap your little head off, green man.

3. Arrow aims at Brick.

ARROW: B—Brick? Jesus...Dragon really called in all the D-listers, didn't he?

4. Suddenly Brick sends a blast of compressed air to Ollie, blowing him across the roof, his bow goes flying from his hand.

SFX: POOM!

PAGE 14.

1. BIG PANEL. Arrow looks up, weak and wounded as KILLER MOTH now appears surrounding him along with RED DART, who aims at him and BRICK.

MOTH: D-Listers? I'm hurt. I'm at least a C-lister.

DART: Oh don't be, *Killer Moth*. He's right, after all.

But the thing is, you know what you get when you add three D-listers together?

2. Widescreen panel along the bottom of the page. Really tight on Dart's smiling lips.

DART: —A real ass-kicking.

PAGE 15.

1. We now cut to RICHARD DRAGON'S APARTMENT. Diggle is still tied to the chair, but now DRAGON punches him hard in the face. Blood and spit fly from Dig's mouth. Vertigo stands behind Dragon.

SFX: THWAP!

DIGGLE: —Ungh!

DRAGON: —In a way Diggle, I do have to thank you for helping to *show me* the way.

2. He punches Dig again.

DRAGON: When I saw you and Green Arrow—when I saw how you dismantled my father's empire through sheer *force of will*—I knew the time for *normal* men like my father had come.

3. Diggle looks up at him through a bruised and bloody face.

DRAGON: I mean—the world was changing all around us. Suddenly men could fly in Metropolis. Space knights with green rings were flying over California.

DRAGON: Yet Green Arrow stood shoulder-to-shoulder with them. A normal man who had made himself into something more...

4. We cut to FLASHBACK. A young RICARDO DIAZ JR. walks through the mountains of ASIA, in a parka, a bag slung over his shoulder. This is still the young, skinny Diaz.

DRAGON CAPTION: He showed me I could do it too.

DRAGON CAPTION: I left Seattle...followed a hidden trail of secrets and legends across the world until I found what I needed...

PAGES 16-17/DOUBLE SPREAD.

1. A massive panel of DIAZ standing before the massive sprawling UNDERGROUND CITY of THE LEAGUE OF ASSASSINS. He stands with another man. A warrior with RED HAIR. This is the real RICHARD DRAGON.

See RED HOOD AND THE OUTLAWS for reference. BRIAN and HARVEY, can you please provide Andrea with proper reference for the Underground City and the League of Assassins.

-Andrea, the real Richard Dragon is just like the original pre-52 Richard Dragon.

DIAZ CAPTION: —Until I found the League of Assassins!

2-4. Three almost identical panels at the bottom of the page. We see Diaz training in a cave with RICHARD DRAGON. In each successive panel we

see Diaz get bigger and more muscular, and add more tattoos with each panel as well.

DIAZ CAPTION: For years I stayed in that underground city. Training and learning.

DIAZ CAPTION: My sensei was a great warrior. He taught me how to leave everything I was behind and become something better...to become a weapon.

DIAZ CAPTION: But Dragon also taught peace, patience, compassion...all things that threatened to corrupt what I'd become. Things that would make *me* soft.

5. Richard Dragon lay dead in the cave, his neck snapped.

DIAZ CAPTION: —So I killed him and *took his name* to honor the strength he had given me.

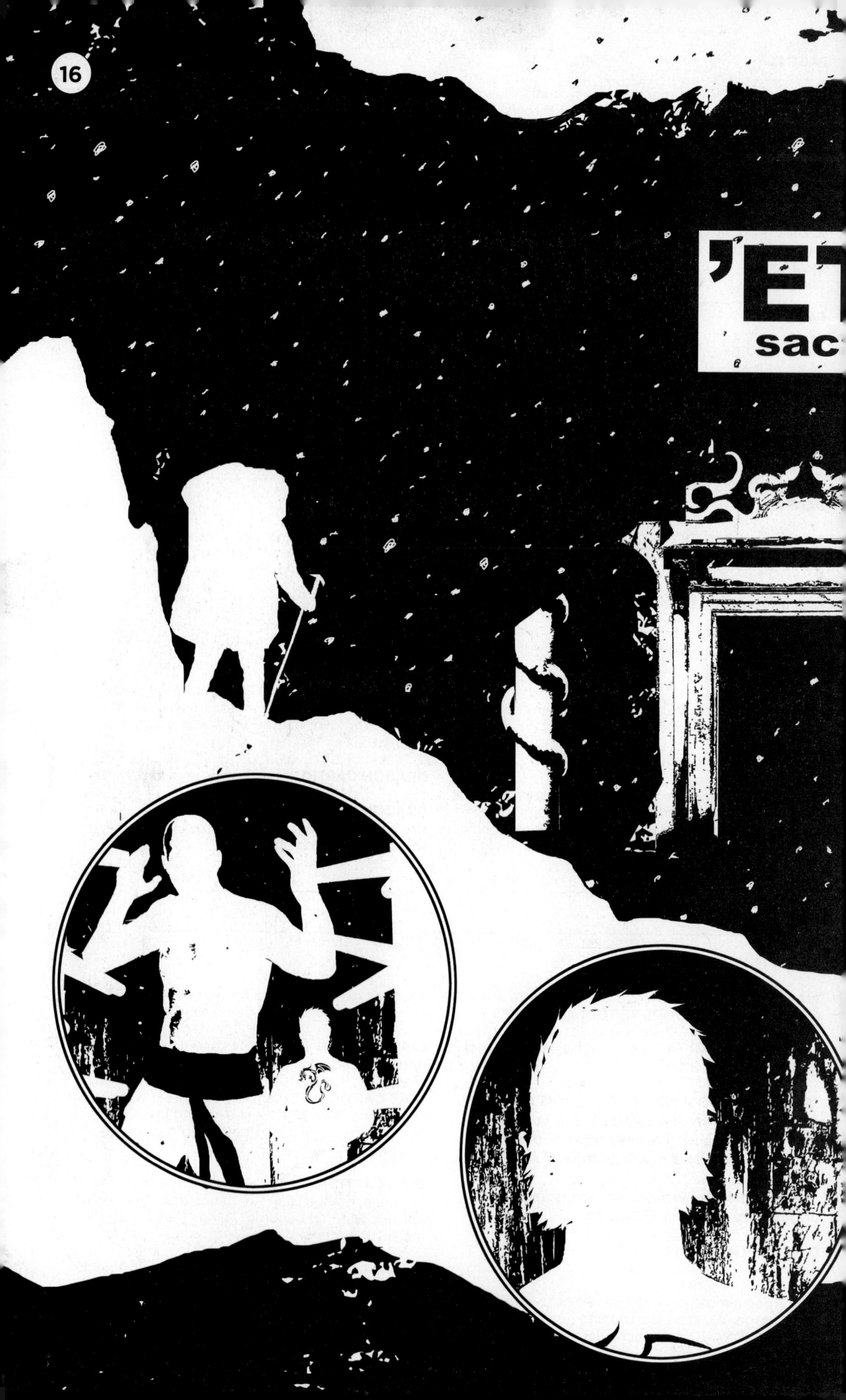
'ET
sac

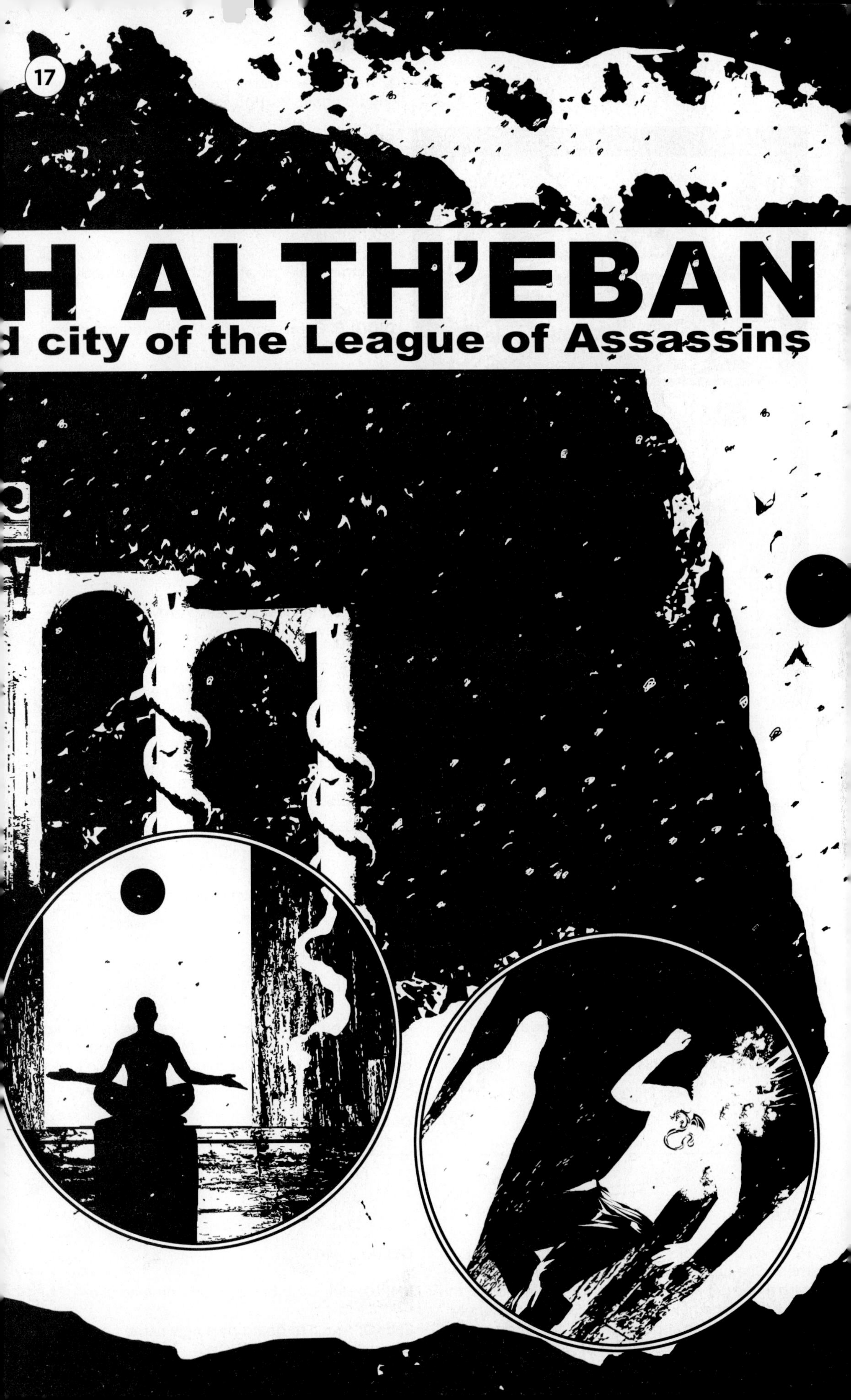
17
H ALTH'EBAN
d city of the League of Assassins

PAGE 18.

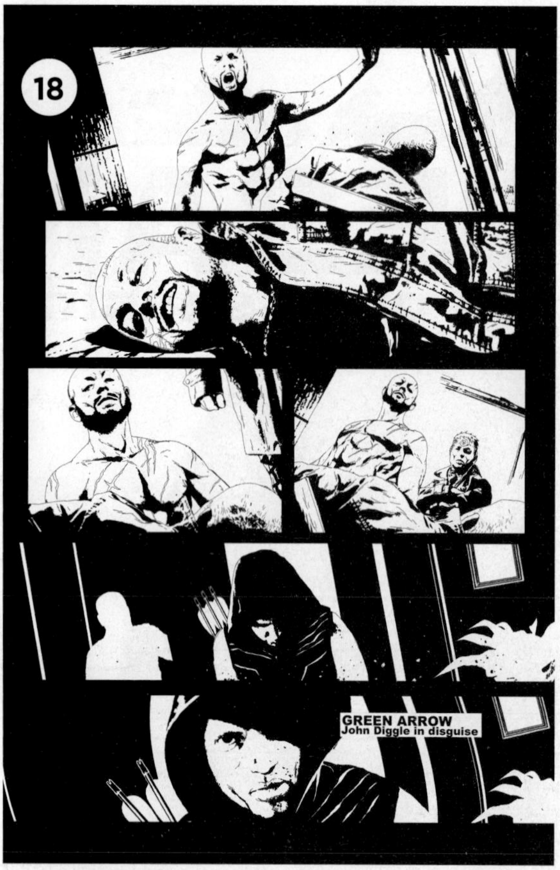
18
GREEN ARROW
John Diggle in disguise

1. We cut back to the present. Dragon punches Diggle again. Vertigo smiles.

SFX: THWAP!

DRAGON: And now, John Diggle, I'm back, and after I've killed you and Green Arrow, I'm going to show this city and then this country what real strength is.

2. Diggle looks up at him through a bloody, bruised face.

DIGGLE: Great story, *junior*...but you got one of your facts wrong.

3. Close on Dragon, who smirks at him.

DRAGON: Really? Please, do tell.

4. Reverse to a surprised-looking Dragon and Vertigo.

DIGGLE: You spent all this time, blood and money going after Green Arrow, but you didn't even need to. See, you already had your man the whole time.

5. Cut to Flashback. Green Arrow stands in the Arrow Cave, full of blood.

DIGGLE: That night Green Arrow stormed in here and whooped your Daddy's ass, *it wasn't the real Green Arrow...*

6. Flashback continues. Green Arrow removes his hood. It's Diggle under the hood, not Ollie!

DIGGLE: —It was *me*.

PAGE 19.

1. We cut to Ollie on the rooftop. BRICK, RED DART and MOTH stand over him, kicking and punching him. They are beating the hell out of him.

DART: This is too easy...almost doesn't seem fair.

2. Close on Brick punching Ollie, blood flies.

BRICK: Forget fair. This loudmouth has it coming.

3. Brick is about to punch him again, but an arrow hits him right in the neck.

BRICK: Arrgh!!

SFX: FWIP!

4. Now a bunch of Arrows fly. Brick grabs his neck and falls from the roof. Killer Moth and Red Dart both dive for cover. Ollie, beaten and weak, looks to see who has saved him...

OLLIE: Wha—?!

PAGE 20.

SPLASH.

Reverse. Ollie looks up to see EMIKO standing there. She has a new costume on. It's all green, with a hood (not up at the moment). Andrea, this will be a brand new design for Emiko in her new identity as Ollie's apprentice. Big full body shot. The bow loaded and ready. She smiles at Ollie.

OLLIE: *EMIKO?!*

EMIKO: Hello, big brother, long time no see.

EMIKO: And, I'm going by a new name now...You can call me *GREEN ARROW.*

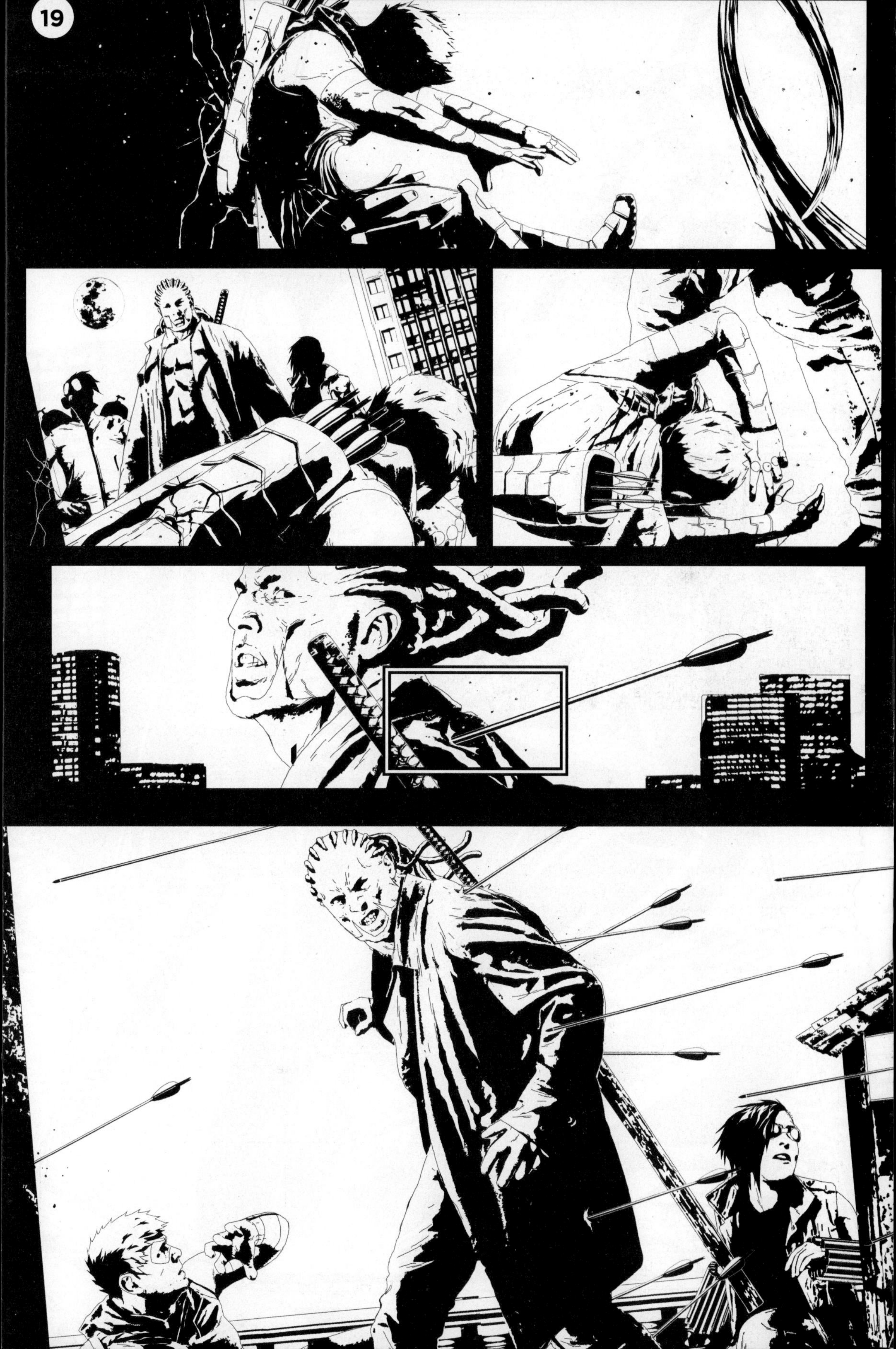

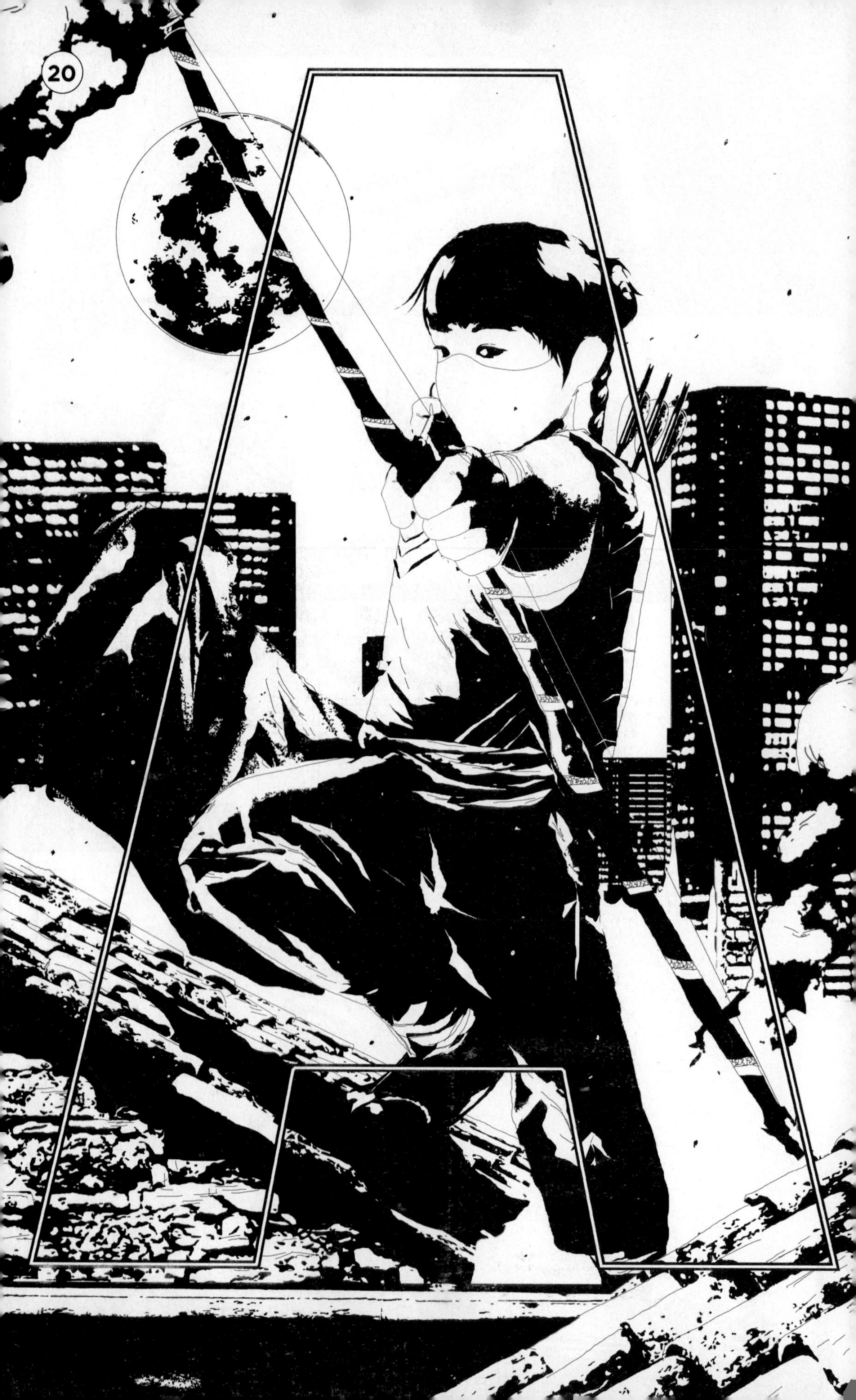
20